PIRATES AND DEVILS

William Gilmore Simms Initiatives: Texts and Studies Series

David Moltke-Hansen and Todd Hagstette, Series Editors

William Gilmore Simms's Unfinished Civil War: Consequences for a Southern Man of Letters

DAVID MOLTKE-HANSEN, ED.

William Gilmore Simms's Selected Reviews on Literature and Civilization

JAMES EVERETT KIBLER, JR., AND DAVID MOLTKE-HANSEN, EDS.

Pirates and Devils: William Gilmore Simms's Unfinished Postbellum Novels

NICHOLAS G. MERIWETHER AND DAVID W. NEWTON, EDS.

PIRATES & DEVILS

William Gilmore Simms's Unfinished Postbellum Novels

Edited by
NICHOLAS G. MERIWETHER & DAVID W. NEWTON

The University of South Carolina Press

Published by the University of South Carolina Press
Columbia, South Carolina 29208

www.sc.edu/uscpress

Manufactured in the United States of America

24 23 22 21 20 19 18 17 16 15
10 9 8 7 6 5 4 3 2 1

Library of Congress Cataloging-in-Publication Data

Simms, William Gilmore, 1806–1870.
[Novels. Selections]
Pirates and Devils : William Gilmore Simms's unfinished postbellum novels / edited by Nicholas G. Meriwether and David W. Newton.
pages cm. — (William Gilmore Simms initiatives: texts and studies)
Includes bibliographical references and index.
ISBN 978-1-61117-456-4 (hardback) — ISBN 978-1-61117-457-1 (ebook)
1. American fiction—19th century. 2. Simms, William Gilmore, 1806–1870—Criticism and interpretation. I. Meriwether, Nicholas G., editor. II. Newton, David W., 1961– editor.
PS2843.M47 2015
813'.3—dc23

2015003054

Publication of this book is made possible in part by the generous support of the Watson-Brown Foundation, together with the Caroline McKissick Dial Publication Fund of the South Caroliniana Library and the University Libraries of the University of South Carolina.

This book was printed on recycled paper with 30 percent postconsumer waste content.

CONTENTS

ACKNOWLEDGMENTS

Anyone who spends time with Simms's writing comes away with a profound appreciation for the importance he placed on friendship. Scholars who study Simms are fortunate to be able to call on the support of a community of scholars, whose friendship and support for this project we are grateful to acknowledge.

James L. W. West III of the Pennsylvania State University Center for the History of the Book provided advice for textual transcription and editorial practices. The research librarians and staff at the South Caroliniana Library at the University of South Carolina provided generous assistance in the preparation of both of these manuscripts for publication. Allen Stokes, the former director, assisted with editing "Sir Will O' Wisp." Allen Stokes, his successor Henry Fulmer, and Manuscripts Specialist Graham Duncan all provided invaluable assistance with conjectural emendations for both texts. John Miller also reviewed sections of the transcription of "Sir Will O' Wisp" and helped with difficult passages.

Work on the transcription of "Sir Will O' Wisp" was completed through the generosity of the William Gilmore Simms Research Fellowship at the South Caroliniana Library. The initial transcription of "The Brothers of the Coast," primarily by Graham Duncan, was generously funded by John Simms.

The University of West Georgia provided funding for graduate research assistantships to support editorial work on "Sir Will O' Wisp." Brooke Sparks, William Manion, and Kimberly Smith assisted with research on annotations for the work. Laura McClanathan assisted with the annotations for "The Brothers of the Coast." Alex Moore at the University of South Carolina Press was a patient champion who never faltered in his belief that these two difficult works deserved a wider audience. David Moltke-Hansen, then director of the Simms Initiatives at the University of South Carolina, created a forum that allowed this book to come to fruition, and he also provided careful readings of the introductory essays for the texts. Any errors are the responsibility of the respective editors.

EDITORIAL METHOD

Both of these works are public texts, intended for publication; the purpose behind this volume is to provide accessible texts that will facilitate the introduction of these formerly unpublished efforts. The editing practices here honor those of The Centennial Edition of the Works of William Gilmore Simms, published by the University of South Carolina Press, and the Selected Fiction of William Gilmore Simms Arkansas Edition, by the University of Arkansas Press, while acknowledging recent changes in textual scholarship that place greater emphasis on readability. This provides an overview of the editorial practices followed here; a more detailed analysis of both works can be made via their online publication, by the Simms Initiatives at the University of South Carolina.

Dialect has been left as Simms wrote it; elsewhere spelling has been made consistent but rendered in accordance with Simms's use. Simms often left compounds such as "any thing," "some body," "day light," and so forth as two words; these have been combined and standardized. Spelling of people, places, and things has been made consistent; in "The Brothers of the Coast," Simms's occasional use of the definite article "the" before "Steel Cap" has also been made consistent and thus dropped throughout. Some archaic spellings such as "sate" for "sat," "gripe" for "grip" have been modernized when leaving them in their original form would have led to confusion.

Capitalization and punctuation have been made consistent and generally modernized. Simms's practice of using dashes to reveal breath-lines, often after commas and semicolons, has been rendered, in most circumstances, as a comma; exceptions have been made when the addition of a new comma would render the sentence too unwieldy. Simms's frequent use of commas has been reduced as well, to better conform to modern usage. Simms wrote quickly and used ampersands (&), Sharfess S's (the German double-S), paragraph marks (¶), and other abbreviations as both shorthand and printer's directives, not intended for typographical transliteration in the published text. These have been spelled out or heeded. Simms provided some paragraph breaks, indicated by either glyph

(¶) or indentation; these have been followed, but additional breaks were also occasionally inserted to improve the flow of the text. Double quotation marks around names and place names have been minimized. Simms usually placed apostrophes before the *n* in contractions such as "do'nt" and "should'nt." These have been made consistent and modernized, for example, "don't," "shouldn't." Italics have been limited to emphasis that Simms intended and to uncommon foreign words and phrases; other instances have been eliminated. When Simms struck out a word, it was omitted. He almost never reinstated a word, once struck out.

The manuscript of "The Brothers of the Coast" was damaged. Missing parts of pages and the obliteration of words mean that the majority of the insertions are conjectural editorial emendations, based on context, physical limits (such as the number of spaces occupied by the missing paper), and general knowledge of Simms's writing. The use of brackets to indicate editorial emendations has been minimized. A detailed, line-by-line transliteration of both manuscripts, along with full textual apparatus, is available online through the Simms Initiatives at the University of South Carolina. The digital facsimile edition of both works, reproducing the manuscripts and accompanying transcriptions, allows this edition to provide a more readable, accessible texts, leaving the digital versions to provide textually authoritative transliterations of the manuscripts themselves.

Introduction

The end of the Civil War found William Gilmore Simms living in a garret in Columbia, S.C., editing—and largely writing—a newspaper that barely afforded him sustenance. For a man who had tied his fate so completely to that of his state and region, defeat was hard enough. Making it personal, was the destruction of his house and library, tragedies that made the burden of his own complicity in the horrors of war and its ravages almost unbearable. Even earlier during the war he had felt his pen stilled, unable to free his mind from the all-consuming conflict that swirled around him and the deep personal losses that characterized his own experience during those four years. But somehow, in the ruins of the city to which he had fled to escape the march of Union general William Tecumseh Sherman, he rediscovered his muse. Despite the punishing heat of Columbia in August, Simms could write his old friend Augustus Everett Duyckinck that "If the publishers could make me these advances, I could begin the world anew, and set my wheels & springs in motion." He continued, "I am conscious of no diminution of powers. My health is good—my frame vigorous, and, once restored to peace of mind,—freed from the terrible anxieties about my children, I believe that I could do better things in letters than I have ever done before. I have my brain seething ever and anon, with fresh conceptions, over which I brood at intervals, with a loving mood of meditation which makes them grow upon me, until the images become as familiar to the eye, as they have been to the mind" (*Letters* 4:516).

It was a remarkable claim for many reasons. That Simms could find himself inspired to write—even in the ashes of a city whose destruction affected him deeply and personally—was almost incredible; that this happened after a protracted war that had devastated him professionally and personally is even more so. What emerges in the letters he wrote that summer and fall is a writer and public intellectual determined to stay in his beloved state and rebuild his name and career, and what he accomplished is noteworthy, a last great surge in creativity and productivity that scholars have been slowly uncovering and documenting since the advent of the aborted Centennial Edition of William Gilmore Simms.

That effort produced Simms's two last great novels, *Joscelyn* and *Voltmeier,* written in 1866 and 1868, respectively, and published in serial form in 1867 and 1869. Publication of these two novels in book form did much to offset the lingering misperceptions of the writer's last five years, a time that, until the Centennial Edition, had been largely defined bibliographically by the dubious 1937 edition of his *The Sack and Destruction of Columbia, S.C.* John C. Guilds, Jr., made plain the appeal of this era for Simms studies in his 1992 biography, noting that "*mirabile dictu,* late in 1867, despite incapacitating illnesses, [Simms's] creativity seemed to explode into one of those marvelous surges that periodically marked his career" (*Literary Life* 304). A careful examination of his postwar writings suggests that this surge began even earlier. And indeed, though Guilds was chiefly concerned with *Joscelyn* and *Voltmeier,* it is interesting to see the degree to which themes and issues Simms explored in those two novels can be discerned, however inchoate, in even earlier postwar efforts. Most recently *William Gilmore Simms's Unfinished Civil War,* edited by David Moltke-Hansen, has done much to explore the significance of this last era in Simms's work, underscoring Guilds's contention and providing a much deeper appreciation for the unexplored riches that remain.

Of those riches foremost are his two incomplete efforts, his pirate romance "The Brothers of the Coast" and his folk fable "Sir Will O' Wisp or the Irish Baronet; A Tale of Its Own Day." No systematic treatment of either work appeared until Moltke-Hansen's critical volume, which contains an essay on "The Brothers of the Coast," and the challenges posed by the manuscripts and their obscurity have skewed our picture of Simms's last years. Left unfinished at his death, these two substantial fragments represent the last of the major primary texts from this final phase of Simms's life to be published. Both deserve attention, and not just for their literary ambitions and achievement, however truncated. Together the texts reveal more of Simms's creative process than scholars have yet been able to uncover, but, more important, they show Simms's commitment to wrestling with the issues he faced in the aftermath of the Civil War, and they document the creativity and courage that his commitment represented—and required. The publication of these fragments makes possible a more complete picture of this last phase of Simms's life, as he struggled with the consequences of a conflict that was the defining event of his life, career, and region.

Simms used his letters, especially to his friends, as a kind of epistolary autobiography, but on occasion he could subordinate their verisimilitude to other causes, such as when he wrote to Northern friends on the eve of and during the Civil War, touting the war readiness and resources of his state and region. But there was no posturing in his postwar claim to Duyckinck that he was "seething . . . with fresh conceptions." One of those conceptions was a long-contemplated novel on piracy. Less than a month later, Simms wrote Duyckinck, detailing his ambition to write "a standard romance of Pirate life & practice": "I propose, if I do not at once come to N.Y. to proceed to the plantation & prepare a new romance, under the persuasions of Smith & Street [sic], which I think I can make equal to any thing I have yet done" (*Letters* 4:519). Writing his old friend and informal literary agent James Lawson that same day, he asked about Street and Smith, requesting Lawson to "ascertain what you can about these parties & advise me" (*Letters* 4:517).

Other work, as well as illness and travel, intervened; three months later Simms wrote Duyckinck that "I hope shortly to begin my 'Sensation' story" (*Letters* 4:528), but by February he had started, writing Duyckinck that he was "also engaged upon my romance, called 'The Brothers of the Coast' of which more hereafter" (*Letters* 4:539). Despite his precarious health and the demands on his time, he made good progress at first. Two weeks later he wrote Duyckinck that "At present I am busy day & night, writing for the bread of the day. I have written some 150 pp. of a MS. Romance anent the Pirates. But I get on too slowly for my impatience, tasked as I am with the sole Editorship of the Carolinian, & writing for that Journal some 3 columns per day" (*Letters* 4:541). The distractions of ill health and uncertain finances continued to plague his efforts, however; he complained to Lawson that he was writing "more slowly than I otherwise should, if my health & spirits were better" (*Letters* 4:545). Other projects, including editing the mammoth *War Poetry of the South,* also intruded, making his progress on the novel fitful. Writing to William Hawkins Ferris, Simms admitted that he was "writing at snatches, when I can, a chapter of my new Romance, which has reached its 9th. Chap. & 173d. page" (*Letters* 4:547). That describes what he left at his death, an amount that he may have believed sufficed to persuade a publisher to sign a contract and begin serialization. In that same letter to Ferris, it is clear that he thought that in two months he would be ready to depart for New York "& possibly be able to start the serial publication of my piratical romance" (*Letters* 4:547).

His hopes did not materialize. Scattered remarks in his letters sketch the manuscript's fate. Simms seems to have abandoned writing it that spring; a month later he wrote Duyckinck and remarked in closing that the story stood at 170 pages (*Letters* 4:550). Worries over family and income were constant distractions, as he wrote Ferris on April 13, and he continued to appeal to his friends for a copy of Johnson's *History of the Pyrates,* a clear indication that he wanted access to this source to continue his work. Anxieties and sources aside, however, the lack of a publisher is what most likely ended Simms's work on the manuscript. Street and Smith did not buy it. Simms pursued at least one other publisher, asking Ferris to tell Cauldwell and Whitney, the publishers of the *Sunday Mercury,* that he was "busily engaged on 'The Brothers of the Coast,' making all the headway that I can—that I have some 200 pp. of MS. written, and hope to be in New York, in *pro. per.* [in person] by the 1st June, prepared to begin the serial publication in their paper" (*Letters* 4:552).

The distractions of anxiety continued, though. Two weeks later he confessed to Lawson that "I have some 170 pages of MS. on a new romance, but I am so distressed in spirit, so worked in brain, so fevered with anxiety & trouble, that I make slow progress. At this moment I have not a dollar that I can call my own" (*Letters* 4:557). Whether his muse abandoned him, his lack of sources thwarted him, or publishers simply encouraged other projects, Simms abandoned the story then. The same fate would befall his second major unfinished opus, "Sir Will O' Wisp," though its circumstances were more turbulent.

While references to "The Brothers of the Coast" appear in Simms's letters following the Civil War, references to "Sir Will O' Wisp or the Irish Baronet; A Tale of Its Own Day" are all but absent. Simms's silence about the manuscript is not entirely out of character. His letters to literary associates and publishers in the North frequently describe his progress on novels such as *Joscelyn* and *Voltmeier* or to other works that he believed would be of interest to publishers and to the reading public. Many other works of varying lengths and stages of completion existed in the years following the war, but Simms rarely mentions these in his surviving correspondence. In his introduction to the Centennial Edition of Simms's *Stories and Tales,* Guilds estimated that, in addition to the works that were published soon after his death, Simms left behind at least eight other significantly developed but unfinished works of prose fiction, of which "Sir Will O' Wisp" and "The Brothers of the Coast" are the longest (xiii). Shorter fiction, articles, poems, and other nonfiction prose works—many never identified explicitly by Simms—also remained, and Simms often referred to these in his letters collectively as "smaller tales" and manuscripts or as "sundry articles for the newspapers" (*Letters* 5:221). That Simms left behind so many unfinished works—many in stages very close to completion—is an enduring testament to the depth of his intellectual and creative powers at the end of his life, even as his physical abilities waned.

While Simms's letters provide few insights into the composition of "Sir Will O' Wisp," he devoted considerable time and creative energy to its development during the postwar years, completing 187 manuscript pages before abandoning work on the project, somewhere near the end of a substantially developed sixth chapter. Written on uniform letter-size stationery, the manuscript contains only minimal corrections in Simms's own handwriting, usually involving words that he edited and interlined in the process of writing the draft. Set in the fictional town of Mongrelia, the story involves a writer named Richard Silex who unexpectedly acquires the services of a well-appointed demon posing as an Irish nobleman who calls himself Sir Will O' Wisp. Lively philosophical discussions between Silex and Sir Will make up large portions of the completed chapters. Other sections involve social satire that focuses on the citizens of Mongrelia, although the development of this satire is uneven in its tone and focus. In the Centennial Edition of Simms's *Stories and Tales,* Guilds grouped "Sir Will O' Wisp" with several other minor social satires that Simms wrote, including *Father Abbot, or, The Home Tourist; a Medley* (1849), "Flirtation at the Moultrie House" (1850), and "Major Martinet; or, the Lost Half Hour" (1870), another unfinished story fragment of which only one chapter was every published (779–80). Simms may have conceived of "Sir Will O' Wisp" as another one of his short novels. In a letter to Duyckinck dated December 6, 1854, he wrote, "My stories, by the way, are regularly planned and are novels in little—not mere scenes or sketches" (*Letters* 3:342). In his biography of Simms, Guilds has concurred, noting that perhaps "more than in the short story . . . Simms excelled in the writing of the short novel or novelette" (*Literary Life* 349). Among Simms's best known short novels, two bear important structural and thematic similarities to "Sir Will O' Wisp." The first is his earliest short novel, *Martin Faber* (1833), which Guilds has described as "his first psychological study in the confessional mode," and the other is *Paddy McGann,* a frontier tale that, like "Sir Will O' Wisp," satirizes the excesses of materialistic greed and superficial social conventions (*Literary Life* 349).

Although "Sir Will O' Wisp" was written during the final years of Simms's life, its origins can be traced to a short story titled "Jack-O'-Lantern: A New-Light Story" that Simms published in the *Southern Literary Messenger* in 1838. The story describes the unexpected meeting between a world-weary writer and a mysterious gentleman demon named Jack-O'-Lantern, whom Simms would later rename Sir Will O' Wisp. Simms published only one chapter of "Jack-O'-Lantern," but returning to a work written earlier in his career was not an uncommon practice for Simms during the postwar era. Guilds has documented in his biography that Simms began writing *Joscelyn; A Tale of the Revolution* before 1860 and returned to complete it after the war was over (*Literary Life* 306). In a letter written to Justus Starr Redfield, his long-standing literary associate and publisher from New York, and dated September 4, 1868, Simms referred to several other works published prior to the war that he believed would be worthy of republication. He went on to state that many of them "are of imaginative, psychological and spiritual character," and concluded with "there are others that I have at home" (*Letters* 5:157). The actual reasons why Simms would return to an obscure, largely unfinished short story during the last years of his life remain a mystery, but one thing is certain: Simms had not forgotten "Jack-O'-Lantern" during the intervening years, and he believed returning to it was worth a considerable investment of his time and creative energies during the final years of his life.

It is not difficult to imagine how such complexities might cause Simms to remain silent about "Sir Will O' Wisp." The story contains a curious mixture of Faustian allegory, folktale, philosophical speculation, spiritual treatise, and social satire and is difficult to characterize. Simms perhaps realized there were few realistic prospects for publishing such a complex, hybrid work in an era when most readers simply wanted to be entertained. In fact Simms's silence may well reflect a different reality altogether: namely that publishing the work was not his ultimate goal even during a time when income from publications meant everything to his family. If this is true, then "Sir Will O' Wisp" can be read as a private confession just as much as a work written for the reading public, the result of an artist wrestling with his own personal demons.

Simms did not abandon these two works lightly. Shortly before Simms died, his old friend Duyckinck wrote to him, urging him to consider writing his memoirs. Bedridden from the cancer that would eventually kill him, Simms wrote back, indicating that he was still writing but that "invention is, even now, an easier exercise than the challenge of memory," and reaffirming his determination to do so: "I prefer, like the swan, to die singing" (*Letters* 4:294). If the memories of a too recent and still painful past surrounded him, then he could, and did, find some surcease in the toils of his imagination. Though the unfinished nature of these two works challenges definitive interpretation, their publication completes a picture of the writer's last years, proof that he did indeed die singing.

Works Cited

Guilds, John Caldwell. *Simms: A Literary Life.* Fayetteville: University of Arkansas Press, 1992.

———, ed. *Stories and Tales. The Writings of William Gilmore Simms.* Centennial Edition. Volume 5. Introductions, explanatory notes, and texts established by John C. Guilds. Columbia: University of South Carolina Press, 1974.

Meriwether, Nicholas G. "An Unfinished Reconstruction: Simms's 'The Brothers of the Coast.'" In David Moltke-Hansen, ed., *William Gilmore Simms's Unfinished Civil War.* 185–201.

Moltke-Hansen, David, ed. *William Gilmore Simms's Unfinished Civil War: Consequences for a Southern Man of Letters.* Columbia: University of South Carolina Press, 2013.

Simms, William Gilmore. "The Brothers of the Coast." Charles Carroll Simms Collection, South Caroliniana Library, University of South Carolina.

———. *Father Abbot, or, The Home Tourist; a Medley.* Charleston: Miller and Browne, 1849.

———. *Flirtation at the Moultrie House.* Charleston: Edward C. Councell, Publisher, 1850.

———. "Jack-O'-Lantern: A New-Light Story." By Eyes-In-Glass. Chapter 1. *Southern Literary Messenger* 4.5 (May 1838): 336–39.

———. *Joscelyn; A Tale of the Revolution.* 1867. In John Caldwell Guilds, ed., *The Writings of William Gilmore Simms. Centennial Edition.* Vol. 16. Introduction and explanatory notes by Stephen Meats. Text established by Keen Butterworth. Columbia: University of South Carolina Press, 1975.

———. *The Letters of William Gilmore Simms.* Ed. Mary C. Simms Oliphant et al. 6 vols. Columbia: University of South Carolina Press, 1952–82.

———. "Major Martinet; or, the Lost Half Hour," *Cosmopolitan Monthly* 1 (January 1870).

———. *Martin Faber: The Story of a Criminal.* New York: J. and J. Harper, 1833.

———. *Paddy McGann; or, The Demon in the Swamp.* 1863. In John Caldwell Guilds, *The Writings of William Gilmore Simms.* Centennial Edition. Vol. 3. Introduction and explanatory notes by Robert Bush. Text established by James B. Meriwether. Columbia: University of South Carolina Press, 1972.

———. "Sir Will O' Wisp or the Irish Baronet; A Tale of Its Own Day." Charles Carroll Simms Collection, South Caroliniana Library, University of South Carolina.

———. *Voltmeier; or, The Mountain Men.* In John Caldwell Guilds, ed., *The Writings of William Gilmore Simms.* Centennial Edition. Vol. 1. Introduction and explanatory notes by Donald Davidson and Mary C. Simms Oliphant. Text established by James B. Meriwether. Columbia: University of South Carolina Press, 1969.

———, ed. *War Poetry of the South.* New York: Richardson & Company, 1866.

Salley, A. S., ed. *The Sack and Destruction of Columbia, S.C.* [Atlanta]: Oglethorpe University Press, 1937.

Schonhorn, Manuel, ed. *A General History of the Pyrates.* Attributed to Daniel Defoe. Columbia: University of South Carolina Press, 1972.

History, the King's Image, and the Politics of Utopia

Reading The Brothers of the Coast

NICHOLAS G. MERIWETHER

Death was much more than a literary theme to Simms. It was a terrible constant in his life, a specter that haunted his thoughts and perdured throughout his writing, regardless of genre. In one of his most poignant wartime letters, death was his house guest, a visitor come to steal another child (*Letters* 4:393). If the Civil War changed the way that Americans understood death, as Drew Gilpin Faust has shown, then that conflict's aftermath added another layer of meaning to the term for Simms (*This Republic of Suffering*). For a writer whose oeuvre had defined a whiggish sense of history as progress, defeat and ruin also represented a profound existential crisis, one that threatened to destroy that view of history (Moltke-Hansen, "When History Failed"). Yet, in the remarkable literary outpouring that marked his final years, Simms never gave into despair, revisiting the touchstones of his critical philosophy and deepening his commitment to a historical perspective that had been profoundly shaken by war and death but stubbornly refused to expire.

We can see that dogged determination to understand in the plots and characters of his postwar novels *Voltmeier* and *Joscelyn,* and it plays out on a broader level in his choice of their subjects, as he returned to the familiar spheres of the violent colonial world of Leonard Voltmeier as it gave way to the equally violent upheaval of the Revolutionary world of Stephen Joscelyn. Simms was also tying up loose ends with these works, finishing projects long contemplated, albeit reshaped by the refigurations that the Civil War and Reconstruction imposed. Another of those long-contemplated projects was a novel about pirates, "The Brothers of the Coast." However, its setting and themes would free Simms from his familiar haunts and allow him to embark on an exploration that suggests how his understanding of history might have embraced the tragic consequences of a war whose advent he had so ardently supported (Meriwether, "An Unfinished Reconstruction").

Simms considered "The Brothers of the Coast" the culmination of a lifelong interest in pirates. He asked his old friend Evert Augustus Duyckinck in September 1865, "Is it possible for you to procure me a History of the Pyrates, the 2 vol. 8 vo. Edition? This, with all my books, has been destroyed. It gives me great material, which I have long desired to work up into a standard romance of Pirate life & practice" (*Letters* 4:519). That desire, or at least a literary interest in the topic, manifested itself early in his career. Stories of Blackbeard's and Stede Bonnet's depredations along the coast of the Carolinas in the eighteenth century were a staple of Simms's boyhood, serving as the fodder for occasional stories before the war, such as "The Pirates and Palatines: A Legend of North-Carolina," first published in the *Magnolia* in 1842, and "The Pirate Hoard," a much longer effort serialized in *Graham's Magazine* in 1856. Book-length efforts such as *The Lily and the Totem* (1850) and *The Cassique of Kiawah* (1859) provided him with venues to explore a number of issues piracy raised as well (Meriwether, "An Unfinished Reconstruction" 188–89). *Southward Ho!* (1854), a collection of stories drawn primarily from magazines, included "The Pirates and Palatines," there retitled "The Ship of Fire," but it also marked the first appearance of Simms's "The Tale of Blackbeard." In one dramatic scene, he used the phrase that would become the title of his unfinished novel: "swear on the bloody head obedience to the laws of the 'Brothers of the Coast'!" Blackbeard tells a captive, followed by the narrator's aside, "such was the name which the pirate fraternity bore among themselves . . ." (*Southward Ho!* 456).

This account, and the book as a whole, presaged several critical themes that would inform Simms's later treatment of the subject. In addition to allowing him to recount some of the history of piracy in the New World, especially in the eighteenth century, fifty or more years before the Revolution, it also gave him a platform to expatiate on the dangers of utopianism. One of Simms's narrators claims that these dangerous theories even inform growing antisouthern sentiment in the North:

> Governed by self, rather than by nation or section, they cry "peace"—all—when there is no peace! When there can not be peace, so long as the south is in the minority, and so long as the spirit and temper of the north are so universally hostile to our most vital and most cherished institutions. Until you reconcile

> this inequality, and exorcise this evil spirit, that now rages rampant through the Northern States—allied with all sorts of fanatical passions and principles—Agrarianism, Communism, Fourierism, Wrightism, Millerism, Mormonism, etc.,—you may cry peace and union till you split your lungs, but you will neither make peace nor secure union. (*Southward Ho!* 394).

Indeed *Southward Ho!* provides the clearest precursor to the political and ideological context that Simms would sketch in "The Brothers of the Coast." In one tale a cholera epidemic in the North gives rise to social experimentation run amuck:

> Society at the North was in Revolution. Old things were about to pass away; all things were to become new. Property was to undergo general distribution in equal shares. Every man, it was argued, had a natural right to a farmstead, and a poultry-yard; as every woman, not wholly past bearing, had a right to a husband. The old Patroons of Albany were not permitted to rent, but must sell their lands, at prices prescribed by the buyer, or the tenant. Debtors liquidated their bonds in the blood of their creditors. The law of divorce gave every sort of liberty to wife and husband. (*Southward Ho!* 391–92)

It was the American equivalent of the French Revolution, a "universal disorder in laws and morals—this confusion of society, worse confounded every day—in its general aspects so wonderfully like those which, in France, preceded, and properly paved the way for, a purging reign of terror . . ." (*Southward Ho!* 392). Social satire aside, here Simms also modeled his earlier advice to Nathaniel Beverly Tucker, whose drama Simms suggested in an 1849 letter could be adapted "to the present state of society in N.Y. City, where the women are regularly engaged in organized cliques & bodies, in procuring converts to Fourierism . . . . By making your drama illustrate the pernicious doctrines of communism, as well as mere fashionable life, you can popularize your subject, and impart to it an additional element of novelty" (*Letters* 2:555). Whether or not a direct reference to *The Communist Manifesto,* it is nonetheless a tantalizing hint of what he would set about adumbrating in "The Brothers of the Coast." No reference to *The Communist Manifesto* appears in Simms's surviving letters, though he may have reviewed it, and certainly could have encountered it in his study of German and German sources (Meriwether, "An Unfinished Reconstruction" 189; Kibler and Moltke-Hansen, "The Man of Letters as Critic" 18).

In "The Tale of Blackbeard," Simms also mentioned a source for his thoughts on pirates, called the *Book of the Buccaneers* in the text but more likely the pseudonymous *A General History of the Pyrates,* which played a major role in his conception of the plot for "The Brothers of the Coast" and clearly served as the source for the chapter on Blackbeard.* His repeated requests over four years after his first appeal to Duyckinck indicate how highly he prized it as a source (*Letters* 4:519; 5:259; 5:262; 5:270). Though not the first book on piracy to captivate colonial and British readers, *A General History of the Pyrates* is considered the most important and is credited with creating many of the popular impressions of pirates, both erroneous and accurate (Cordingly, Introduction, vii–viii; Woodard, *Republic* 6, 325). Earlier generations of scholars tended to be more impressed with its relative accuracy than later ones, though that view still has adherents (Hughson, "The Carolina Pirates" 72–73n1; Schonhorn, *A General History* [663]; Gosse, *A General History* 2; Cordingly, Introduction ix). Colin Woodard's recent assessment sums it up, calling the book "an impressive work of scholarship, skillfully integrating documentary records with materials clearly gathered from interviews," but noting that "It is, however, riddled with errors, exaggerations, and misunderstandings . . ." (*Republic* 329). That could also describe the debate over its authorship, misattributed for decades to Daniel Defoe and more recently ascribed to noted London Jacobite printer Nathaniel Mist, the book's publisher.† The fascinating, labyrinthine connections between Mist, the book, and British politics and publishing at the time—its two volumes first appeared in 1724 and 1728, respectively, shortly after the setting for Simms's pirate story—and the issues Simms was exploring in his own tale exceed the bounds of this introduction, but they are part of the historical backdrop that informs the most significant symbol in the text, the tavern called the King's Image, discussed below. And the broader point—that Simms believed the book to be accurate—demonstrates the degree to which he found the book's fictitious

*The title probably refers to Alexandre Olivier Exquemelin's *History of the Bouccaneers of America,* considered one of the most important works about seventeenth-century piracy, and one of the most bibliographically complex works of that century. Though its numerous translations, impressions, and editions complicate the text's history, its first English publication (1684) preceded Blackbeard (1680–1718). For more see Latimer, 256.

†The pseudonym not only lent authority to the work, it protected Mist as the publisher from government reprisals as a result of his known Jacobite sympathies and strong opposition to the Whig government of Robert Walpole. The choice of pseudonym was shrewd: a Captain Johnson was an actual Caribbean pirate in the 1680s. The evidence for Defoe's authorship was both historical and literary. Although the latter appears speculative and nugatory in retrospect, the former is no less confused: Defoe even worked for Mist until 1724, when the first volume of *A General History of Pyrates* was published. For more on Defoe, see Schonhorn; for more on Mist, see Bialuschewski, Black, and Rogers.

account of one Captain Misson appealing. He was one of many readers who over the years would single out those chapters as the best in the book (Novak, *Daniel Defoe* [i]).

Those chapters recount the story of a French pirate named Misson and his friendship with a defrocked Catholic priest, Caraccioli, and the pair's efforts to found a democratic utopian pirate republic on Madagascar. Misson's conversion to Caraccioli's deistic, socialist outlook provides a platform for the author's critique of British society, as well as a template for the pair's experiment in governance, the short-lived republic called Libertalia. Though the colony fails, destroyed by a surprise attack by natives, one aspect of Misson and Caraccioli's plan made it especially apropos of a post–Civil War perspective: their stance against slavery. When they take a Dutch ship, Misson orders the slaves found on board to be dressed in the clothing of the sailors, telling his men that "the Trading for those of our species, cou'd never be agreeable to the Eyes of divine Justice," with the author making the point explicitly that Misson "hop'd, he spoke the Sentiments of all his brave Companions, he had not exempted his Neck from the galling Yoak of Slavery, and asserted his own Liberty, to enslave others" (Schonhorn, *A General History* 403). The avowed abolitionist aspect of the pair's plans, along with the socialist government they establish, provided a compelling model for what Simms wanted to explore.

The author of *A General History* may have intended the story to be a veiled allegory indicting the Walpole government and, more generally, the "hypocrisy, injustice, and cowardice of his English society," as one critic put it (Schonhorn, *A General History* xxxvii), but Simms and other readers would have easily been misled about its veracity. The story opens with the bald assertion that it is drawn from "a *French* manuscript" (Schonhorn, *A General History* 383), and it closes with how that document was passed to the author (438). Simms referred to these directly when he had his character Caraccioli urge his friend Steel Cap to "read these letters to Misson, and note what they say. You will see what is expected of you, and what can be done" (61). Moreover the end of Misson's story occurs in the following chapter on Thomas Tew, a real privateer-cum-pirate (Schonhorn, *A General History* 419–39). Readers would have also been misled by the general tenor of the two chapters, which skillfully incorporate facts of pirate history along with explicit condemnation of British government corruption, attacks against slavery and the mistreatment of sailors, and a basic critique of poverty, all of which lend an air of verisimilitude, since these critiques inform the rest of the book as well (Novak, *Daniel Defoe;* Schonhorn, *A General History*). Additionally there are several historical figures named Caraccioli who could have inspired the depiction given in Misson's narrative, and the heresies ascribed to him are historically plausible if perhaps concatenated. No French pirate by the name of Misson has been identified, however.

The book may have supplied Simms with deeper insights as well. After a brutal fistfight, Steel Cap muses, "Fight! Fight! The perpetual thought of Englishman and Dane . . . as if all virtue lay in strength of muscle, and the will to inflict pain and suffering" (76). Thus the stage is set for a deeper clash between him and Caraccioli, not just over ideology, but methods. Here *A General History* might have supplied Simms with another useful example, Governor Woodes Rogers, who is credited with having ended the golden age of Bahamian piracy. Rogers created his plan for quelling the pirates after visiting Madagascar, site of Misson's fictional Libertalia but also a very real pirate haven, historically. His experience with the pirates there cemented his conviction that, as one historian put it, they were "lonely, forlorn men desperate to return to the motherly embrace of civilization, bowing again to the dictates of their country, Crown, and God" (Woodard, *The Republic* 163). He firmly believed that pirates could be cajoled, enticed, and if necessary punished into accepting the yoke of society once more; Rogers "was sure that with a careful combination of carrot and stick, a pirates' nest could be quelled, and a productive law-abiding society would rise in its place" (Woodard, *The Republic* 163). His approach did not entail the creation of a socialist utopia, but the parallels with what Simms sets forth in his story are intriguing.

Simms's repeated requests to northern friends for *A General History* clearly shows that he wanted to refresh his memory before continuing his story—as he noted in the first chapter, his intention was to write "a history," although as Sean Busick has observed, his use of that term encompassed a broad swath of literary efforts, including his fiction (*A Sober Desire* xii, 9). What he completed, however, was compelling.

When Simms set aside the manuscript of "The Brothers of the Coast" sometime in March 1866, he had reached a good stopping point. Though not technically a cliff-hanger, the close of chapter 9 was a fine hook to prompt a publisher to purchase the novel, and it marks a point in the narrative in which Simms had established his characters, plot, and major themes. Set in the failed British colony of the Bahamas in the early eighteenth century, the action takes place on the island of Nassau, in the town of New Providence. Simms's characters represent the gamut of European interests in the New World, hailing from Britain, France, Spain, and Portugal, along with Denmark, Italy, and Ireland; the range of countries makes the point that piracy is a universal response to European corruption. Piracy and outcasts are linked together, as responses on a meta level to the problems of the Old World, grown intractable and rotten—as the existence of piracy proves.

The plot plays off of the pirate confederation that flourished in the Bahamas during that time, a topic that enjoyed wide popular appeal among English and American readers in the eighteenth century and after (Woodard, *The Republic* 4, 26–27). Simms chose his title from the term adopted by those early Bahamian pirates, who called themselves *les frères de la côte,* the brothers, or brethren, of the coast, or just brethren (Latimer, *Buccaneers* 75). Brethren ships were famous for their democratic rule, a source of both their romanticized, popular appeal as well as their actual success: when Brethren ships attacked, often a part of the crew of their victims defected and joined the pirates. It was a powerful indictment of the privations and deep inequities of maritime service and is a principal theme in *A General History* as well.

Simms depicted New Providence as a settlement on the cusp of emerging into a society, a frontier beset by conflicting forces—and a topic long familiar to him, explored in so many of his works (Guilds and Collins, *William Gilmore Simms*). His protagonists range from commoners to pirates to merchants to exiled nobles, with a full range of humanity expressed within those strata, from virtuous to evil, with many complex shadings between those poles. All have one trait in common: each is missing something vital, whether physically or psychologically, and this loss drives their agendas and interactions. The story revolves around an exiled British nobleman, Edward (also called Mortimer) Cavendish, nicknamed Steel Cap, and his association with Caraccioli, called "historical" in the text based on Simm's reading of *A General History.* The heretical doctrines espoused by Caraccioli are the driving mechanism in the plot, forming the basis for what Steel Cap and he hope to accomplish: a democratic, egalitarian republic that will transform the pirates into law-abiding enlightened citizens, and Nassau —or another suitable site—into an independent socialist utopia.

The tensions on the island are legacies of its history, that of a failed plantation colony and a long-contested site of rival European imperial powers, and those provide a somber, cautionary backdrop for Simms's tale. The lawlessness of the island predominates: robbery and murder are never far from the surface, whether in the form of brigands—pirates operating on shore—or shrewd, amoral merchants, who also navigate the continuum from the legal but unethical to outright collusion with piracy. Indeed Simms's New Providence is a petri dish for emerging civilization, where the liminal space of the frontier contains all of the competing, contradictory impulses that define human nature, from an urge toward nihilistic freedom from all restraint to the expression of the highest bonds of responsibility and humanity.* Each character sketches part of that continuum. Cicily, the barmaid at the King's Image, is an orphan whose natural intelligence and inherently virtuous outlook vie with that of her employers, the shrewd and amoral Harridick and his wife. Their counterpart is the French merchant Le Vasseur and his wife. Le Vasseur's talents for trafficking with the pirates provide him with profits that he can log as entirely legitimate, and his association with Blackbeard provides one of the book's compelling, unresolved mysteries. Le Vasseur's wife is also a master of duplicity; she is the town's social maven, whose parties represent an uneasy neutral ground for her polyglot guests, masking the social tensions among inhabitants and also generating a comfortable income for their hostess from gambling and the sale of exclusive wares. And the constant presence of pirates, from commander to common seaman, provides the undercurrent of mystery and cloaked identity that creates much of the text's power.

The apex of that mystery is Steel Cap himself. The book begins with a plot by a trio of pirates to gain access to his stronghold, which is thwarted by Cicily's intervention, and ends with Madame Le Vasseur's partygoers escorting Steel Cap's wife back home in hopes of piercing the secrets of his domicile and presence on the island. In the intervening chapters, Simms illustrates his broader theme of the tensions of an emergent society with clashes and conflicts between his characters: Caraccioli's theories and Steel Cap's ambivalent acquiescence; Le Vasseur's trafficking with Blackbeard and his agenda, only obliquely revealed to his wife; Cicily's defense of right against the blind depredations of commerce; Steel Cap's exile and the privations it imposes on his beloved Geraldine. The pirates are no less nuanced, from Captain Ferrand's competition with Lieutenant Leonard to Thorfinn the Dane's inner turmoil over his occupation. For scholars the subtext of honor is especially telling, contributing to our understanding of the centrality of that idea as it played out in Simms's thought and work after the war, as Todd Hagstette has usefully explored ("Private vs. Public"). Several supporting characters make intriguing appearances, with enough of an outline to suggest roles that Simms may have already had in mind when he introduced them. But, in these nine chapters, what we have are the contours of a fine story with well-developed characters, one that may well have met the expectation that

*Here I am using *liminal* in the sense described by Victor Turner in his *The Forest of Symbols.*

it would be "equal to any thing I have yet done," as Simms wrote Duyckinck so excitedly in September 1865.

Simms reported to William Hawkins Ferris on March 24, 1866, that he had finished what exists today in the South Caroliniana Library. It constitutes nine chapters (the first labeled an introduction) spanning 173 pages (*Letters* 4:547), totaling 28,268 words.* Those small, fragile pages, a little over five by eight inches, many of them damaged by insects and age, tell much about the writing.†

In August 1865 Simms wrote to Duyckinck that "I have my brain seething ever and anon, with fresh conceptions, over which I brood at intervals, with a loving mood of meditation which makes them grow upon me, until the images become as familiar to the eye, as they have been to the mind" (*Letters* 4:515–16). It is a remarkable letter for many reasons, not least for its proximity to when he would begin to write "The Brothers of the Coast," but it also suggests that Simms tended to think his way through a story long before he set pen to paper. A comprehensive analysis of the manuscript exceeds the scope of this introduction, but a number of useful points emerge from a survey.

The first chapter of the manuscript shows few corrections: a steady, strong hand throughout suggests that the first fourteen pages were produced in one session, with increasing numbers of revisions, corrections, and interleavings beginning a third of the way through. At the end larger, darker letters and wider lines with minimal emendations show Simms's confidence: this is thoroughly thought out, with the lines showing a pen rushing to get the words down. The change in hand between those lines and chapter 2, whose hand also matches the revisions to the end of chapter 1, suggests that Simms reread the end of the earlier chapter before embarking on the second. Now into his plot, this chapter and its

*There are three prefatory pages that Simms did not count in this total, as well as some complicating aspects of paginating the manuscript, such as one page of extraneous essay material, clearly intended for another work, along with some extensive revisions that continued on the verso of some sheets. A full explication of these textual issues will be made possible by the digital edition of the manuscript to be published by the Simms Initiatives at the University of South Carolina.

†A total of 42 pages show damage that obliterates some part of the text, necessitating 305 conjectural editorial emendations. Fifteen pages contain one or two errors, and 27 contain three or more errors, 11 of which have ten or more errors. In a majority of instances, the context makes things clear; a small number required greater conjecture. A complete list of these emendations can be found online at the Simms Initiatives.

successor are in a tighter, smaller hand, as if he were writing carefully and more deliberately, a point emphasized by the revisions, which tend to be expansions.

Throughout the text, Simms revised for clarity as well as for aesthetics, and occasionally for organization, striking a paragraph or entire half page and then reworking much of the same material for later inclusion. It suggests that he had a range of modes or moods, from fast to measured, though more the former than the latter—a reflection of the difficult circumstances in which he had to work, buffeted by ill health, anxiety, and the demands of other writing. The revisions often differ in penmanship, showing that he tended to reread and revise earlier chapters while writing later ones, perhaps before embarking on them, or perhaps after, to bring earlier ones into line. Most of all, however, his revisions are thoughtful and consistent—and even more significant, they are comparatively rare: he did not rely on his muse to move his pen; he knew what he wanted to say before he put pen to paper, the result of the "loving mood of meditation" that he mentioned to Duyckinck.

There are exceptions. As the manuscript progressed, the revisions were occasionally more extreme. More words were struck out, but often in the same hand, suggesting that he revised more heavily as he worked, and larger pieces were elided, such as at the end of chapter 4, where he needed to set the stage for the introduction of Caraccioli. This is no surprise, and it shows how much Simms thought about charged issues like staging. There are even evocative expressions of those issues, when the power and emotion of the topic at hand weighted his pen strokes and tightened his hand. The materiality of the manuscript is palpable and revealing here.

Overall the handwriting suggests that Simms tended to write only one chapter at a sitting, though occasionally more; and in general he was indeed rushing to complete this first section of the book in a bid to secure serialization. What the manuscript reveals is proof of the contentions Simms made in his letters: that he rarely had time to devote sustained concentration to the project, but that he had indeed thought about it a great deal over the years—and, most incredibly, that his powers of concentration were capable of overcoming the privations and distractions of his straitened circumstances to a remarkable degree.

If the manuscript is revealing, the text is more so. Tracing the progression of the novel fragment demonstrates the sophistication and complexity of the themes that Simms was assaying. The text opens with the best chapter in the fragment. Adopting a bird's-eye view, the narrator provides a fine overview of the Bahamian archipelago, tracing its contours and touching on major events in its encounters with humanity, from the Mayan ruins of Cape Catoche to Columbus's arrival. It is significant that Simms joined those two events here: Columbus's voyage ended a mystery—what lay beyond the reaches of the Old World's maps—while the Mayan ruins of the Yucatan peninsula enshrined another. Like the cycles Simms saw in his reading of history and that he expressed so powerfully in his own work, the appearance of these mysteries is cyclical and inevitable, similar to the conflict and competition that define nature itself.

The chapter makes that point explicitly, drawing a reductive parallel between the pirates who populated the seas and their animal counterparts, the predators that form a natural part of any ecosystem. It is a portent of the conflicts that drive the plot of the text, along with the broader contexts—nature, geography, history—that Simms depicted here as governing those conflicts, impelling while encompassing their scope, defining their impact, and framing their meaning. Those conflicts and their contexts take place in a set of nested sites, beginning with this largest arena, the Bahamas themselves, where the struggle for empire between rival European powers gave rise to the pirates who form the subject of this story. From this macro view, the battle for empire, for dominion of the sea, or simply for plunder is nothing more than the struggle for supremacy that defines the clash between predator and prey. Nature colors all such conflict in the same shades, reducing it to the same primal binary of survival or death.

There is a neutrality to that view, making pirates appear no different than sharks or eagles, and in the second chapter the plotting of three pirates occurs on the water, in the harbor of New Providence. This is the second site of conflict: the seas that link the Bahamas and form this terraqueous landscape. One of the trio, Thorfinn the Dane, abhors violence and eschews drink, yet is a formidable fighter; this chapter revolves around the rules of piracy, which Thorfinn feels have no place on land, where his companions seek to murder and rob. On the open ocean, piracy makes sense to Thorfinn: there are rules, even if they are little more than those followed by any predator. But on land, even in a rough, lawless frontier such as Nassau, the rules of piracy do not obtain, as Thorfinn's uneasiness with his colleagues' machinations suggest.

Nassau is where all rules are in play, where society itself is in flux. The town of New Providence represents the last arena for struggle and contains the three primary sites of the text's action: Steel Cap's castle, Le Vasseur's house, and the tavern called the King's Image. Steel Cap's castle is the setting for the better part of two chapters, providing a stronghold that contains, barely, the stormy relationship between Steel Cap and his wife, Geraldine, as well as the complex interplay between Steel Cap and Caraccioli. The clash between Steel Cap and

Geraldine represents the tensions between civilization and exile, between society and the frontier, that Simms explores here as he did in so many of his works; but the erosions that Nassau's isolation imposes on Geraldine, and Steel Cap's obduracy in resisting those forces, suggest that new currents had emerged in Simms's thought. Scholars have argued that Simms's postwar novels represent a deeply pessimistic view of history that departed markedly from his fundamentally whiggish antebellum perspective (Moltke-Hansen, "When History Failed" 28–30); the chapters of "The Brothers of the Coast" underscore that reading, exploring how individuals navigate the demise of empire and maintain their humanity in a withering, debilitating social context. That context might contain signs of health—expressed in the form of individuals, endeavoring to behave honorably—but their efforts here appear to be ultimately doomed by a hostile environment, whose lawlessness represents a nihilistic entropy that threatens to consume all virtue, even as it provides a breeding ground for destructive philosophies, making them appear rational and appealing.

That seductiveness lies at the core of the complex relationship between Steel Cap and Caraccioli, whose interactions occupy chapter 5, the crux of the text. Another struggle plays out here, pitting Caraccioli's ideology against Steel Cap's philosophy, with the latter's unjust exile forcing him into an uneasy alliance with Caraccioli, whose deliberate, studied heresy precipitated his defrocking and excommunication. Simms created the book's most telling aside when he described the heart of Caraccioli's heresy: "It was the doctrine of Caraccioli that this evil [original sin] was solely the result of human training, false laws and habits of society, a corrupt religion, and the perpetual wrongs done, by authority, in the name of law and government. His doctrines, followed up in detail, would suffice to illustrate some of the more pernicious of our own times, which are indeed likely to obtain a fatal currency" (59).

Against this Steel Cap defends a natural, spiritual view of humanity that prizes friendship and places selflessness and reciprocity at the core of a philosophy that abhors force and abjures manipulation; this places him in conflict with Caraccioli's socialism, with its overlay of Communist utopianism that rationalizes the need for a war machine to defend and control the early stages of the experiment. This is the choice Simms presented with his pirates: to allow the natural progression of civilization to unfold—a process that has already turned Harridick from pirate into a landlord and caused Steel Cap to question his former occupation—or force its development, embracing an unnatural philosophy that portends only suffering, failure, and ruin.

Le Vasseur's house is the second site of conflict on the island. Its upper stories house his wife's grand parties, where pirates pretend to be gentlemen until the clock and the bottle erode that veneer, and the basement hides his shadowy business, allowing time and secrecy to transmogrify blood-soaked pirate booty into legitimate wares. Those themes also inform the last and greatest site of struggle on the island, the King's Image, the most complex symbol in the text.

Simms chose the name of his tavern carefully. The King's Image is both a historical reference and a literary allusion. It refers to John Milton's *Eikonoklastes,* a 1649 polemic indicting the *Eikon* (The King's Image), a book that venerates Charles I. Simms's reference is itself complex, filtered through his own attitude to Milton. As a poet Simms revered Milton, urging young poets to study him, among other greats, and always with a focus: to understand "by what art they evolve all the secrets in a subject" (*Letters* 6:237, 239). That line is revealing, explaining how, in Simms's view, poetry is designed to go to the heart of a subject, not skate lightly over the surface—and an especially telling injunction when considering the centrality of appearances and deceptions in "The Brothers of the Coast."

Milton remained a life-long influence on Simms (Brennan, *Poet's Holy Craft* 46–47). It is interesting to speculate that a younger Simms, especially during his brief foray into politics, might have found appealing Milton's stature as a polemicist—or at least the idea of the poet as a writer and shaper of public opinion. Still, if Simms was repulsed at the idea of the literary artist as pawn and propagandist, he may have been mindful of Milton's polemics when he wrote his own political sonnets, most notably his "Progress in America" series of poems penned in 1846, as Matthew Brennan has noted (*Poet's Holy Craft* 74–77).

Yet, however admirable Milton's poetry, the excesses of his politics were deeply troubling to Simms. *Eikonoklastes* is Milton's greatest polemic, his revolutionary treatise that systematically destroyed the *Eikon Basilike*—including the image itself, which Milton decried as "the conceited portraiture before his Book, drawn out to the full measure of a Masking Scene, and sett there to catch fools and silly gazers" (Hughes, *Complete Prose Works of John Milton* 3:342). Milton's obloquy does more than merely dismiss fools, it inveighs against those who "imbastardiz'd from the ancient nobleness of their Ancestors, are ready to fall flatt and give adoration to the Image and Memory of this Man, who hath offer'd at more cunning fetches to undermine our Liberties, and putt Tyranny into an Art, than any British King before him" (3:344). Ultimately *Eikonoklastes* makes the case for iconoclasm as fundamental to Milton's view of history, destroying the image of Charles I visually as the frontispiece and rhetorically in the text in an attempt to "free history from the tyranny of the king's image," as David Loewenstein has concluded: "Iconoclasm for Milton is consequently a profoundly radical, creative, and liberating response that cannot be divorced from his sense of history: it represents his attempt to undermine an entrenched ideological and historical perspective, so as to bring about a regenerated social order and a whole new mode of social vision" (*Milton and the Drama of History* 51). And that is precisely how Simms depicted Caraccioli and his seductive, utopian fallacy—and, closer to home, how he described the North's conquest of the South in the Civil War, in his *Sack and Destruction of the City of Columbia, S.C.* (Meriwether, "Simms's Civil War"). No wonder he chose the King's Image as the name designating one of the primary sites of struggle in the text.

Milton's sense of history was radical; Simms's was not, but they did share deeply held beliefs about the importance of the process of history and the power of the poet to engage with it. This engagement was more profound than just topical. Milton's radicalism was an expression of "his sense of active performance in the contemporary historical moment," as David Loewenstein has stated (*Milton and the Drama of History* 1). Both writers saw themselves as active shapers of historical consciousness, and that activity was not removed, but immediate—what Loewenstein has said of Milton applies equally to Simms, that his work shows an "acute sense of the urgencies and conflicts which both generate and thwart historical renovation in his age—and with the literary responses that historical consciousness provokes" (*Milton and the Drama of History* 1). But where Milton's iconoclasm was direct, deliberate, and revolutionary, reclaiming the king's image from idolatry and defacing it, Simms's king's image—the sign outside of the tavern—is faded by time and the erosions of the elements. It is defaced by nature, not people, as surely as nature eroded the Mayan ruins Simms shrouded in mystery in the opening chapter, a somber reminder of the dust that will inevitably reclaim all human effort.

Milton's polemic was itself the product of the kind of clash that Simms depicted between Steel Cap's and Caraccioli's views of history and humanity. Simms used Steel Cap's wife, Geraldine, to summarize the pair's aims, responding to Steel Cap's remonstration: "Why do you persist in reminding me, Geraldine, that I am an exile, that—but enough! You already partly know my objects here" (54). Her knowledge of those plans may be incomplete, but she knows enough to retort:

> Yes; and think them a sort of madness. Between you and this Italian Signior, you dream dreams which will sink your vessel. You would change the world

> would you, with your philosophies. You think man may become a perfect creature under your wise administration. You would emancipate him from all the restraints of law and the teaching of all the ages and peoples for a thousand years. You ascribe all his vices and misfortunes to the vice of authority, the tyranny of rulers, wicked counsellors and stupid laws. And you would persuade the lawless men who gather here, to become virtuous under your wiser maxims. You would convert these thousand islands into a commonwealth, and realize every fancy of your Platos and Sidneys. And so, between you and this Italian Signior, this priest whose philosophy has got the better of his religion, you lose yourselves in dreams which you can never realize in action. (55)

Simms's point is clear: ideology will never succeed. It echoes his dismissal of another utopian scheme, much closer to home: John Locke's *Fundamental Constitutions of Carolina* (ca. 1669), which Simms labeled "the crude conception of a mind conversant rather with books than men—with the abstract rather than the practical in government and society" (*History of South Carolina* 48). For Simms, any attempt to implement ideology is doomed. Nature, whether in the form of time's passage or as an expression of the immutable laws of human and animal behavior, will always resurface and ultimately prevail—which is why the signs the Spanish conquest rule of New Providence have decayed, leaving only ruins and the palimpsest that appears on the other side of the bleached sign identifying the King's Image. That decay is a sign of what is already happening to British rule as it sinks beneath the weight of its own moral turpitude and corruption. No imposition of ideology is necessary to facilitate the process.

Caraccioli's views are not just divorced from history, they are also deeply iconoclastic. The king's image, as a phrase, literally means the face of rule. The threat of iconoclasm is the danger it to the rule of law itself, not just to royalty. Lana Cable has explained, "As royal advisors had uneasily sensed at least as early as the reign of Edward VI, icon-manipulation entails great risks. On a purely practical level, once the iconoclast succeeds in rupturing primitive or naïve belief in the icon, no rationale and no substitute icon can be assumed to recapture the same quality of belief. If the worshipper can witness demolition of the crucifix, he can conceive as well destruction of the King's sign, and ultimately, destruction of the King himself" ("Milton's Iconoclastic Truth" 135). The text makes the same point about the vicissitudes of politics, which branded a hero, Steel Cap, with the stigma of exile. Steel Cap's castle is a mausoleum of lost nobility, where aging mirrors mock him and Geraldine with a faded reflection of their former status, which is described in a telling passage:

> A lute in a corner, a few books upon tables, indicated, or would seem to indicate, unwonted taste for such a region; and yet the anomalies are not infrequent which require us to recognize the assassin in the sentimentalist, the midnight burglar occasionally in the guitar or flute player, and the bookworm in scores of Eugene Arams. At all events, the ordinary and natural thought wonders to see the evidences of taste, art and a high civilization in the wild region of the Bahamas some two hundred years ago. Yet despotisms which drive heroism, patriotism, and all the virtues into exile, may also be supposed to expel from its domains the cultivated tastes, the fine fancies, the highest attributes of art and genius. (52)

Once the natural order is upset, the ensuing destruction cuts deeply, and this is what Simms suggested will result from Caraccioli's schemes. However appealing those schemes may be to someone who has lost his religion, such as Caraccioli, and however understandable their appeal might be to someone who has lost his country, such as Steel Cap, these utopian theories are only that, notions, born of an ill-conceived and deeply flawed view of history, that appeal only to damaged, flawed adherents. Indeed the danger of those theories stems from their beguiling seductiveness, which Simms likened to a serpent's eyes, with the same outcome, death, as foretold by the ruins he describes in the first chapter, stern and silent and imposing.

Simms set forth several other themes in his nine chapters, chief among them the idea of humans' social roles and its complex relationship to identity, anonymity, and agendas. Each of his characters has a role to play in this emerging society, just as do the sharks and predators focused on in the opening chapter; what those roles could accomplish, and how that could appear in the eyes of history, was what Simms was exploring.

In the text names and anonymity underscore the theme of roles and identity. When the three pirates are plotting their crime in chapter 2, one of them exclaims, "Steel Cap can't be his real name. It's a shy!"—prompting the response, "And who's got a *real* name among all these people here?" (42). Some characters have only a given name, some only a surname, some several names. Simms listed Steel Cap twice in his list of characters that precedes the first chapter in the manuscript; later in the book, after noting that Caraccioli addresses him as Mortimer, he remarked in an authorial aside that "there is a mystery in all these several names which we cannot yet fathom" (60).

Just as names may obscure identity, anonymity obfuscates accountability, making it a highly prized commodity in criminal enterprise. That defines the economy of New Providence, from the pirates drinking away their spoils and guilt in the King's Image to Blackbeard's collusion with Le Vasseur's mercantile trade. Names only signify roles as flags do ships, however, often hiding agendas like cargoes—or their origins. Barney Britton is also called Harridick, the landlord of the King's Image; his loss of a leg "had the effect of converting a bold boarder into a shrewd and money making landlord" (38). His deeper loss—that of his homeland—can be seen in the way he prized British newspapers (and yet another interesting connection with Nathaniel Mist and British printing at the time, which Simms praised in an aside as more advanced than in other countries). Steel Cap defines the other pole of British exile, that of a lord whose noble service as a privateer was later branded by politics as piracy, and like Harridick his loss is symbolized by a physical one, the loss of part of his skull from a combat wound. Steel Cap's injury is one that human surgery could not heal, though Simms pointedly noted that nature is slowly doing so; until then it leaves him prone to devastating seizures.

Steel Cap's is the most graphic weakness, but each character projects the vulnerability that stems from loss. Cicily is an orphan, attempting to cobble together an education from the rude circumstances of her surroundings. Harridick's wife is overly fond of her own rum punch—and her role in her husband's shady, frontier business also echoes with the theme of concealed roles, as she excels in obscuring the defects of local fare in her cuisine. Clym, Steel Cap's servant, lacks judgment, a defect that in him occasions the same unintended and potentially disastrous outcome that Caraccioli's own lack of judgment portends on a much grander scale. Caraccioli's is the worst defect; he is someone who has learned the wrong lessons from his own mistakes, and from those that he has observed, and who tries to persuade himself as well as others of the rectitude of his extremism. When he ends his peroration to Steel Cap, describing how "our empire shall be one of unmixed freedom, and unblighted innocence, such as made the fabled happiness of Eden, and constituted the secret of the fabulous Age of Gold!," Simms made his self-delusion clear: "His eye was bright as that of the serpent . . . Here was the enthusiast, in conflict, as well as unison, with the philosopher!" (60). Caraccioli's ability to persuade the pirates to his way of thinking is proven; as Thorfinn tells Steel Cap, "He's a fine talker. He's got the heart, and the sense" (75). But Caraccioli's real plans—his actual agenda—remain concealed, like the plot to rob Clym.

Thorfinn and his two comrades are pirates, but Thorfinn alone possesses the moral insight to question his occupation, even as he upholds what he views as the tenets of its code. That is why he refuses to participate in his companions' plot, but will come to their aid if need be—and never reveal their names to the authorities. What he lacks is knowledge of an alternative worldview: when Steel Cap lectures him on friendship, he responds positively, saying "You talk strange things, but your voice is honest as a clear bell, from a great church tower, high up in the air, with its gold peak pointing to the stars" (75). It is an exchange that also underscores the gulf between Steel Cap's sermons and Caraccioli's heresies.

What Thorfinn is missing can be supplied; this is what a healthy society can do. For Simms this was how a frontier could develop into a successful society and ultimately become a proud civilization, by strengthening its citizens, shoring up their weaknesses, compensating for or filling in what they are missing. A nation or state may succeed for a time despite its shortcomings, but if it lacks that firm moral compass, then even the greatest empire can fall, just as the American colonists could defeat the vastly superior strength of Great Britain because they had right on their side. When Simms wrote of Le Vasseur, "He could have carried his books into the Admiralty with safety, even while his customers were hanging at the yard-arm, and been absolved from all connection with them" (79), it was more than just a classic expression of the Jeffersonian view of England's debasement: it suggests how a successful empire nonetheless incubated the seed of its own destruction. In this Simms was expressing a central tenet of his approach to writing history, which was the cyclical nature of a society's moral progress: societies went through periods of greater and lesser morality, even though their material progress proceeded unabated. Similarly his depiction of England's corruption, from the injustice of Steel Cap's exile to the amorality of Le Vasseur's quite legal commerce with English banks, describes the Jeffersonian belief that England represented both the peak of civilization's technological and industrial prowess and the nadir of moral bankruptcy (Busick, *A Sober Desire* 4). This plays out on a microcosmic scale, as well in the King's Image itself, a neutral site where competing interests can play out their hands, side by side: one, toward stability and society; the other, toward drinking and cards—vice. Simms was making the point that capitalism is ethically neutral, with the potential for both good and evil.

That potential could be difficult to see. The play of image over substance, appearance versus reality, is a constant theme in the text, highlighted by the prominence of masks, names, roles, and identities. Insight is what allows us to discern the difference between appearance and reality, which Simms drove home in his opening chapter by noting the continuing value of the Spanish piece of eight. Spanish rule may have decayed, but the old Spanish coin, the piece of eight, was still valued, suggesting that underlying kings and reigns are the constancy of human nature and fundamental needs. Silver's value is real, unlike paper currency, which relies on "plausibilities in pictured papers" (38). Though Simms had lived through the hyperinflation and collapse of Confederate currency, his point was that silver is authentic, enduring, substantive: everything that contrasts with kings, nation states, and signs, which are all imagery—surfaces, not substance. When those bills bear the face of a sovereign, it powerfully connects to the idea of the king's image, the portrait of Charles I that Milton attacked in the most visible and visceral argument in the struggle to define the British monarchy and the nature of government itself in seventeenth-century England. The American Civil War defined the nature of government in the United States, destroying the South's bid for independence as it did the value of Confederate currency. "The Brothers of the Coast" asks how government can be defined in the wake of empire, probing the deeper nature of the rule of law as it relates to nature, human nature, and history.

The text suggests three possibilities. The first is lawlessness: crime is one response to the loss of rule, symbolized by the attack on Clym by Thorfinn's comrades and, significantly, by their ultimate purpose, to rob Steel Cap's castle, a last outpost of European culture and refinement. Without law, force is the only rule: this is why Harridick sees no reason to intervene in the plot to rob Clym until Cicily points out the consequences of incurring Steel Cap's wrath. Harridick may be on shore now, but he still respects only power, reminding us of the pirate he once was. A second possibility is the disastrous scheme of Caraccioli, a corrupt manipulation that exploits the voids that the lack of civil government provides on the island and that the practice of piracy has created in the inhabitants. The third possibility is that in time a healthy society may emerge. Simms provides a glimpse of this with the final image of the first chapter, the inchoate and ambiguous symbol of a tavern. It is an early sign of stability, where a seaman comes to shore and a pirate becomes a tavernkeeper, a continuum Simms made explicit. Neither is that continuum necessarily external. When Simms described Steel Cap's furnishings, he invoked one of England's notorious criminals, Eugene Aram. Human nature spans good and evil, often in the same person, as Aram proved: what is his identity—great scholar or common murderer?

The text makes the point that the King's Image, like New Providence as a whole, is a site where the illicit becomes licit, where piracy becomes commerce as ill-gotten gains get spent legitimately, where sailors gamble and drink to oblivion, and where crime is plotted and thwarted. Ultimately the chapter is about the frontier of civilization, the borders of empire, where good and evil coexist and contend in a neutral site, where the rule of law is as faded as the reign and face of the king.

This is why "The Brothers of the Coast" shows the potential for becoming what it did not: Simms's most trenchant example of what Sean Busick has correctly identified as his concern with "portraying the clash—and sometimes the decline—of civilizations" rather than "progressive nationalist narratives like those of George Bancroft" (*A Sober Desire* 91). After the Civil War, a Bancroftian view of the conflict, and perhaps all of American history, was impossible for Simms. At heart "The Brothers of the Coast" is about government—or, rather, the politics and ideologies that shape governments—but Simms framed this as a deeper search for perspective: how do humans respond to and understand tragedy and defeat, both individually and collectively? Everyone in the novel is damaged in some way; all represent responses to the stresses of their circumstances. Beneath their foibles lies a greater, universal need for stability and protection. As Simms made plain in the book, this can be found only in cooperation: society requires a gestalt, one that must be moored in the arts and in farming and legitimate commerce, to thrive—which is the only way for people to heal and to fill in those missing pieces. All that is required to see that is the right one: the one with which he opened the book and which gathered the Bahamas together and allows us to see time and history and nature as interconnected—and, most significantly, that could calm "the most feverish and impatient heart," for his readers and for Simms.

Death haunts "The Brothers of the Coast" from its introductory chapter till the end of the fragment. It opens with images of death and decay—the Yucatan ruins and the predators, human and animal, that populate and define the area—and ends with dire hints of Lieutenant Ferrand's impending demise, part of the barely repressed violence that threatens even the most civil gathering in Nassau. Death is the inevitable end of all human projects, just as it is of all life, as Simms commented to Lawson in late 1869: "Death is of course. Life & Death are but chapters in the same volume" (*Letters* 5:287). If death was no secret to Simms, he had a keen appreciation for how its appearance could create one, making lives disappear and civilizations vanish. This is why the text opens with a secret—the profound mystery of the Yucatan ruins—and ends with an assault on one, as the partygoers approach Steel Cap's castle, bent on unmasking the secret of that house and its owner.

Simms abandoned the story there, enshrining that secret in the most palpable way possible and leaving readers to ponder, with so much of the story committed to paper, why not finish? Given what we know of Simms's circumstances, it is tempting to speculate that the task of resolving the novel was too arduous: the allegory was too direct; the outcome too painful. And, too, he wanted to consult *A History of the Pyrates* before continuing, as he made plain in so many letters. But economics provide the best answer. His letters reveal an author looking for a publisher for any story: *Joscelyn* and *Voltmeier* proceeded because they had publishers willing to pay. Perhaps Simms was the victim of his own success, for the market for those kinds of historical romances was well established; perhaps publishers felt that a war-torn populace simply craved a sense of continuity, an escape into a comforting past that presaged a positive future, as opposed to a doomed one. That may have been true of their author as well: it was easier to root stories in familiar soil, at a time when the concentration necessary for new imaginings was so precious, buffeted by anxiety. As late as December 1866, Simms complained to Duyckinck that "I have on hand several chapters of a Pirate Story,—and I have in my head the plan of another tale of the Revolution. Nothing but the anxious, desultory and comfortless life which I have been living since the war, could have kept me from the preparation of both of these stories" (*Letters* 4:625).

However true, what is likely is that, given a publisher's commitment, Simms would have returned to his pirates: as his postwar output demonstrates, a contract produced concentration. Even before the war, this was often his process, writing enough of a work to tempt a publisher to offer a contract and finishing only then. It is also important to keep in mind that it took him twenty years to mine successfully the materials he gathered on his 1847 hunting trip, which fueled *Joscelyn* (1867), *The Cub of the Panther* (1869), and *Voltmeier* (1869). "The Brothers of the Coast" provides another indication of his creative process: he would work until concentration was broken, either by the fulfillment of the original burst of inspiration, a logjam in the narrative, or the demands of another deadline—or just the anxieties and privations of postwar South Carolina, as he remarked in his letters.

That process also tells us something of Simms's powers of concentration: once engaged, those powers allowed him to return to a story much later and complete it. He first mentioned *The Cassique of Kiawah* in 1845; twelve years would pass before he completed it. He also left *Vasconselos* for a lengthy break before finishing it; indeed the parallels between it and "The Brothers of the

Coast" are obvious when we read his letter to Hart in 1851, where he admitted that *Vasconselos* "is about one third written, and has been for some time lying by me; but if encouraged, I should resume the story and press forward to conclusion" (*Letters* 6:117–18). This is not to deprecate the very real concern he showed for refreshing his memory of *A History of the Pyrates* before continuing "The Brothers of the Coast." As a historian, Simms relied on his sources for information, just as a writer he found inspiration in those sources as well. When he finally got his copy of *A General History of the Pyrates* in October 1869, he wrote to Duyckinck to thank him, saying that "My brain still seethes with thought, and my designs fill my dreams. I am temporarily forbidden to endeavor to develope them at the desk. It is possible that the world will see them yet" (*Letters* 5:262).

That did not happen, but his letter shows that he was still thinking about the novel only months before his death, and that seems to indicate more than just an author who wanted to tie up loose ends. It suggests how powerfully the story appealed to him and how important its resolution was despite his infirmity. That may be the most important aspect of "The Brothers of the Coast" to scholars: as the last, most important unfinished artistic business of its author's life, a responsibility to his muse, to the sweat equity of his concentration, that he sought to honor and fulfill even on his death bed.

Throughout his postwar writings, we see Simms grappling with the aftermath of the war and the lessons he sought in the wreckage. But there is more than just an allegory of the Civil War and Simms's own role in it animating the story set forth in "The Brothers of the Coast." Like the sites of struggle for his characters in the book, the text was itself a site of struggle for its author, a narrative whose creation represented a major part of his postwar thought. Though unfinished, the narrative shows Simms weaving anew the diverse strands of his theology, philosophy, and sense of history, refracted by the baleful lens of Reconstruction, but determined, as always, to look unflinchingly at human behavior and wrestle sense from it. The haunting aspect of "The Brothers of the Coast" is that we have only a sketch of what those lessons might have been for him and for us.

Works Cited

Bialuschewski, Arne. "Daniel Defoe, Nathaniel Mist, and *The General History of the Pyrates.*" *Papers of the Bibliographical Society of America* 98, no. 1 (2004): 21–38.

Black, Jeremy. "An Underrated Journalist: Nathaniel Mist and the Opposition Press during the Whig Ascendency." *British Journal for Eighteenth-Century Studies* 10, no. 1 (1987): 27–41.

Busick, Sean. *A Sober Desire for History: William Gilmore Simms as Historian.* Columbia: University of South Carolina Press, 2005.

Brennan, Matthew C. *The Poet's Holy Craft: William Gilmore Simms and Romantic Verse Tradition.* Columbia: University of South Carolina Press, 2010.

Cable, Lana, "Milton's Iconoclastic Truth." In David Loewenstein and James Grantham Turner, eds., *Politics, Poetics and Hermeneutics in Milton's Prose.* Cambridge: Cambridge University Press, 1990. 135–51.

Cordingly, David. Introduction. In Charles Johnson, *A General History of the Robberies and Murders of the Most Notorious Pirates.* 1724. Reprinted, Guilford, Conn.: Lyons Press, 2010. vii–xiv.

Exquemelin, Alexander O. *The Buccaneers of America.* Trans. A. Brown. Mineola, N.Y.: Dover Publications, 2000.

Faust, Drew Gilpin. *This Republic of Suffering: Death and the American Civil War.* New York: Alfred A. Knopf, 2008.

Gosse, Philip, ed. *A General History of the Robberies and Murders of the Most Notorious Pirates.* By Daniel Defoe as"Captain Charles Johnson." Kensington: Philip Sainsbury, 1925.

Guilds, John Caldwell. *Simms: A Literary Life.* Fayetteville: University of Arkansas Press, 1992.

———, ed. *Long Years of Neglect: The Work and Reputation of William Gilmore Simms.* Fayetteville: University of Arkansas Press, 1988.

Guilds, John Caldwell, and Caroline Collins, eds. *William Gilmore Simms and the American Frontier.* Athens: University of Georgia Press, 1997.

Hagstette, Todd. "Private vs. Public Honor in Wartime South Carolina: William Gilmore Simms in Lecture, Letter, and History." In David Moltke-Hansen, ed., *William Gilmore Simms's Unfinished Civil War.* Columbia: University of South Carolina Press, 2013. 48–67.

Hughes, Merritt Y., ed. *The Complete Prose Works of John Milton.* Vol. 3: *1648–1649.* New Haven: Yale University Press, 1962.

Hughson, Shirley Carter. "The Carolina Pirates and Colonial Commerce, 1670–1740." *Johns Hopkins University Studies in Historical and Political Science.* 12th series (May–July 1894): 241–370.

Kibler, James Everett, Jr., and David Moltke-Hansen. "The Man of Letters as Critic." In James Everett, Jr., and David Moltke-Hansen, eds., *Literature and Civilization: Selected Reviews by William Gilmore Simms.* Columbia: University of South Carolina Press, 2014. 1–12.

Knachel, Philip A., ed. *Eikon Basilike: The Portraiture of His Sacred Majesty in His Solitudes and Sufferings.* Ithaca, N.Y.: Cornell University Press, 1966.

Latimer, Jon. *Buccaneers of the Caribbean: How Piracy Forged an Empire.* Cambridge: Harvard University Press, 2009.

Loewenstein, David. *Milton and the Drama of History: Historical Vision, Iconoclasm, and the Literary Imagination.* Cambridge: Cambridge University Press, 2009.

Marx, Karl, and Friedrich Engels. *The Communist Manifesto.* Trans. Samuel Moore. Notes and introduction by Gareth Stedman Jones. New York: Penguin Books, 2002.

Meats, Stephen B. "Artist or Historian: William Gilmore Simms and the Revolutionary South." In Samuel B. Proctor, ed., *Eighteenth-Century Florida and the Revolutionary South.* Gainsville: University of Florida Press, 1978. 94–109.

Meriwether, Nicholas G. "Simms's Civil War: History, Healing, and *The Sack and Destruction of Columbia, S.C.*" *Studies in the Literary Imagination* 42, no. 1 (2009): 97–120.

———. "Simms's *The Lily and the Totem:* 'History for the Purposes of Art.'" *Long Years of Neglect: The Work and Reputation of William Gilmore Simms.* Ed. John Caldwell Guilds. Fayetteville: University of Arkansas Press, 1988. 76–105.

———. "An Unfinished Reconstruction: Simms's 'The Brothers of the Coast.'" In David Moltke-Hansen, *William Gilmore Simms's Unfinished Civil War.* Columbia: University of South Carolina Press, 2013. 185–201.

Moltke-Hansen, David. "Ordered Progress: The Historical Philosophy of William Gilmore Simms." *Long Years of Neglect: The Work and Reputation of William Gilmore Simms.* Ed. John Caldwell Guilds. Fayetteville: University of Arkansas Press, 1988. 126–47.

———. "When History Failed: William Gilmore Simms's Artistic Negotiation of the Civil War's Consequences." In David Moltke-Hansen, ed., *William Gilmore Simms's Unfinished Civil War: Consequences for a Southern Man of Letters.* Columbia: University of South Carolina Press, 2013. 3–31.

———, ed. *William Gilmore Simms's Unfinished Civil War: Consequences for a Southern Man of Letters.* Columbia: University of South Carolina Press, 2013.

Novak, Maximillian E., ed. *Daniel Defoe of Captain Misson.* 1728; reprint, Augustan Reprint Society Publication 87. Los Angeles: William Andrews Clark Memorial Library, University of California, Los Angeles, 1961.

Rogers, Pat. "Nathaniel Mist, Daniel Defoe, and the Perils of Publishing." *Library: Transactions of the Bibliographical Society* 10, no. 3 (2009): 298–313.

Schonhorn, Manuel, ed. *A General History of the Pyrates.* Attributed erroneously to Daniel Defoe. Columbia: University of South Carolina Press, 1972.

Simms, William Gilmore. "The Brothers of the Coast." Charles Carroll Simms Collection, South Caroliniana Library, University of South Carolina.

———. *The Cassique of Kiawah.* New York: Redfield, 1859.

———. *The History of South Carolina, from Its First European Discovery to Its Erection into a Republic: With a Supplementary Book, Bringing the Narrative Down to the Present Time.* New York: Redfield, 1860.

———. *Joscelyn; A Tale of the Revolution.* 1867. In John Caldwell Guilds, ed., *The Writings of William Gilmore Simms. Centennial Edition.* Vol. 16. Introduction and explanatory notes by Stephen Meats. Text established by Keen Butterworth. Columbia: University of South Carolina Press, 1975.

———. *The Letters of William Gilmore Simms.* Ed. Mary C. Simms Oliphant et al. 6 vols. Columbia: University of South Carolina Press, 1952–82.

———. "The Pirate Hoard. A 'Long Shore Legend." *Graham's Magazine* 48, (January 1856): 54–59; (February 1856): 124–31; (March 1856): 224–29; (April 1856): 344–51.

———. "The Pirates and Palatines: A Legend of North-Carolina." *Magnolia* 1 (July 1842): 32.

———. *Southward Ho! A Spell of Sunshine.* New York: Redfield, 1854.

———. *Voltmeier; or, the Mountain Men.* In John Caldwell Guilds, ed. *The Writings of William Gilmore Simms.* Centennial Edition. Vol. 1. Introduction and explanatory notes by Donald Davidson and Mary C. Simms Oliphant. Text established by James B. Meriwether. Columbia: University of South Carolina Press, 1969.

Turner, Victor. "Betwixt and Between: The Liminal Period in Rites de Passage." In Victor Turner, *The Forest of Symbols: Aspects of Ndembu Ritual.* Ithaca, N.Y.: Cornell University Press, 1967. 93–111.

Woodard, Colin. *The Republic of Pirates.* New York: Harcourt, 2007.

The Brothers of the Coast

A Pirate Story

CHAPTER I

Introduction

Could we command the wings of any one of these great white sea birds which we behold, continually hovering around us, and rise to the adequate elevation, we should behold a picture of these Bahama islands such as would fill the heart with content, the most feverish and impatient heart; and enliven and unkindle, to activity and delight, the most languid and unimpressible Fancy.

Assuming for a moment, the possession of this wing, and having attained this elevation, we behold spread before us a thousand miles of islet and island, and grey key and bald rock, half-buried, each in the embrace of its own billows, as with a belt of blue; and rejoicing in such fruits and flowers, as might well compensate the most heroic enterprise and excite the most languid spirit. Far as the eye can sketch, following the flight of flocks of great sea birds, all bound as if it were to some chosen and well known realm of their own, these little coral gems of land and rock rise suddenly out of the deep, to intercept the horizon, already on the strain, and to rest the wing already wearied from its flight. Some of them are simply gray specks upon the surface of the sea, to be submerged by inrolling waters, when the ocean swells with storm and dilates in fury; others are long lines of habitable realm; covered with shrub and fruit trees, filling the air with fragrance, which the winds shall waft in blessing to less favored regions.

From that eminence you gain glimpses, on one hand, of the lovely shores of the Cuban; on the other of the long and narrow capes of the Floridian; and, if your elevation be sufficiently great, and your eye sufficiently keen, like that of pelican or osprey, the horn of Yucatan, or Cape Cotoche, projects beneath your gaze, a sad realm of mystery and shadow whose wondrous ruins enshrine a secret of probably five thousand years!

Verily, a spacious and beautiful empire; an archipelago second to none, of lovely retreat and loving solitude; a vast empire of the sun, upon which, pouring down his most fruitful beams, he grafts his flowers upon the *basserest* of rock, and from their clefts, draws out the slender tree which brings the fruits of the tropics to perfection in the progress of the briefest season.

Follow these thousand avenues of sea, through these myriad barriers of rocky islet, and you penetrate from realm to realm, finding in each some compensation for your toil, and rewards in the survey alone, by all the charms of a full-bosomed beauty, reposing in the embraces of a voluptuous sun. Mark now the progress of this grand procession of white birds, great winged creatures that swim and soar, and dive and run, alternately, as they wind their way through narrow channels, among scores of these rocky islets, or dunes of sand and sea shell, on and on, steadily pursuing a fixed route, as if to a select and long inhabited empire of their own. They conduct you finally to a region to which we propose to direct our own step, one of equal obscurity and notoriety, as well in past as in present times. You pass with them into the channels which lead immediately to a little realm, an island of small size, but large in comparison with hundreds in the same region; which the red man held to be one of his paradisal domains, but which the white man soon converted into a seat of sin and suffering. Yet he, too, because of the rest it gave him, and the peace it promised, called it his Providence; and there, without a law, he planted his habitations; and there, without the banner of a nation, he revelled in all the insolences of a prince!

Pursuing your objects of vision, from your ideal height, you suddenly behold a great white form, looking very like a sea bird also, with immense white wings outspread, rounding one of the thousand islands which present a front, at once wooing and defensive, to the billows of the gulph; a long slip of land or rock, utterly obscure, yet singularly powerful in recalling a grand history. That islet is Guanahani, San Salvador, or Cat Island, the first spot of the new world which held out a feeble light, at midnight, to the straining eyes of Christopher Columbus, making his way blindly, but with heart of faith, through the uncertain channels of the unknown deep. Even now, that which seems to your remote vision a great bird, is a war ship of Europe, filled with European men; and she presses forward, making her way to one of the several passages which conduct to New Providence. And, as you gaze, you behold another, and yet another, of these great vessels, though from opposite courses, and far apart from each other, all tending in the same direction.

And, were you on board one of these vessels, you would behold, even as you are about to enter one or other of the channels which are to conduct you to your port, another of these goodly looking ships; and she would appear, framed to your eyes, as by the framing of a picture, through a vast opening in the solid rock. Such is the picturesque medium through which you look forth upon the ocean, through the arched passage of abaca, and behold, possibly, in the approaching vessel, an enemy whose rival cannon you run, and prepare yourself to encounter with the broadsides of your own.

Briefly, your eye, surveying the vast amphitheatre which groups together, in one grand frame work, the Bahamas and the Great Antilles, takes in a wondrous panoramic procession of white sails, (as of white birds) all pressing forward, though from opposite points of the compass, in the one direction of New Providence. That island, at the period of which we write, was the great harbouring place for all European birds of prey. It was this grand receptacle for the pirates and discontents of the Old World; the bold, audacious, reckless adventurers, who grew finally to be so strong as to write themselves into a powerful fraternity, calling themselves the Brothers of the Coast. They are trooping forever in their ships to and fro, giving themselves but little rest, and denying rest to others. They come and go, perpetually, rounding the Capes of Florida, from the British colonies along the Atlantic; from the golden realm of the Spanish main they make their way; from a thousand regions which, like many of these *Cayos* (keys) and islets, seem designed only for the harbourage of birds of prey; moral sharks, and eagles, and cormorants; vultures of all degrees and sizes, from the little hawk that preys upon the sparrow to the mighty Condor of the Andes, which carries off, on great pinions, the fattest ewe of all the flocks! They are then, at the period through which you take your survey of the scene, speeding or hovering in scores along the deep; seeking each some spoil or victim; frequently singly, and with a desperate hardihood, that goes forth even in a cockle shell, or cutter; slight of build, and conveying its ten men only; to the great ship of thirty guns; and, anon, uniting their beaks and talons in a savage foray on some common prey. Thus uniting their powers, they have on occasion come forth, with a grand armament, sometimes of no less than fifty war vessels in a line.

These, under names of different nations, are the lineal successors of the Vikings, the Sea-Dragons of the Northmen; having all their keen appetite for plunder; their reckless hardihood; their audacious courage; their unscrupulous avarice; their utter scorn of human sensibilities and suffering. And though the skies thicken, so that we may no longer trace their progress along the deep; and the winds rise and threaten the ocean with their lash; these scattered prowlers whom we have watched will all soon congregate together safely in the harbour of Nassau. Well do they know these avenues of sea. They have mapped each one in blood! They knew them as well three hundred years ago as we do now. Nor were these spoilers then held to be the criminals which we should pronounce them now. Great kings gave them, in many cases, their credentials to persecute and plunder! Under the Great Seal of State, they were commissioned to open the arteries of rival nations. The blood of princes and nobles has not unfrequently filled the veins of their chieftains, and the honours of knighthood were not unfrequently accorded to some of their most savage leaders, as a reward for deeds of as much infamy as *valeur.* It was the season when "deeds of derring-do" were deemed sufficiently to atone for the atrocities of the outlaw; when it was proclaimed, "There is no peace beyond the line;" and when one powerful European nation, like some great leviathan, had outraged the rest of Europe by its power of excesses, that, as by common instruct, they all seemed to single her out as a common enemy; and, like a sword fish armed against the whale, lost no opportunity to pierce her sides with their sharp weapons, making up, by their celerity and audacity, for their lack of bulk and armament!

Nassau was then but a scattered hamlet. Its dwellings dotted hills remote from each other; were scattered over the long stripe of line fronting the harbour entrance, without plan or uniformity. There were no streets. The buildings were generally small, rarely exceeding a single story, and built, in the Spanish fashion mostly, of the composition tapia, or the soft stone common to the region. Here and there might be seen a dwelling of two stories, standing upon some loftier spot, and looking more like a huge barracks, or fortress, rather than a merely human habitation. And, verily, these habitations had need to be fortifications, each well manned, with a garrison of its own, watchful against all surprise. There was no law in the island. There was no municipality. The population lived mostly in the violation of law. They profited from the spoils of violence. The strong arm was the best security for life and property, and, indeed, the spot was not often employed for the preservation of those spoils which were yet brought hither for distribution. The birds of prey might gather here for a season, nay, for many seasons, but they simply rested here for a night, as will those great sea birds whom we behold, to take their flight, seeking other prey, by the dawn of another morning.

Yet there were some small scattered groups in this wild abiding place, families disposed to rest, who had sought the region as one of refuge, and did not share the objects of those who used it for the purposes of crime. Men of broken fortunes and attainted blood, from Europe, were here united to maintain a monotonous existence, glad to find repose from the strifes of European society or politics, and escape from dangers which they had incurred in the civil wars of their several countries. Here and there, and now and then, would the whisper go through the settlement, of this or that banished noble, the son of a lord or earl or duke, and possibly his lordship himself, only too happy, if let alone when identified; housing himself, perhaps, from sight, whenever a king's cruiser came into these waters, in the interior of the island. Some of these refugees had brought wealth with them; did not, at all events, seem needy; and their dwellings were generally the most select, and the most secluded; guarded by equal reserve and vigilance. Society, if the irregular intercourse known among the residents might deserve the name, was something of a medley; there were a few groups of English and French, some Irish, and occasionally a family of Portuguese or Spanish. But these, in large degree, were not wholly independent of those adventurers who sought, in these waters, to carve out their fortunes with the sword. The dashing English buccaneer, the French corsair, the Spanish or Portuguese picaroon, the Dutch *Flibustier* were in the ascendant; and though willing to forbear toward those residents who were disposed to show them a friendly countenance, were yet apt, upon occasion, to show their teeth and assert their powers of mischief, at seasons, if only for the continued practice of authority. There were taverns and pot houses in the place, in one of which we propose to open the details of this history. Let us proceed to enter that which stands most conspicuous before us; a great, broad dwelling of soft stone, just fronting the harbor, and not more than two hundred yards from one of its landing places. It is called the King's Image, and has for a sign a circular plate of brass or tin, rudely painted to resemble a large piece of golden coinage, on one side of which, a something vaguely like a crowned head is barely perceptible, while on the other some few traces remain to mark one of the pillars, the sign of the Kingdom of Spain, though nearly obliterated by exposure to the weather. The idea was probably borrowed from the ordinary Spanish milled dollar—a piece of eight—a coin not altogether extinct; the value of which, in these times of plausibilities in pictured papers, is by no means under par. The King's Image consists of a long lumbering range of houses of a single story, but consisting of narrow apartments that seem rather to have been thrown than built together; addition upon addition having been made according to the growth of the place, and the increasing demand for shelter. Its landlord was supposed to be an Englishman—he had been a pirate doubtless, certainly a sailor, and had lost a leg in the service; a loss which had the effect of converting a bold boarder into a shrewd and money making landlord. But we must reserve our introduction to him and his hostel for another chapter.

CHAPTER 2
Three in Council

It is dusk, and the stars are already coming out in heaven. The winds are rising. Lights glimmer from the houses scattered along the heights. Lights gleam from boats and vessels in the bay. Sounds of merriment, rude, hoarse and wild, arise from some of the ships that lie at anchor. Like sounds arise in the distance, from a remote dwelling on the hills, mingled with the faintest sounds of the violin. Everything denotes the spirit of revelry, if not of peace and happiness. Boats are busied still in passing between the vessels and the shore. Parties ascend from the beach, and glide towards the hotels, or fathoms. An occasional group may be seen, standing apart, and engaged in private conversation; and, in one of the boats, lying a hundred yards from the shore, three seamen are resting on their oars, employing them only at intervals, as if simply to keep the boat in her present position.

Two of these are light-limbed sailors, more lithe and active apparently than strong; but the third is a giant in bulk. He lies at length, his legs across the thwarts, and his eyes cast upward meditatively, as if counting the stars as they come out. His hair is black, his cheeks brown from exposure, but exhibiting, when you have seen him in the daylight, the rich red blood of the extreme north. He is a Dane; of stature far beyond the ordinary size of man; long limbs, of great bulk and muscle; and like men of such structure commonly, lethargic of movement.

But he is a person of terrible passions when thoroughly awakened, and his companions address him in the language of deference. His courage and capacities for strife are well known to them; so also do they well know the ordinary sluggishness of his temperament. He answers them carelessly, and somewhat impatiently, like a person conscious of his manners. He is a man of blood, free to use the dagger, and they know it. But, in his calm moments, he himself revolts at his own practice. His fits of stagnation are periodical. So are his passions. Fire these and he is the Birserker—the human tiger—blinded with ferocity! He never drinks, yet, in his passions, he rages, like the demonic under drink. Even now he seems to baffle the counsel of his companions who would egg him on to some deed of violence.

"I tell you, no!, Heiligrath. I want sleep more than money. I want to lie down for a month and just feel the breeze and sleep in it under the cocoa nut trees. I've done enough work to give me a right to a month's sleep. What do I care about the money? I have three hundred pieces, stowed away, where no rascal among you can find it; and while that lasts, I want my sleep, with nobody to come between me and the wind."

"But when the money is gone, Thorfinn?"

"Then time enough for another cruise. I don't like this working for it on shore. Give me the deep sea, then, a Spanish galleon close ahead, and my boarding pike! Whenever I have had an affair on shore, I have slashed some poor devil's throat, who had nothing but a throat to offer. There was the poor Spanish pikeman Lopez—what had I to do with him. It was your business! I have felt ashamed ever since I whet my knife on his gullet."

"He was nothing but a Spaniard."

"No matter what! He was a poor devil, and not the man for me to strike. But twas done in the dark, and he might have been a Dane like myself; might have been my own brother! Why, Heiligrath, do you come stirring up this devil's blood in me? If the thing's so easy, go and do it yourself. You and Holt are surely enough. It's but one man or so you've got to avenge."

"One! Three! Three of them! There's the Steel Cap himself, the Englishman, and old Harridick says he's as strong as a horse, and he looks so; and he always goes around with a small sword by his side, and a big knife in his bosom. Besides, who knows but he's got a pistol about him?"

"Well, there's two of you, and that should be enough for any three of these shoremen!"

"Enough! When there's his servant, and that priest."

"Pooh! Pooh! A servant, and a priest!"

"Yes, indeed, and both look as if they know how to fight. The servant's a stout clean-limbed fellow, broad shouldered, well set, rounded and narrow at the hips like a lion, and bow-legged in the bargain, with arms as long as an ape's. He's no trifling customer."

"That is, if he's got the pluck!"

"We must take that for granted. Steel Cap wouldn't have him for servant if he hadn't. That house on the hill is full of treasure, and the men who watch it will fight for it, let me tell you. That priest will fight too! He's an Italian, and he's young, and he wears a sword, too, and no doubt he knows how to use it. Those Italians are great with the small sword."

"Yah! Yah! Yah!"—yawning—"I never heard you make such nice calculations before, Heiligrath! What do *you* say, Holt?"

"Well blast my eyes, I'm willing to take three on my own one pair of shoulders, but Heiligrath is scary, and if I didn't know *you,* Thorfinn, I'd think you scary, too. But you are always slow."

"That I am, when I'm not in the humour for a thing! Who's this Steel Cap?"

"An Englishman; that's all I know. Old Harridick says he's a lord, and as proud as the devil! Carries himself with an air, bold as to say, 'I'm your master, whoever you may be.' Harridick says he's rich as a king—he's got any quantity of silver plate, and coin, and he spends his money like a Spanish grandee. He goes every day to the King's Image, calls for his bottle, and reads the English papers. Whenever Harridick gets a paper he sends him word. Harridick swears he's a lord or earl, or something like it, and that he was run off from England for treason, or petty larceny, or some other blasted ugly matter. But he's got the money, and there's no good reason why we shouldn't help him spend it. The truth is, I'm nearly out."

"You don't borrow any more from me!"

"Wait till I ask you, Thorfinn."

"Ay, indeed, and you'll have to wait, long after asking, before you get an answer. But listen my boys. This Steel Cap is the husband of that great black-eyed woman that the Captain is so thick with. He goes to her almost every night when he's in port at Madame Le Vasseur's or some other house. There they dance, and waltz, and have devil-fine fun in the fandangos. They're at it this very night. You can hear the fiddle now!"

"That's it! She's the very woman! He's the very man, Steel Cap! And this should be the very night for us, now when Steel Cap visits the Frenchwoman's with his wife."

"But how do you know he's there?"

"That's to be found out! His servant, Clym, is at Harridick's. He's there always when his mistress is at the madame's. He carries a lantern to show her the way."

"Good! But what will the Captain say if we dip a spoon any where into his dish? We know what he's after."

"And don't much care! But he needn't care who plunders the house. Let him carry after the woman if he will; and if he and Steel Cap cross swords, what matter if both throats are slashed? We've as good fellows left in the ship as Captain Ferrand."

"Yourself, eh, Heiligrath?"

"In place of a better, Thorfinn! Certainly not you! You've got the bulk, but not the brains. You can carry out, but you can't lead. Give us your bulk now, old boy, and I'll tell you such a plan as shall make us rich for life."

"But I don't want to be rich! I want to rest easy. I want to sleep when night's on me and not be troubled thinking of my riches!"

"As if one could be easy, and sleep when he would, if he hadn't money! No! Shake off this lazy fit, and be a man!"

"This Steel Cap—this Englishman—what's his name? Steel Cap can't be his real name. It's a shy!"

"And who's got a *real* name among all these people here? That's almost the only one they know him by, for he wears a bonnet of solid steel, with a peak to shade the eyes. What he wears it for, no one knows. It's his fancy, perhaps, or maybe he has worn it in some of the wars in England, or somewhere, perhaps among the Turks. But he wears no other armour, except his sword."

"He may have a corslet under his coat?"

"Perhaps! Harridick shakes his head whenever he speaks of him. Says he's a most powerful fighting fellow; how he knows, I don't know; and I've heard some people call him Howard, and others Cavendish, and still others Marston, but—."

"And Harridick says he's a powerful fighting fellow, does he?"

"Equal to any man that ever lived of his size."

"And what are his inches?" asked the Dane, withdrawing his legs from the thwarts, and slowly lifting himself up to sitting posture, while he stretched his brawny arms above his head, and yawned without cessation for a minute and more.

"Some few less in height than you but quite as broad in the chest. He's young, too; I should think hardly more than thirty or thirty-five."

"How should Harridick know he's a fighting fellow?"

"He's seen him, perhaps, in England. He speaks shy of him—and in such a way as to make one think he don't know him, and is yet afraid of him."

"I'd like to see this fellow—jest see him for myself—this Steel Cap! A lord, too, you say."

"Some say a duke! Go with us now to the King's Image. He's almost sure to be there; him or the servant; and the man Clym, he carries the keys of the house—it's something of a castle."

"I won't dip finger in that bowl."

"Well, you can look on, at least should see a good chance to relieve Clym of the keys of Steel Cap's castle."

"If I'm not asleep on the sands," said with a dreary yawn; "I'll look and listen."

"Have you the lariat?" said Heiligrath, in a whisper to his companion, Holt; he was answered in the affirmative. The former then added, *sotto voce,* "We shall find Manuel at Harridick's. He's on the watch. Let's pull in shore now."

And a few strong pulls led the boat head up upon the gravel shore, where the party, having secured, proceeded in the direction of the King's Image. Heiligrath and Holt entered the building without delay; Thorfinn, the Dane, remained without, whistling a nautical air, and yawned at intervals.

"See if the man is there," said Thorfinn as they passed in, "I don't drink, you know, and will not enter unless to look upon this famous fighting Englishman."

"But there are dice, Thorfinn, cards—you know."

"See if the Steel Cap's there," said the other bluntly. The parties separated, and the Dane stretched out his arms, awaiting the embrace with an enemy. He was rejoined in a few minutes by Heiligrath. The Dane immediately asked, "Steel Cap—is he there?"

"No! But his man Clym is."

"Oh! D—n Clym! I have nothing to do with him," said he, as he turned off whistling.

"Whither do you go?" asked the other.

"To the boat! To the shore, and aboard."

"What! You leave us, and don't care to see what will happen."

"What have I to do with that?"

"But suppose we want help?"

"It is your own business."

"That's not like a comrade, Thorfinn."

"Perhaps not, yet what would you have? I tell you, I don't want to step in this business, and you would force me into it. But you shan't say that I deserted you. If you're in trouble, make the signal, and I will help you out of it, though I put myself in; and you don't deserve that! I should not count on you in a dark night with an ugly customer."

"You'll not be out of hearing?"

"No! I tell you! But I might be asleep." And he moved off without farther leave taking.

"A d—d obstinate bear, as ever. But he will hold fast," muttered Holt as he re-entered the King's Image. We may state that all of these parties, during their conferences, freely lauded their speech with oaths of gross and horrid character. We have preferred to divest them of this sort of grumbling. The imagination of the reader will supply them, if he keeps in mind that these men were all pirates, sailing under the diabolical black flag, with its ominous and spectral skull, decorated with the usual feared cross, delineated in human bones! Let us follow the two into the tavern, and behold the aspects of those who usually gather there in revelry and debauch, staking at dice and cards the profits of their bloody traffic, and drinking till all sense of loss is quieted in the oblivion of drunkenness.

CHAPTER 3
Clym and Cicely

A long low hall, an oblong block with coarse walls of stone, pierced by a few small windows, and sundry doors opening, here and there, into other apartments, crypts, perhaps, or chambers; we follow our visitor into the domain under the special auspices of the King's Image. There was a long counter, a portion of which was railed in—a bar, in modern parlance—behind which two of these doors might be seen. There were some rude benches against the opposite wall; a few dilapidated chairs and common tables, mostly small, about the room, at which two or four persons might sit and regale.

There were three stalls, occupying a range to themselves against one of the walls, each capable of containing a group of four persons. Briefly, the hall and its annexes were not unlike what we see even today in taverns, ale houses and pot houses, dedicated to the uses of the humbler and ruder elements of society. A round table in the centre contained a well thumbed and greasy collection of newspapers from Europe, generally six months or even a year old, for information from the Old World came, in those days, very slowly to the New, and, in such a place as Nassau, the newspapers were only such as were gathered by the pirates from their trade lines.

Our host at the King's Image was an Englishman, though the fact was sometimes doubted or denied; and he had an appreciation of a newspaper, such as was possessed neither by Spaniard, Frenchman, German or Portuguese, in that day at least. The newspaper was already an English institution. Barney Britton—Harridick was the name by which he was generally known—was always eager to procure newspapers. He searched all vessels as soon as they came into port, and as, from his character as publican and his former life as pirate, he had any number of friends among captains as well as crew, all these parties were solicitors to gather and to save for him such papers as came with their possessions. These he filed and adjusted every morning, and was always ready to exhibit the latest to these customers to whom they were most especially an object.

Barney Britton was a shrewd landlord. His pirate experience had not made him reckless of his fortunes; and the loss of a leg in battle, with the growth of a beard, now thoroughly gray, which completely masked his chin and cheeks, were so many counsels to prudence, and the propriety of accumulating was now his *sine qua non* of life. His profits now must come from care, economy, and the passions and appetites of others rather than any active exercise of his own. He could no longer afford their exercise himself. Enough, however, that he was still a vigorous fellow; not active, but strong; capable to hold his own, as well as make it; and his wife, for he maintained that luxury, if not older than himself, was quite as shrewd, and a shade or two more shrewish. She had her infirmity, however, and esteemed rum punch, which she manufactured to perfection, to a degree which sometimes disturbed her equilibrium on her way to her chamber and bed at night. But she was readily forgiven this weakness, in consideration of the justification that lay in the punch itself. That carried a renown second to none in the island.

Mrs. Barnaby Britton was also great as a cook. She had an almost French genius for converting the obscure into the distinguished; for manufacturing dishes that the main taste of the original element was no longer recognizable; and this was no small facility in a region where the fish and oysters were somewhat insipid, and characterized, naturally, by a briny flavour, the result of the coral harbours where they bred and grew. Her turtle soups, and steaks and fins, calipash and calipee, were great successes; and even the little muscle, which was called *par coutere* an oyster, she dressed in soups and salads to perfection; the conch, one of the most delicious of the bivalves of that region obtained by diving, became, in her hands, a dish eagerly sought after by all tastes. The crayfish salads of our hostess were in constant demand; and her stews of the baracouta, the cavalli, the dolphin and other fish, all silvery to the eye, but naturally flabby and insipid in that region, were made so to harmonize, in stirs of red wine, that the King's Image was famous for its cuisine among all the Brothers of the Coast, within that vast area of island and shore which we have already endeavoured to group together into relative dependency within a single grasp of the map.

Mrs. Barnaby had the benefit of a barmaid, whose very great merits, however, she was not fully prepared to acknowledge. Cicily—she had no other name—was an orphan; an English girl of seventeen; one of those naturally gifted creatures who grow superior to circumstances; who grow superior to what is ordinarily called education; who gather by absorption; who hear nothing without sifting and solving it, as by a sense of natural chemistry; storing away in memory all the valuable residuums, and dismissing all the rest as dross. She was wonderfully quick and clever; shrewd and virtuous; yet nice and sensitive. She had need to be all this, living in such a region, and among such associates. She was tall and slender, but well formed; graceful and good natured; was quick at reply, at repartee, and could parry offence with good humour, and disarm impertinence with a smile. She was not fair, but brown; not handsome, but very comely to look upon. And she had an eye, very large, black and lustrous; and, we may add, a very large organ of veneration, which, in the peculiar world in which she finds herself, is not too often exercised. But it is exercised, and Cicily has her favorites among the mixed multitudes who make the King's Image the place of habitual resort. She reads books, too, when she can get them, and thus nurses her veneration.

Crowds come and go. Barnabas, wife, and Cicily are all busy as Heiligrath and Holt enter the hall. There are groups at several tables. Two or three men, in a partial state of inebriety or stupor, are stretched at length on the benches, which span one entire side of the wall. Some of the groups are eating—all are drinking. Oysters, conchs, fish, in stews or salads, are in demand. Huge pewter flagons foaming with British porter cluster on some of the tables. More potent beverages, white and red, garnish others. Smokes arise from formidable pipes of tobacco, and the hall is darkened by their fumes.

There is little talking, and that is chiefly done by a restless person, whom we see carrying a lantern in one hand and a flagon of porter in the other, and passing with incessant motion around the hall. He chats with everybody; passes from table to table; has a devil-may-care spirit for all parties, landlord and wife included; and is evidently a little the worse for his potations. He is a genuine Englishman, a person of good figure, if we excuse a certain pair of bow legs; and good features; a fine Saxon stamp of God upon his broad high forehead; clear blue eyes; with great breadth of nostril; large mouth, shaded by as yellow a moustache as ever yet made saffron about the face of a setting September sun. His hair is of the same colour—a rich generous auburn growing into gold; and he had a full shock of it, falling in massive curls, upon a pair of the broadest shoulders in the world. This is Clym of Rydon, who, when he writes his name in full, is Clym Royston of Rydon. Clym has some special claims upon our attention now, as he is the very party upon whom Heiligrath and Holt have set eyes of calculation, which, with such parties, always mean eyes of mischief.

Clym is unconscious of their interest in him. He sees them enter the hall, it is true, but gives them no heed. He does *not* see when they approach one of their comrades, who seems to have been sleeping upon the bench where he has been for some time stretched at length. The two whisper but a few words in the ears of this comrade, whose answer shows that he has been wide awake all the time. The parties then separate. The two late comers, leaving the other and proceeding to a table, call for a stew and a tankard each.

Meanwhile, Clym of Rydon talks and drinks. He slaps Barnaby, the landlord, on his back. He speaks civilly to Mrs. Barnaby. He has a whisper over the counter to Mistress Cicily, as he calls upon her to refill his tankard. She does not at once comply with his demand, but answers him, with a sly whisper in return.

"Go home, Clym, and don't make a fool of yourself! You are talking too much for your own good. Look out! You have no friends among these people."

"Friends!" he cried, "friends, my dear girl—all the world's my friends. I'm generally beloved wherever I'm known, more especially by the women kind. My friends—."

She clapt her hands boldly upon his mouth, and fixing her great black eye upon him sternly, said in low tones,

"You've drank too much, Clym! You're in danger! Begone, while you can!" All this, in the lowest possible tone, one of such concentrated earnestness that the half drunken man was instantly made conscious, in some degree at least, of his folly.

"Cicily!" roared the landlord.

"Cicily!" the landlady.

The girl hurried to her duties, giving Clym of Rydon another look of mixed caution and reproach. He stared at her for a moment, with a stupid face of wonderment mixed with pleasure, then suddenly, with the newly awakened spirit of a half drunken man, he cried out,

"But where's my drink? You call off the girl just when she's serving me my liquor!"

"Serving you!" cried the hostess, "pretty serving, indeed, and you keep her talking all the while, and doing nothing for anybody else."

"Well, can't a chap talk with a pretty girl, I want to know, mother?"

"No time for that!" answered the shrew. "Besides, Cicily's *not* a pretty girl, and you mustn't put that nonsense into her head!"

"Cicily not a pretty girl!" Then with an oath he roared, "Cicily's the prettiest girl in all Providence, ay, and all the islands, too, and all the main; and I'll break any man's head that says she ain't! Who dares!" looking around fiercely.

"You're right, comrade! We're agreed there; and I'm your backer, though you march into a fight!" cried Heiligrath, coming up and slapping Clym on the shoulder. "Let's have a drink together, my brother."

Heiligrath was not the comeliest person in the world. His face was broad, but not fleshy. His nose was huge and disfigured by the slash of a cutlass right across. His eyes were small, and of the palest gray colour, almost whitish. His beard was red; his skin cadaverously white. He was not comely to the eye, and Clym rather recoiled from the unwanted familiarity with which he made his acquaintance, and he was just drunk enough to be fully tenacious about his dignity. He drew himself up stiffly, as he said,

"Oh! Who are you?" This was spoken with all the stateliness of a genuine John Bull. But the other was resolved to take no offences and he replied good humoredly,

"Any sort of a good fellow, my friend, who has an eye to a pretty girl; and Cicily is all that, just as you've said it; and I have a taste for good liquor; and so, my worthy brother, let us drink to the health of pretty Cicily."

"That will I do, comrade. Though I don't know you! Here, father Barnaby, let's have the stuff, and let Cis serve us."

"No! No! *My* shot this time!" quoth Heiligrath. "Your turn next. We shall crash many a cup together as I take it, before the swallow flies."

"Well, as you please, comrade. So, let the pledge be in porter."

"Agreed! Ho! Mistress Cicily; the liquor's doubly sweet when you are the tapster. Isn't it so, old Harridick."

"To be sure it is," growled the landlord.

Cicily obeyed the summons, and stood before them, behind the bar, her eyes as watchful as that of a black snake going into the nest of the young mockingbirds. She looked warningly to Clym; but he took no heed of the expression in her eye. He had set down his lantern, which was unlighted, upon the counter, and, feeling in his pockets as if in search of money, he had drawn forth a pocket knife, a pipe and tobacco box, and finally, a large bunch of keys, followed by a single, but very massive one. These he laid down beside his lantern upon the counter, while extending his hand for the mug of porter, which Cicily had just filled. The foaming beverage completely filled his eye; but the eye of Heiligrath was eagerly set upon the keys; and, while, with one hand he grasped the pot of porter, and was hob-nobbing with Clym, the other hand, as if carelessly thrown out upon the counter, was extended towards the keys.

But, in that very moment he met the keen glance of Cicily; her eye steadily watching his every movement, while a slight smile of derision seemed to curl her pretty, pulsing lips into an expression which might soon rise into that of scorn. The pirate withdrew his hand and arm, and turned his eyes once more upon Clym; and the two touched once more their only half-emptied mugs, and with a maudlin sort of dignity, Clym drank to their better acquaintance; to which Heiligrath responded in a gracious echo; and swallowing his porter hastily, he demanded that the two pots should be refilled.

Clym offered no dissent; and when Cicily turned to the tap, the pirate drew nigh to the counter, and while his eye and tongue kept his drunken companion in full exercise, his hand was once more extended toward the keys. But the celerity of the girl was superior to his own. He had just laid his hand upon the massive single key when her glance confronted him; the pots of porter were placed before the two, and the opportunity was lost. And while, standing in the floor, the two drank gazing into each other's eyes, and bowing and smirking, with whatever they could command of dignity and deference; she contrived, with wonderful boldness and dexterity, and without noise, to sweep her sleeve and hand over the keys and quietly remove them. This done, she disappeared for a moment, and re-appeared only to seize the chance, while Heiligrath drew aside to Holt, and Clym still hung above the counter, to whisper to him once more the words of caution.

"You are in danger, I tell you! Be off and take the hills. Beware of the rope—the rope, mind you! The rope! You are not too drunk but you can yet save your neck, especially as you have now nothing else that you can lose!"

The last member of the sentence was spoken rather in soliloquy than to him. And, with these words, she went to the landlord, and whispered to him, "There's some mischief a foot! Get Clym off—send him to the French madame's where he's to see after the lady. He'll be in trouble before long."

"And what do I care about that? And why should I send a fellow off so long as he can pay for his liquor."

"He can't pay much longer; and he can't drink much more; and he's drank more than enough already, for his own safety. Eyes of mischief are upon him. So look to it. I tell you there's mischief; and whether you care about Clym or not, you do and ought to care about Steel Cap; and you will know what his thanks will be, if you make his man drunk here and get him into danger."

"He makes himself drunk! But I'll get him off. Get along, hussey. You know too much for a girl, Cicily. Steel Cap—yes! To be sure." And the landlord bestirred himself, while Cicily disappeared. Meanwhile, Clym was stirring also.

"Ha! Cis! What's that you say, my beauty?" asked the serving man, suddenly rousing himself up, after a few moments of stupor.

But the girl was gone; she had disappeared through one of the doors in the rear of the bar, and was no longer in the hall.

"Drunk!" quoth Clym, muttering to himself. "Drunk! It is a hard speech, Mistress Cicily. But if I'm not drunk altogether, I'm in a fair road to be so! Ah! What's next? What's that? *Beware of the rope!* heck! Very d–d unpleasant associations! Where's the man I drank with? Off! It's time for me to be off, too! I'll drink no more tonight! My head feels a little bit uneasy. It can't be the liquor! It's only excitement. It's in the narves. D–n the narves! I never could see the use of them. I must cool 'em off. Look you father Barney—Barnabas—let me have your bucket of water over my head. Come to the door, old fellow, and give me a souse! It's needful to my legs, for I must travel. Cool head, light legs they say. Cool head, father Barnabas!"

The landlord was now very ready to assist him. A bucket of water was poured over his head and neck; into another he plunged his massive shock, head and hair, and kept it immersed for several seconds, then shook himself like a water dog, and wiped off, and declared himself ready for departure. The landlord lighted his lantern; showed himself somewhat solicitous; conducted him outside of the dwelling, and put him on his way, whispering in his ear similar counsels of caution, but equally vague, to those which had been said by Cicily.

"Ay, ay, father Barnabas; I thank you. I know it all. The rope's the thing—the rope, the neck! You say!"

"What rope! What neck! What did I say?"

"No! Twasn't you; twas Cis, the girl! Sharp girl! She knows something. Hold off Barnabas till I get steady. And—where's my knife? Oh! Here!" and he drew the belt around him, which carried the knife, the usual companion of the sailor, and which he wore in sailor fashion. It had worked round behind his back. He brought it conveniently to his grip, in front, a great broad blade, the genuine *couteau de chape,* of the English hunter.

"Head feels cooler, old Barney! Legs more sure! I'll do now! There's the house over the hill, the French madame's—I can see the light. I can hear the violin. They're at it yet, and will be so till the small hours. Steady! So! Goodnight, father Barnabas! Good night!"

"Goodnight!" said the host; "and keep an eye to every point of the compass."

"So I will!" and he stepped off, slowly but surely enough, and feeling himself somewhat cooler of brain, and trying, however imperfectly, to work out some logical notion of the danger in his way, of which he had been warned, and how he was to escape them. This process began, strangely enough, by his singing aloud, "Over the hills and far away!"

The landlord muttered, "music drunk," as he re-entered the hotel. When there, he looked about him, and again muttered,

"Heiligrath gone; Holt gone; and that bloody Portuguese, Manuel! *They* are the fellows on his track! Lucky if he gets off with a whole skin. Cicily must have heard something. Sharp ears, that girl! But where's she gone? Cicily! Where's Cis?" to his wife.

"Where? Who knows! She's not in the house. I've called her a dozen times."

Cicily was gone also—was at that very moment speeding also across the hills, and far away, but not in the same direction with Clym, towards the gay revel of Madame Le Vasseur. She took an opposite course, now running, now walking, in the most direct route to the sombre dwelling known as the castle of the mysterious Steel Cap!

CHAPTER 4
Steel Cap and the Lady Geraldine

It is time that we ourselves should make the acquaintance of Steel Cap. To do this, *selon les regles,* we must go back to a period somewhat in advance of the several scenes in which we have been occupied with other and inferior parties. But this period we shall anticipate by a few hours only. We return to the afternoon of this very day, the night of which promises to be so full of events. It is a golden afternoon, covered exquisitely by the glorious flush that precedes the sunset and the starry dusk. The dying sun has pumped all the western walls of the sombrous castle of Steel Cap. It shines through the narrow windows of the basement—apertures rather than windows, in the outer walls, and lights up the gloomy chamber with a solemn radiance which tells, with grand effect, upon a goodly collection of ancient but well kept furniture.

It would seem that considerable sums had been expended to impart to this lone and comparatively lowly habitation the aspect of those splendors to which the eyes of the highly born are accustomed in the courtly halls of Europe. There were two rich steel mirrors against the walls; their clearness and polish well preserved, with gilded frames elaborately wrought, though now tarnished with age and dust. No less than two score of antique portraits, the costumes of which carried you back for two centuries in English history, had place in line with the mirrors against the walls; and these two were encased in heavy frames of fine workmanship, tarnished almost to blackness also by antiquity alone. Some fine but faded damask hangings depended from and over the narrow windows, looped aside for free admission to the sunlight. The chairs and tables were of ancient patterns also, massive, rich, ornate, stiff and stately, of a date which might be followed up to the times of Henry the Eighth and Anne Bulleyn. There was a stately harpsichord of large size that occupied fully a quarter of the room. On one side stood a spacious sofa, half resembling a couch, adown the back of which, held up by gilded knobs against the wall, depended a massive crimson curtain, richly figured, but showing visibly the fading impress of age and wear. There was no carpet to the floor, which was made of planks finely smoothed, apparently of Spanish cedar. The building might have been a hundred years old. The island of Nassau was not without several of these antique habitations scattered over the island, especially in those regions where coffee plantations had been established. Even now the traces of these and the plantations also, are to be found by the traveller who rambles over this pretty province. A lute in a corner, a few books upon tables, indicated, or would seem to indicate, unwonted taste for such a region; and yet the anomalies are not infrequent which require us to recognize the assassin in the sentimentalist, the midnight burglar occasionally in the guitar or flute player, and the bookworm in scores of Eugene Arams. At all events, the ordinary and natural thought wonders to see the evidences of taste, art and a high civilization in the wild region of the Bahamas some two hundred years ago. Yet despotisms which drive heroism, patriotism, and all the virtues into exile, may also be supposed to expel from its domains the cultivated tastes, the fine fancies, the highest attributes of art and genius.

But if you glance upon that gorgeous sofa you will not wonder to find these proofs of grace, taste and art, such as Europe makes its boast and pride, here, in the desolate but lovely world of the Bahamas. Very beautiful is the woman who now half sits half reclines along that sofa; her dainty fingers playing with her parrot, alternately teasing and soothing the favorite, while in her large and lustrous eyes you behold an expression of excited feeling and of a very impatient nature. The face is a very fine one; a perfect oval but of somewhat oriental type. The features are not perfect, tried separately, but they harmonize with a wonderful effect. The eye is as restless, as it is large, with just enough of humidity to lend additional luster, to the deep keen, fiery glance which it shoots out, momently, like sudden flashes of summer lightning, in a dark night. The nose, of Grecian shape, is capable of dilation to the fine scorn of a lofty nature, as you may perceive now, that while playing with her pet, she really regards it not; the expression of the eye being elusive, and the dilating nostril declaring an emotion which at present finds no other mode of expression. The mouth is soft, admirably cut, with an exquisite curve to either corner, not wholly lost, just now, in the somewhat close and stern compression of the lips. The chin is full, the cheeks forming a beautiful curve to the line of intersection with the chin, which carries one pretty little dimple in the very centre. Over all, a high, and not too broad forehead, black masses of blended braided and falling hair, black as night, and showing with fine effect, from the serpent-like loopings of great strings of pearl which secure it, several waves and ripples, each in its appointed place. Over all, and in some degree the result of the harmonious grouping of all, was the happy play of animation in the glorious face and head which might have been those of Zenobia, when, in her power, she dared, in the haughty pride of a great soul, to brave with defiance the dreaded power of Rome. The figure was large, and superbly habited, as if for a ball, in the gorgeous silks and satins of the time, rather of Mary Stuart, fresh from France, than of the dynasties which succeeded her in England. She possessed that half voluptuous style of beauty which the poets so much praised in Mary; but, in the case of the lady before us, it was raised perhaps in command, and imposing persona, without losing any of its charm, and winning effect. There was a blending of hauteur and tenderness, or rather, a rapid fluctuation of expression in her mobile countenance, between the two, which was at once the source of as frequent pleasure as surprise to the beholder.

The lady was not alone. Opposite to her, at the other extremity of the room, stood, half leaning against the wall, a male figure quite as imposing of presence as her own. This was the Steel Cap, so called because of the skull cap which he wore, close fitting to the head, having a small peak in front which did not suffice to shelter his eyes. The cap was a well known headpiece without visor and without ornament. On the left side however a close inspection would show a slender tabulated ridge, which might carry a bunch of sable plumes, it is more than probable that it had borne them in times not long past. A leather strap passing from the sides of the cap secured it effectually beneath his chin.

The figure of this person was tall, erect, symmetrical in high degree, of easy and graceful carriage, and in well fitting costume of sable, English cut, of that day, he seemed one who had figured equally in court and field. His face, was a blending of the Norman and Saxon, with the lofty, eagle like aspect of the one race, the stern, fixed, firm and tenacious expression of the other. He wore a light moustache, and beard of a dark brown; his beard peaked, in the manner of the time of Charles the First, and the slight locks of hair which escaped from beneath his cap, were of the same colour. He might have been thirty- or thirty five years of age. The lady was probably somewhere about twenty-five, though this was rather to be inferred from her full development of figure, her ease and aplomb, than from the lines of her face, the *tout ensemble* of which expressed only youth, and all its eagerness and impulse.

It might be seen that she glanced obliquely at her companion, with an expression of displeasure and solicitude in her face. He, on the contrary, had concentrated his eyes upon her, and they wore an aspect rather of sadness than of anger. She toyed with the parrot, then said,

"Poll, pretty Poll, who is a bad man?"

"Bad man, Cavendish," replied the parrot promptly, in an awkward imitation of the English.

"Who is very wicked, Poll."

"Wicked Cavendish!" was the reply of the parrot; and so the dialogue, question and answer through some half dozen sentences to the same effect.

"Do you hear, Edward? Pretty Poll, she knows what a brute you are."

"Geraldine!" was the only word.

"Well," languidly, "what next."

"Am I to be always answered in this manner."

"What would you have? Am I always to be a subject of reproach."

"Not reproach, Geraldine. Expostulation."

"And why expostulate."

"Verily, you may well ask the question, since no good seems to come of it."

"And how should it Edward? You tire me with complaint."

"Even as you tire me with offence."

"Offence!"

"Offence!"

"And why should you be offended because I dress gaily, dance gaily, and love to be amused. Am I a prisoner or not?"

"Surely not! But why persist in seeking forbidden or suspicious places and persons? This French woman, Le Vasseur, is a coarse, vulgar creature, of whom no one knows anything."

"She is neither coarse nor vulgar, Edward Cavendish. She is a very clever, pleasant, and good creature, and as for knowing anything about her, who in this place knows anything about you or me?"

"We ourselves know, Geraldine, and that should suffice us with regard to ourselves. This woman has a husband or not, and who, and what, and where is he?"

"Really, I cannot answer that question as regards anybody here. Why did you bring me here, to this desolate region, Edward Cavendish."

"Why do you persist in reminding me, Geraldine, that I am an exile, that—but enough! You already partly know my objects here."

"Yes; and think them a sort of madness. Between you and this Italian Signior, you dream dreams which will sink your vessel. You would change the world would you, with your philosophies. You think man may become a perfect creature under your wise administration. You would emancipate him from all the restraints of law and the teaching of all the ages and peoples for a thousand years. You ascribe all his vices and misfortunes to the vice of authority, the tyranny of rulers, wicked counsellors and stupid laws. And you would persuade the lawless men who gather here, to become virtuous under your wiser maxims. You would convert these thousand islands into a commonwealth, and realize every fancy of your Platos and Sidneys. And so, between you and this Italian Signior, this priest whose philosophy has got the better of his religion, you lose yourselves in dreams which you can never realize in action. Such followers as you find here will sooner turn you into a pirate, than you turn them into saintly citizens."

"You are irreverent, and know not what you speak. Consider rather what I have said to you, and do not cheapen yourself and me by such free intercourse with such people."

"And why, then," she answered rising quickly and throwing the parrot from her wrist, "why, I repeat, have you brought me here? I loathe these people, despise them, perhaps, just as much as you do; but I must live, I must breathe, I must have air and motion; and enjoy some intercourse with what has, at least, the appearance of humanity. I do not call it society. As society, it does not compensate me. What! O, what will compensate me again, Edward Cavendish, for what we have been forced to abandon of that grand old world in which I have lived, if not a queen or princess, at least a lady with all a woman's consciousness of what belongs to the affections, the sensibilities, ay, and the higher aims which they inspire. And I a Geraldine, kinswoman to princes, if none myself!"

Her magnificent form, lofty, grand in attitude, with right arm outstretched, now in the direction of Steel Cap, and now pointing as it were to Europe, while her left hand pressed convulsively against her heart, and every muscle of her features was alive in the most passionate play, constituted a glorious study of the artist. Yes, she was a Geraldine! And had in her veins the noblest blood of Ireland. It declared itself in voice, tone and gesture. She was an Irish princess, though one utterly discouraged.

Her husband, for such he was gazed upon her with a blended visage of sadness and admiration. He said mournfully,

"And you reproach me with all this, Geraldine?"

"I do not—I would not reproach you, Edward; but I will not submit to reproaches. If you bring me here, I submit, but here or there, or anywhere, you must have that faith in me which forbears every show of suspicion."

"Suspicion!"

"Ay, suspicion! Jealousy, Edward Cavendish, because I dance with a French, or Spanish, or English gallant, and laugh merrily at his jest, and seem pleased, and do not scowl upon the courtesy which seeks to give me pleasure."

He strode towards her, grasped her wrist in his hand, and said his eyes settling upon her with a degree of sternness they had not shown before,

"Never use such language to me again. You are speaking those things in your passions which you will bitterly repent when this fit is over. It is not of your virtue that I am jealous; it is of my dignity. I know that you would not dishonour me, but you must not trifle with my honour. You must not cheapen me by cheapening yourself in the market place. You may not be guilty, but if, in your levity or recklessness, you give occasion to the finger point of scandal, the shame attaches, though the honour be wholly free from blame. Opinion must have no leave for censure, where the chastity of a woman is the subject."

"And who dares impugn it here? And what care you for the sort of opinion which prevails here?"

"Mark you, you have been the subject of comment at the King's Image by loose revellers; and this Captain Ferrand, and another, one Leonard, who appears to be an Englishman, a lieutenant, I hear, have been your escorts. They have boasted of it—."

"Ha! What?"

"Nothing much; save that you are a gay lady, perhaps; and—but enough, that I have my eyes upon them, and my ears will be sufficiently open should one insolent tongue dare to utter that which my wife's levities are supposed to provoke."

"Well! Well! Captain Ferrand, Captain Ferrand—and Lieutenant Leonard, that willowy whipster. Very good, very interesting. You shall see that I do not fear them, or their tongues—."

"No! But you may compel me to cut theirs out."

"Nay, now, Edward, no violence. Trust me. Leave it to me, Edward. You have no reason to fear."

"Fear, Geraldine! I love too much to fear! But wherefore not be wise? Why not break off from this woman's associations? Her house is the harbour for all this class of people!"

"The very class out of whom you and Signior Caraccioli propose to manufacture a model republic. Oh! Cavendish."

His face became suffused.

"Your sneer might be spared me at this moment, Geraldine."

"No! No! I can spare you nothing when you goad me on this subject. I tell you, I will not surrender my liberty—the privilege to look on Humanity, no matter what its aspect. Heaven knows, it has but little charm here. Oh! Edward, why have you chosen this bleak desolate empire. Why not Europe. If the doors of Britain are closed upon you, there is the continent. There are the Turks with whom you fought. Even were it that you should take up the sword as a profession, I would say not nay, so that you leave these miserable associations in which you think I so much delight. I will go with you. I will bundle on armour myself. I will fight—die by your side—a thousand times rather than wear out life in this miserable world which you have chosen. One year more of life, in Europe, or the East, and I will cheerfully give up all the rest."

He shook his head mournfully.

"Dream, as you call it, Geraldine, it is now my life. I must have a purpose, if I would live. Bear with me and my experiments patiently. The trial will be made ere long, and—."

"Say no more! I will resign myself as I can. You are my fate!"

"And will you break off from these connections?"

"No!—Yes! When it shall please me to do so!" stamping her foot upon the floor. "I go to Madame Le Vasseur's this very night, though I never go again! I must enjoy this felicity of dancing with the admirable Captain Ferrand! Do you hear? Yes, and I will tread a measure with the placid Lieutenant Leonard! And so—and so! Yes, Edward, I must look once more upon these worthy gentlemen who fancy they have claims upon my consideration; and whom you fancy have claims upon yours."

"You are perverse, Geraldine."

"I am a woman, Edward Cavendish, and she, according to my notion, should be something of a man herself. I will not usurp *your* rights, Edward—no, nor sacrifice them, or in any way, imperil them; but you shall see that I can assert my own!"

"Beware, Geraldine!"

"On! No cautions, no warning fingers, Edward, above all no threats!" And, as he gazed earnestly and sadly upon her, the passionate woman, with a sudden burst of tenderness, rushed to him, threw her arms about his neck, laid her head upon his bosom, and burst into a flood of tears! He pressed her fondly to his heart, kissed her on her forehead, released her, and left the room without another word. Her eyes followed him out with a sad expression.

The parrot flew to her shoulder, and cried out,

"Bad Cavendish." She threw off the bird from his perch, with a sudden crash to the floor, and stamped at the astonished offender, with her pretty foot; then murmured,

"Poor Cavendish! And he to doubt me! But no! He does not doubt! He knows me too well. Should he doubt me, I must die or madden! So, so Captain Ferrand, one captain grand, with his corsair, adonis whiskers! So! So! I shall not fear, even though Cavendish should doubt. And the pleasant smirking Leonard too! Well! Well! And one French madame, good bustling, shrewd, silly Madame Le Vasseur! All in good time, Edward, all in good time."

And so speaking, she touched her little hand bell, and as it tinkled sharply, a servant girl appeared, a diminutive little creature, a child in size but a woman in development, whose features showed her to be probably quite as old as her mistress, and perhaps more shrewd.

"Ursula," said Geraldine, "see that you tell Clym of Rydon to get his lantern tonight. I will go to Madame Le Vasseur's."

The girl smirked; it was scarce a smile. It argued a sly sinister thought, or feeling, and had it been perceptible to the proud passionate mistress, it must have conveyed some doubts of the girl's fidelity—must have prompted at least, an annoying impression. But she saw nothing without. The eyes of her maid were just then turned inward though her large black eyes were taking in the full proportions of her own majestic figure in the gratefully reflecting mirror.

CHAPTER 5
Caraccioli

In an adjoining chamber in the same dwelling, which is so furnished as to seem at once a studio and a laboratory, we find Steel Cap now seated and in close conversation with another party, whose presence was scarcely less imposing than his own. This person was habited somewhat in the style of a priest of the Catholic Church. He was probably forty years of age, through from the subdued and habitual gravity which became his face, he might be supposed to nearer fifty. He was tall, somewhat lean, but of good figure and lofty carriage; with that noble head of the Italian, which is still so fine and frequent a study with the painter, which seems to blend the massive characteristics of the ancient Roman, in beautiful harmony with the delicate contour of outline, and sweetly chiselled features of the modern Tuscan—the somewhat stern aspects of the former, toned admirably down by the actively developed sense of art and beauty, in the latter race.

The person is historical, Caraccioli *had* been an Italian Priest. But he had been excommunicated for heretical doctrines. He had anticipated much of the

French philosophy of a subsequent period, and his opinions were in remarkable unison with those of a modern German school, which equally undergoes the ban of the Christian church. He was, nevertheless, a pure, and, according to his ways of thinking, a pious person. But his piety partook of a political aspect, was in fact largely political, and contemplated the possible perfection through government, of that race of which most religions insist upon the inbred deficiencies, the natural deformities, the hated incapacities arising from the presence, in their moral constitutions, of a natural element of evil.

It was the doctrine of Caraccioli that this evil was solely the result of human training, false laws and habits of society, a corrupt religion, and the perpetual wrongs done, by authority, in the name of law and government. His doctrines, followed up in detail, would suffice to illustrate some of the more pernicious of our own times, which are indeed likely to obtain a fatal currency.

But we need not continue this subject in this manner. It will, perhaps, suffice to follow the conversation in which we find the two now engaged so earnestly. Whether this companion of Caraccioli had been inbred by him with his views of man and society, or inclined, of himself, to the same way of thinking, it is impossible to say. There was perhaps a decided tendency on his own part to what may be called socialistic views of morals and religion; but it is equally certain that he was very far from any full concurrence with his companion, in that wide sweep of vision which characterized the philosophy of the other. Indeed, the views of Steel Cap seemed rather to contract his objects wholly to political considerations, only so far considering religion and moral philosophy as these might serve to illustrate or influence the tendencies of the human race in a common government.

"I confess," said Steel Cap, as if in reply to or in continuation of a frequent argument before, "that my difficulty lies in any generalization which shall undertake to consider the race as a whole; and this appears to me to be the weak point in all the arguments to which I have listened on the subject. We take up individual cases and argue for the family, or race, though the experience, in every household, state or nation, shows the absurdity of that assumption of equality, in their behalf, upon which all the reasoning depends. I see no such equality among men, as the argument assumes. I see nothing but inequalities everywhere. The capacities and susceptibilities of men are wholly different in the different individuals. There is no classing them. We must make a law, for each; and that law must contemplate the uses to which each shall be assigned in the social state. To do otherwise is to wrong the most intelligent and highly endowed by confounding him with the mean and inferior; and such debasement as naturally elevates the base and inferior into a rank superior to the intrinsically superior. Equality of social condition is lost, in the very social equalization of the parties; and in the establishment of equality, we make a tyranny—the inferior necessarily becoming usurpative of the proper rights of the superior."

"The race rights itself in a few generations!" was the ready reply. "We cannot contemplate mere individual cases; in considering the condition of the whole human family. Necessity establishes its own laws in time; and the classes gradually attain their several levels. Were it not for the despotisms of class, government and religion, all would be right in a few seasons. It is the crime of government, and of all select orders in society, that they grow into despotisms, and, for the maintenance of power, strive continually for the perversion of the race."

"And so the race dies out; and the republic; after a certain time of glorious struggle, and miserable strife, and wretched abasement, and final prostitution! This has been the unfailing history, even where the promise, at first, was the most pure and brilliant."

"We shall cure this, my dear Mortimer, in an experiment. Once we people these thousand islands, and they will maintain their hundred thousand souls; bring them together under an authority which not only contemplates their good exclusively, but is conversant in those grand philosophies which shall best shape government for good; and you will see the fruits of an experiment which shall shame all that has ever been done, or sought for, in all the fine-spun theories of ancient times. Yes, over these islands, we shall extend our sway."—and the speaker rose and stretched forth his hands, as if already grasping all the regions of the Bahamas and Antilles—"and here, under the benign influences of nature, we shall accommodate our laws to those of nature, and our empire shall be one of unmixed freedom, and unblighted innocence, such as made the fabled happiness of Eden, and constituted the secret of the fabulous Age of Gold!"

His eye was bright as that of the serpent; his cheeks glowed, and his whole frame quivered with excitement. Here was the enthusiast, in conflict, as well as unison, with the philosopher! Steel Cap, whom, by the way, Caraccioli addresses as Mortimer—there is a mystery in all these several names which we cannot yet fathom—Steel Cap looked at him with sadness as he replied,

"Alas! My friend, once again, this material? How shall we subdue these Brothers of the Coast to meekness, to that gentleness and simplicity of heart which shall bend their hard and iron natures, soften the rigours of their inveterate habits, and bring them to the consciousness of that charm in well being, and love—creating society, which is our aim and purpose."

"Do I not see them daily, nightly? Do I not discourse to them? Do they not listen with patience? I have made many friends among them; have many admirers among them; and many have declared their conviction of the truths which I deliver, and express a desire to realize the condition which I describe. We must have shipping, Mortimer;" and he placed his hand familiarly and earnestly on the shoulder of the other, as he added—"vessels of war! We must be prepared to defend and maintain the realm which we propose to establish; and it is through their habitual occupations, that we must gradually reconcile these mariners to the new condition which shall make them free and happy."

"Think you these people comprehend you, Caraccioli?"

"And have you so long known me, Mortimer, as to doubt that, on this subject, so close to my heart, I should speak vaguely or in vain. No! No! I am winning my way to their understanding; through their hearts; the proper secret of preachers, teachers and orators. You must take the sea again; Mortimer read these letters to Misson, and note what they say. You will see what is expected of you, and what can be done. As Misson, you will renew these achievements upon the sea, of which Europe has so glorious a memory, in your conflicts with the Moor and Algerine. The sea must needs be our field for a season, until we can people these islands; or, if, need be, plant our colony of the Brothers of the Coast upon some genial and productive shores, where a native population may share in the blessings of that government which we shall be well able to give to the race, so wretched now!"

Steel Cap did not answer, but, taking up a telescope, passed to one of the narrow openings of the hall which was only a substitute for a window, and looked forth towards the sea. The sun was at his setting, and his beams were beautifully spread over the white canvas of a goodly looking ship, about to enter the harbour.

"A man of war, standing in through the northeast channel."

"What! A royal vessel?"

"No! She carries, wide-spread, that hateful sign, the crossbones and the skull! From her thin and rakish set, I should almost take her for the "Revenge.""

"What! Blackbeard again? That devil of all the devils, the worst and blackest!"

"Even so! He will probably mar, in a week, all that you have been doing for a month! But hark! A gun!"

"Another, and another!"

"It is a salute from the ship of Ferrand; and there go Blackbeard's cannon in reply. If it be he, Carracioli, his arrival is unfortunate."

"The clouds sometimes obscure the sun, Mortimer, but he does not go back! I have learned to recognize in patience one of the best securities for progress."

"At all events, while this loathsome fiend is here, it will be well that you should not be too active in your demonstrations. It is in his power to be very mischievous, especially if he fancies that your teachings may beguile him of his men."

"Have no fear, Mortimer! Caution is the elder sister of patience, and both equally well know how to wait upon time."

Their conference was continued into the night; meanwhile, the Lady Geraldine kept her purpose, and, under the escort of Clym, bearing his lantern, made her way, at the appointed hour, to the dwelling of the dashing, flashing French madame of whom nobody knows anything, save that she gives very pleasant parties and gorgeous feasts, which readily reconcile her guests to their continued ignorance of her status.

We have seen how the lantern bearer disposed of himself at the King's Image, after having safely lodged his lady. We will suppose several hours to have passed, when the conference between Steel Cap and the philosopher, Caraccioli, was interrupted by the sudden entrance of Cicily, the barmaid of the King's Image, who appeared before them, hatless and almost breathless, habited just as we saw her, when she suddenly disappeared from behind the tavern bar.

We have seen how she possessed herself of the keys, which Clym, in his drunkenness, had so incautiously laid down. We have gathered from what she said to Clym herself, and to the landlord, what were her suspicions, upon these she seems to have acted with a rare decision of character, the result of early employment, among men, and in situations which familiarized her mind to peril and performance; without, as we believe, impairing the integrity of her mind, or the native purity of her soul. There are characters who can preserve fine souls even when surrounded by contamination; and who acquire strength and courage from their sympathy with the suffering and feebleness which they behold. This girl, but seventeen—taught in no schools but those of hard toils and a rough future—seems to have been of this description of character. She had run and walked, alternately, over the space that separated Steel Cap's castle, from the King's Image, and half breathless had opened the gate, pressed to his presence, and, apologizing for her inter-ruption, had given the keys into the hands of Steel Cap; while, in brief tones, all to the point, she described the situation of Clym, and declared the suspicions which she entertained of the principal trio, Heiligrath, Holt, and the Portuguese, who had seemed so profound a sleeper. She gave no counsel as to what should be done; merely stated the facts, and, hesitating for a moment, with a profound courtesy, she prepared to withdraw.

"Cicily, my good girl," said Steel Cap, "I thank you very much. You have shown equal goodness of heart, good sense and courage. Take this, my good girl."

And he would have pressed a doubloon into her hands; but she recoiled, and looking up half reproachfully, sadly at least, into his face, she murmured,

"Oh! No, sir! Oh! No, my lord, no! How could you think, sir?"

"Call me by no titles, Cicily. I am no lord! If I continue to be a gentleman, I shall be satisfied. But I must thank you, as a gentleman, and acknowledge your services tonight in my own way."

And, drawing a ring from his finger, he took her hand into his, passed the ring over one of her fingers, and, stooping, pressed his lips upon her forehead."

She murmured, inaudibly, and her face, which was a fine one, though not beautiful, was suffused with a crimson flush which might be pleasure or surprise; then she turned and sped away, with fleet foot steps which Steel Cap found it impossible to follow, as he made his way to close the entrance after her.

She was gone, skimming the white chalk-like plains, glaring beneath the stars, with a fleetness of footsteps that was accelerated by a certain fresh invigorating lightness of heart. She reached the tavern from the rear, only a moment after Clym of Rydon had taken his departure from the front.

Steel Cap meanwhile, having closed the door, returned to the apartment in which he had left Caraccioli, and, buckling on his sword, was preparing to leave the castle. The latter was already armed, and appeared about to accompany him, but Steel Cap arrested him.

"You must not go, Caraccioli. These fellows may attempt the house while I am gone. You are the only person to take care of it. You cannot rely on Brereton alone. He is already asleep and is always in a stupor when he wakes. Better wake him up at once, and keep good watch while I am gone. You have the petronels all loaded, and by sousing Brereton with a bucket of cold water, he may be made useful in a few minutes."

"But there are *three* of these fellows, my lord," said the other.

"Yes; there are three; but, my good Caraccioli, were there thirty, do you not see that I must go, and go alone? The house, the treasures, are all here, needing a protector! Who but you now? See to it, and I will see to these rascals! Do not fear!"

And he half drew forth his rapier, and he thrust a dagger into his vest; felt at the fastenings of the cape beneath his chin, and hurried forth; Caraccioli carefully locking and shooting all the bolts behind him.

CHAPTER 6
The Lasso

Half conscious only of his situation, half conscious of a lurking danger—yet uncertain of the quarter whence it should come—the words of Cicily, in warning, still sounding in his ears; and somewhat troubled with the reflection that he had, in some way, endangered the security of his master's house; uncertain of his footsteps, and conscious of the fact; uncertain of his brain, yet trying to task it to regular duty; Clym Royston of Rydon took his way, unsteadily, but with a very dogged resolution to walk upon the square, from the King's Image, where he had been playing fool and culprit, in the direction of Madame Le Vasseur's dwelling, when he had a shrewd suspicion that his Lady had been playing the fool in her own fashion, if not the culprit also.

Clym was not a bad fellow; he was really a good fellow; and, but for that "one rascally weakness," as Steel Cap described it after Cicily's departure, would have been the most admirable steward and butler that could be found in courtly family, but for the single imperfection in his tastes of the strength of his appetites. He, too, thought upon his "rascally weakness," as he passed from the shadow of the King's Image into the open highway, a blank tract of chalky limestone before him; without streets, or ports for guidance, or lights save those of the melancholy stars; the plain, dotted here and there, by plantain or cocoanut trees, that grew in groups, and now and then relieved the monotony of a tract utterly wasted; which, in the daylight pained the eye with the intense glares reflected from the sun. Clym staggered onward for a few paces over this desolate plain, and then deliberately sat himself down upon the ground!

It was, perhaps, the very best thing that he could do. He was coming to a resolution; and meditation demands physical rest. He was struggling to recall his mind.

There is a process of self-soberizing which an innately strong and well poised mind can, when the inebriety is not too great, command, under a very strong effort of will. Clym was exercising his will. But he was one of those persons who can only reason or think, while they converse aloud with themselves. Even when quite sober he was given to soliloquy; when drunk, he was not likely to forego the habit; the only difference, lay in the quality of the thought on such occasions; the quality of utterance being somewhat disproportioned to the degree of sense which it was apt to involve.

He sat himself down, as we have said, to do his thinking more at his ease, and then, by soliloquy, began the attempt to soberize himself.

"Drunk!" quoth he, "and upon British porter! The liquor is genuine! That's certain! It has the proper body to it! I feel it! Barney Briton keeps the best! *That* is some excuse for me! That's clear! British porter is—British porter! Nothing like British porter! I don't care the valley of a Cheapside d—n, for any of their French and Spanish liquors! I've drank 'em all from the wines of Alicante to Bourdeaux. What says the 'Postle? Milk for babes, meat for grown people. Then these light wines will do for such people as Frenchmen, Spaniards, and Portuguese and other sucking babies; but, for a good strong British stomach, they're but shams, and begits emptiness! I could ha' drank forty quarts of *them* and never been the worse for it! It's a pity I hadn't! I'm a sort of baby, tonight, in the hands of British porter! I'm opset! I'm in a heap; and, as for the limbs, I don't feel any call to move 'em. There's a pretty heavy feel, like a lead weight, under the hollow of each foot. I could just now stretch off here, where I am, in this little lime hole, where I am, and, axing for no blanket but the green skies, and the blessed blue stars, I could take as sweet a sleep as I ever had with a nice counterpane atop o'me, and great flowing curtains all hanging down about the bed, and shutting out the impudent daylight.

But I can't and mustn't! Sleep! What have I got to do with sleeping now? I must wake up—wake up, with that ringing in the ears! What's that the girl said—that nice girl, Cicily? Something about danger; and a fool; and a rope; and a neck! It was *my* neck she was meaning, all the time. But about the rope? Ah! Ha! I have it! Neck! Rope! It's the lariat! It's the lariat; and I'm to catch it, she thinks, and I guess it must be here, on the very way home! Eh! They choked off a Spaniard a month ago, in that very fashion—choked him down, dead; caught him by the coffee plantation of Trowbridge, by the lake, and wound him up, out of breath, in little more than the twink of an eye! Then they emptied his pockets! Took all he had, solid goulden doubloons! Blast 'em, they'll find no doubloons in my pockets! No, indeed! Clean, I think."

And, suiting the action to the word, he searched his pockets, and immediately started up, staggering the while, to his feet! He had, in that one moment, taken a long leap in the direction of sobriety. He had made a discovery.

"Great God! The keys are gone! That d–d overpolite German son of a _____ has picked my pocket! *Somebody* has picked my pocket! The keys are gone! Lord save us! They may be robbing the castle now."

"One stupid moment motionless he stood;" and then the will grew more powerful than the liquor in the brain. He stood fast, stood firm, steadied himself for a moment, then strode forward, doggedly, with the determination of one sworn against his enemy—sworn to his overthrow—and mustering all his energies and powers to his support.

Verily, the will is a god! Supreme; a rock against the ocean that mocks every wind and billow! On a sudden Clym hears a whistle. It is echoed! His senses are all quickened. His eyes peer out on every side!

"The rope—ah! The lariat! Well, I'm not drunk no longer! I have my legs! I have my arms! Where's my knife? Ah! I've got that too. They left me that."

He laid down his lantern; opened it; blew out the light; felt for his knife; made it bare in his grasp; and, leaving the lantern where he had laid it down, he strode forward, not now for Madame Le Vasseur's, but in the direction of Steel Cap's castle!

"The keys are gone!" He muttered, "but I'll be there in time if they'll let me. Lord! Lord! hold 'em back only a little while!"

The rogues were on his track. The path had been waylaid. But his change of course, which had not been anticipated, had prompted a change in theirs, also, and hence the signal whistle. Clym naturally supposed the keys to be already in their possession. The brigands as naturally supposed them to be still in his. *We* know where they are; but the game of both was played with regard to their own conjectures, and not as to the facts. Had Heiligrath and his companions known what we know, no attempt would have been made upon Clym. As it was, their plans were pursued as originally made, and with the tenacity of the tiger on a hot scent of blood.

Clym pressed forward, guided only by the starlight. The way was rough, uneven, and he stumbled more than once. His diversion, from one route to another, had taken him out of the beaten track. He was pushing obliquely to recover it. A clump of orange trees stood up before him, and was one of his guide points. He made for that. Beyond, there was a group of cocoanuts. He might next gain that, and he thus counted his stages.

Another and another whistle!

"I hear you," he muttered. "You blasted Algerinos!" He grasped his knife firmly, set his teeth together, and strode forward eagerly though still unsteadily. He had nearly reached the clump of orange trees, when he felt himself hurled to the ground, as if brought down by a stone.

He was half strangled, but he comprehended his situation in an instant. The meaning of Cicily's warning was not lost upon him.

"The rope! The neck!"

His instant thought was action. He had been brought down by the lasso. The Portuguese had a reputation for flinging it equal to that of any thug in the East. Cicily knew that! She had rightly conceived the plan of the robbers, and

Clym, as we have seen, drunk as he was, had comprehended her warning fully, though but lately.

Clym succumbed; but, half strangled and dragged several paces along the stony ground, he was collected; grasped the rope by which he was drawn; held it firmly with one hand; while with the other, which grasped his knife, he severed it with a single stroke, taking care to cut the brief section between his neck, which it encircled, and that which his left hand grasped. This grasp he still maintained; and, as the robbers drew upon it, he yielded to the strain, and submitted to be drawn still further. The natural conclusion of the thug was that the victim was incapable, by reason of his strangulation, of any resistance, in that he had been effectually surprised and was now wholly in his power.

With this conviction, Heiligrath rushed forward, and threw himself upon the only half recumbent Clym. But, in an instant after, the assailant arose with a shriek crying out,

"Himmel! He has slashed me to the bone!"

With a chop, rather than a stab, Clym of Rydon had relieved his enemy. He smote him through the fleshy part of one arm and shoulder, the weapon gliding down along the back and sides, inflicting an ugly and painful, but not a mortal wound.

With the instinct of an old combatant, Heiligrath at once called for succour, by a peculiar whistle through his hands, while he still continued, though at a decent distance, to confront his opponent, still lying upon the ground. He had his policy in this.

But Clym did not keep this posture long. He too, rose to his feet, as he beheld the other parties approaching; and, flourishing his knife, sharp as a razor, he first made a dash at Heiligrath, who retreated, and then, his diversion being successful, made his way in a few bounds to the cover of the orange clump before him. Here he prepared himself, as well as he could, for a renewal of the attack.

Holt soon after made his appearance, joining Heiligrath, with whom he had a brief conference, succeeded by a volley of signals, exceedingly shrill and sharp, and calculated to reach quite across the island. The Portuguese, Manuel, meanwhile, had caught up the rope which Clym had abandoned, and, keeping cautiously aloof, seemed to be busied in preparing a new draw-loop for the renewal, if possible, of his lariat practice; a game, however, which the sheltering clump of orange trees, in great measure served to defeat.

But, though Heiligrath was wounded, and Manuel was cowardly, there were three to one, and Holt was fresh; and how armed, Clym knew not. He had, by this time become very tolerably sober, and though somewhat fatigued was still unbowed. The loop of the rope still hung about his neck; he had no time to remove it; and he prepared himself, with all the resolution of a genuine John Bull, to make fight to the last extremity, seeing that his enemies showed no purpose of withdrawing from their game.

Their signals were repeated; and then, both Heiligrath and Holt, as by concerted arrangement, made a rush towards him.

But the former was rather demonstrative than desperate. He did not come up to time, had lost some blood, and was somewhat enfeebled. Besides, he felt that he had to do with a desperate man, who had become unexpectedly sober, and was now upon his guard. He might be conquered, but he could give savage blows; and these were no ways welcome. Heiligrath, accordingly, making a circuit, sought to effect his approaches towards the rear of the trees under which Clym had sheltered himself; while Holt made his demonstrations in front.

Clym conceived the game. He saw that the two were separated; and, to the equal surprise of both, he made a sudden dash at Heiligrath; and, with a loud halloo, and a terrible rush, waving his knife aloft, he left Holt to follow, while directing a vigorous effort at his companion. Heiligrath fairly took to his heels, but fell; and Clym was almost upon him when compelled to turn, by hearing, close in his rear, the footsteps of Holt. Then he turned upon him, with the conviction that he now had to meet his ugliest customer.

Holt was an old salt, though not an old man. He was a veteran in piratical conflicts. He had been at the sacking of many a Spanish town along the coast; knew well how to use his cutlass, and had borne a boarding pike against a score, plunging headlong among them, yard arm to yard arm, and, by sheer dint of pluck, driving them below hatches, or overboard. But he had grown cautious of late. He had calculated the heft and inches of the broad-shouldered Briton who now confronted him, and simply prepared to stand upon the defensive, until Heiligrath and the Portuguese should be able to come up and make a diversion in his favor.

There were no weapons but their knives among any of the parties. Not to provoke suspicion of their objects, the pirates had left cutlasses and pistols aboard ship. They had not anticipated a fight. They had purposed nothing but a robbery.

Clym, now as fully recovered from the effects of liquor as he could well be, was on the alert. The vigorous, broad-shouldered fellow was now in full fighting trim, and he was not the man to wait upon the signals of his assailants. He now boldly advanced upon Holt, who gave way before him, seeking to withdraw him from the shelter of the orange trees, so that the Portuguese, who held aloof, and where no persuasions of his comrades could bring to a closing struggle, might renew his attempt with the lariat.

But Clym had his wits about him now, and, contenting himself with driving the foe immediately in front to a decent distance, he suddenly wheeled about, and took to his heels, going at full speed, and aiming for the shelter of the clump of cocoanut trees, upon which he had fixed his eyes before.

There was a wild yell from his assailants, as they gave chase. The Portuguese was fleeter of foot than the other two, and while running, flung his lasso, which fell short, the noose barely striking the shoulder of the fugitive. In a few moments, Clym had gained the cover of the trees and stopt for a breathing spell, meaning to take another run as soon as he could recover. But the brigands were now heated, and resolute to prevent this policy. Heiligrath, though feeling an increased feebleness from the loss of blood, concentrated his will upon his purpose; and, hewing himself to a desperate effort, was the first to make towards him. Holt was a heavy man, and no runner, and had been thrown out in the chase. The Portuguese even was in advance of him; was at first in advance of Heiligrath, and, dropping his lariat, as of no more use at present, was brandishing his knife, and making forward with quick steps and a sharp low cry, like that of a wounded cur.

"Ah! Rascal! You come on now!" muttered Clym. "You get bold as you see my back—as you see me run, do you! Look out for my teeth before I run again!"

And, almost as he spoke, he darted suddenly forth from his covert, with a terrible British yell, and bounded towards the Portuguese. The cowardly villain did not wait to encounter that huge form, and that fiercely flashing knife blade. He turned about and incontinently fled, pursued by the bitter execrations of Heiligrath, who was making up to his support.

Then Clym turned upon Heiligrath and with three successive bounds sprang upon him, sprang over him, striking him as he went, and in dodging the stroke, Heiligrath went down, stumbled, fell flat on his face, while the iron-heeled shoes of the Englishman struck him heavily in the loins. The impulse of his rush carried him still forward, and he felt himself confronted on a sudden, by the knife blade of Holt. The fight somewhat resembled that in the classical legend of the Horatii and Curiatii, one man making severally his conquest over three.

And, with blood terribly excited, and thoroughly roused to the conflict; roused by the sense of the success he had had, and stimulated by considerations of equal pride and passion, Clym was not to be confronted! With a tremendous stroke, which no skill of Holt could avoid, the Englishman wielded his *couteau de chape* above the head of the pirate. It flashed doom in his eyes, and he recoiled, with a feeble throwing up of his own blade for the parry; but in vain, as he felt assured. Another moment would have seen him slashed down from throat to abdomen, but for the unexpected interposition of another party from the rear. The arm of Clym was caught from behind, and he found himself fast fettered in the iron grasp of Thorfinn, the Dane!

Holt was saved, at the very moment when he looked upon death as inevitable!

"I have you my chicken!" Cried the giant, whom the signals of the pirates had summoned to the scene. "I have you and shall keep you fast! What! You play with a knife like a Malay, and you hurt my little peoples! You must not hurt my little peoples! I must take your knife and put it up in a basket. It is too sharp for a little boy like you."

Clym struggled terribly, writhing as in a vice; but the iron muscles of the Dane did not relax, and he proceeded in the endeavour, not only to hold the Englishman fast, but to take from him his weapon. Poor Clym felt that he struggled uselessly. He was in the hands of his master. He was, indeed, fast fettered, and considered himself as lost.

But, even in that instant, he was released. A sudden terrible buffet from an unknown hand, that sounded very much like the report of a pistol, brought the Dane to the ground.

Clym was again free, and with a triumphant yell, his knife still safe and flashing in his grasp, he rushed toward Holt, who had recovered himself, and was again approaching in front. Heiligrath lay insensible on the ground. The Portuguese was no longer visible, and Holt was considerably cooled by what he saw. He fled before the Englishman, and Clym stood up, and crowed as lustily as the cock of St. Peter.

Meanwhile, the Dane had sprung to his feet also, and confronted his unknown assailant.

"Thunder!" he cried. "What was that! Who was that! Who shot me to the ground!"

Steel Cap stood before him. The Dane had never seen him. But he had heard of him, and the bright cap of steel glittered in the starlight, and taught him who he was. It made him cautious.

"Was it *you*?" he cried. "Well it was a good blow! It was a grand tumble! But all is not over yet, my friend. No! No!"

And with these words, without more preface, he grappled with Steel Cap! With his long, heavy, muscular arms, he embraced him, as with the clasp of a lion; and rejecting the use of his sword, which he had cast down in the fray, Steel Cap accepted the sort of conflict which the other forced upon him.

The two rocked to and fro, for a few moments, in the stern embrace of the wrestle. But not for long. To the astonishment of the giant, he went down, incapable of keeping his legs, in the conflict!

He rose again, and this time, in rage. But he rose, and confronted his opponent, only to encounter a new form of assault. Blow upon blow encountered him as if delivered by a mallet! In a few moments his face was covered with gore. His eyes were both closed, as if with a curtain of blood. His cheek was scored as with the cut of a knife, and his breath driven from his body, by three successive blows, planted in his chest! He was insensible, motionless certainly, on the white ground, life being only evident in the frequent groans which broke from his throat.

Steel Cap stood over him a moment, then turned to the examination of Heiligrath. The German, weak from loss of blood, severely bruised, and trodden under the iron hooves of Clym, was *hors de combat.* Holt had followed the Portuguese in his flight; both pursued by the eager Clym, now thoroughly sober and anxious to do mischief. Steel Cap had his mode of signaling also. With a silver whistle at his mouth, he summoned Clym to come in, and stay all farther pursuit. The Dane and German were to be cared for.

CHAPTER 7
The Mystery of the Steel Cap

Steel Cap now proceeded to an examination of the prostrate body of Heiligrath. He still remained insensible; and it was evidently impossible that any examination of his hurts could be made in his present situation. He must be removed to the castle.

Steel Cap impatiently repeated his signal for the return of Clym. Meanwhile, the Dane made a feeble movement, and partly raised himself upon his side and elbow; finally, as the former approached him, with some caution, as not knowing what his temper might be, and what degree of power he might still possess for injury, he raised himself to a sitting posture. Steel Cap drew nigh and stood before him in a menacing attitude.

"I hear you," said the Dane, "but I can't see you. I'm blind!"

"Are you much hurt, my good fellow."

"Hurt! Are you the man that killed me?"

"Killed you!"

"Thunder! Yes! I'm as nigh being killed as I wish to be, and a good deal nigher! You've knocked daylight out of my eyes, and starlight too, and you've knocked the breath out of my body! Are you the man that did it."

"Yes! I was the man that struck you!"

"And with what? You had a mallet—a handpike—iron it was, and round, a handle with a bullet head."

"No! Nothing but my fists."

"Don't believe it! Don't lie to me! No man can do such things with a naked fist! I'm a strong fellow myself—strong as a horse! Thought myself the strongest man on the island—ay, in all these seas! And I've a fist, too—feel it! Look at it if you can. I can feel it still, but can't see it. God! Am I blinded for life?"

"Not so! Your eyes are only bunged—that's all."

"Bunged! Do you call it? Blast such bunging I say! And what do you mean to do with me?"

"Take you home to my house."

"What!" with a sort of howl, "Make me a prisoner; and the next thing, blast you, you'll be for having me tied and hung—hung in chains, eh!—for the carrion birds to pick at! Sooner than that, we'll try it again, for life and death! Better die in the track, and in close hug, than be hung up to dry in the west wind, with the crows saying grace over the meal!"

And the Dane made a desperate struggle to rise. The hand of Steel Cap was placed firmly on his shoulder, and he pushed him backward without difficulty upon the ground.

"Be quiet!" said he, "and no harm shall come to you. Show any more signs of fight, and I shall have to finish what I began."

With a groan, the Dane replied:

"Ah! you're the man for it. You're my master. Someday every man meets his master! One day, you'll meet yours! But them mallet blows, and that fling! And I with such limbs! Where did you get the strength? It was trick—not strength! Let me get my eyesight, and you shall show me. I'll go with you. I'll trust you; you're terribly strong. Let me feel your grip. Ah! Enough; I'm all over sore. I'm nothing but a boil. Enough! Enough! Stay, I hear footsteps. Some one comes. Look out for yourself, master, there are many of us—keen dogs—and sharper than myself if not so strong."

"This is a friend," said Steel Cap, and he was joined by Clym.

"They're out of sight," quoth the latter, "down by the landing. I thought better to let well enough alone, and was coming back when I heard the whistle."

"You were right."

"But I've made a mark on one of them, will save him from any mistake among his acquaintances. I gave him a slash in the face that won't make him any handsomer. But who's here?"

"No matter to look: Hurry to the house, and bring Brereton, and the light hurdle in the gallery. One of these poor fellows seems in a bad way. He is still insensible. You and Brereton can take him on the hurdle. As for this man, he will soon be able to walk, with my support. Let Father Caraccioli give you a bottle of rum, and bring it along with you. Hasten now."

Clym disappeared, and Steel Cap continued his watch, dividing his attention between the two wounded men, and occasionally examining the still quiescent form of Heiligrath. In the case of this man, he exhibited some considerable anxiety; and, with finger pressed upon his pulse, and occasionally upon his breast, he at length satisfied himself that the German still lived. But he was impatient for the return of Clym. Meanwhile, the Dane had raised himself again to a sitting posture, and he called to Steel Cap.

"Look here, master—you're my master now, you know; I feel it in all my bones! Do you say that you can save my eyes? I can't see no more than a bat. Will I ever get my sight again?"

"Oh! Yes! I tell you they're bunged up only. In English fighting, that's a common thing. We strike at the peepers, as we call them, and for the bread basket."

"The bread basket? Ah! yes! Them were the blows that knocked head and breath out of me! Look you, master, you're the Englishman they call Steel Cap?"

"Yes!"

"I've heard a good deal said about you; yet nobody seemed to know much. Hark you, one thing: stoop down, bend your ears. Now."

And, in lower tones, the fellow continued:

"One thing they do say, and all believe it, that you've got a world of money, and silver plate, and jewels, and somehow I believe it too; and that's the secret of our affair tonight. They laid their plans to make your man drunk, and rob him of the keys. But I had no part in this plan, I wouldn't agree. I didn't say anything, or do anything to stop 'em, and wasn't with 'em, at the beginning; only come up, as I promised, to help 'em in their difficulty; and I've got myself sweetly sauced for it. I was lying along the beach, and looking up at the stars, when they sounded the distress signal; and so I ran up, thinking to brush off the flies only, and instead of that, here I am seeing sights without ever an eye to open!"

"And who were the fellows concerned in this transaction?"

"Oh, fair play, master! Can't tell that! Mum's the word! Honour among thieves you know! That's English law they say! I'm done with them. I'll ship with you, if you'll take me; and when Thorfinn takes service, he signs his name in a bloody cross. But he don't 'peach. I've ate and drank with them fellows, and we've had many a bloody match with the cross'd pikes and the cutlass, when we've stood beside each other, and so my tongue's as good as fastened to their necks. I'll dance in the air, without shoes or stockings, sooner than be King's evidence. I know how they do things at the "Old Bailey," master, and I keep a still tongue, in a hard head, and even though they crack the one, they can't get at the other."

The Dane was garrulous; but much that he said, was said at intervals; we have thrown together much that simply trickled from him at moments, the taciturnity of Steel Cap affording him free opportunity for the exercise of a faculty which seemed to be one of very active and habitual use. He had a tolerable command of the English—was familiar with the strong phrases of the lower orders, and with those of the pirates, but showed himself equally intimate with the idioms most common among the ordinary English.

At length, Steel Cap was relieved of his watch, if not of his curiosity. Clym came with Brereton, bringing the hurdle, upon which the German was lifted with proper tenderness, and borne off by the stalwart arms of the two English servants.

"Now, my good fellow," said Steel Cap, "I think, with my help and guidance, we can get you to my home. You will find your own legs, and I will find the eyes so as to keep you in the path. Lift your feet high, for the ground is very irregular, and lean on me. Here's my arm."

He helped the Dane to his legs. The latter struggled feebly, to and fro, for a moment, then, taking the proffered arm of the Steel Cap, the two set forward together.

"And it's no prison you're taking me to?" demanded the Dane.

"No! You shall be free as air, as soon as you can see your way, and get over your hurts."

"That comforts me. I believe you. You've got an honest voice. It is a man's! There's no sneak in it! How far have we got to go?"

"Do you feel too weak to walk?"

"No! I only asked."

"Not far; and I've got a good surgeon in my house—Father Caraccioli—who will cure you as soon as any doctor in Christendom."

"I know him. He preached to us at the coffee plantation of the Welshman, Jones. He's a fine talker. He's got the heart, and the sense. I like him; and he lives with you?"

"He's my friend!"

"Ah! That's a good thing to have, though I don't know what it means exactly."

"He'll teach you! I'll teach you. Where there's a heart in a man he's capable of friendship. Friendship is the purest kind of love. There's none of the animal in it."

"I think I understand you. There's a something in what you say, that sounds like daylight in the senses. I'm a rough man, a very strong man, and I've lived upon my strength. I know what I could do, and I made a calculation. I could fight, and did so without shutting my eyes, and I always got a good share of prize money. But, look you, master, I always had to hide my money for I had no friend. I made my prize money my friend; and I spent him, whenever I got a chance; so you see I couldn't love him."

"Thorfinn, the Dane! You shall have a better friend than money."

"How! You know my name—you know me."

"Well! I have known you long as too good a man to be so naked."

"Naked! What do you mean?"

"The man who lives without a friend, is always naked. He puts a fig tree between himself and God. He hides himself from his own heart. He does not believe in himself, because he does not believe in his fellow. You believed in nothing but your own strength, and you only knew that by using it on your fellow. You knew not love, or faith, or confidence, in anything but your own strength or cunning. So you fought for money, and you hid it; or spent it; and you lived without friendship or love, and so you lived without God. My poor friend, God lives in our friends, even as he lives in stars and suns, and winds and skies, and all the beautiful things he puts before us, to show us how beautiful is the love that can believe, and trust, and be faithful."

"You talk strange things, but your voice is honest as a clear bell, from a great church tower, high up in the air, with its gold peak pointing to the stars."

And the giant rested heavily on the arm of Steel Cap, and he groaned bitterly as he said:

"It's so sad to think that I've lived so long, and only begin to see now when I'm blind!"

"You're not blind, except for a day or two, and when I send you forth, I hope it will be with your eyes of the heart opened, as well as the eyes of your face."

"Master, I'm not going to leave you. I believe in you. I'll follow you, and fight for you to the last."

"Fight! Fight! The perpetual thought of Englishman and Dane," exclaimed Steel Cap, musingly; "as if all virtue lay in strength of muscle, and the will to inflict pain and suffering."

"What's that you say master?"

"Why fight, Thorfinn? Why not work? Why not be at peace, fighting with an enemy that cannot suffer—a stubborn soil; fighting in such a cause as makes friends of castle and air; and subdues man to meekness, and gentleness and goodness; makes beauty a common thing; and wins friendship; and compels love; and gives security; so that you shall no longer need to regard gold as the only object of life and worship; so that you shall no longer need to hide it; distrustful of yourself and your comrades; distrustful of God; and having no refuge, save in your own perpetual watch, anxiety, care, struggle, and brute strength! There will come a time when you will be no longer strong—when you will be feeble—when the boy will overthrow you—."

"Let me die first! Let me die in battle, my good master, first wielding a cutlass by your side!"

"We are here, Thorfinn. You are now about to enter a house, not a prison. You will see that there is a friendship which never seeks to rob or injure; a friendship upon which you can always lean; nor apprehend the dagger-stab in your side, when you are most ready to believe."

"Lead in, Master. I have your voice in my ears; I believe you!"

And the two entered Steel Cap's castle, following close behind the hurdle which bore the still inanimate form of Heiligrath, the German. Caraccioli was an experienced chirurgeon of that day. He soon reassured Steel Cap, in regard to the condition of Heiligrath. He next attended to the Danish giant. Steel Cap was quite reassured when he said that the former, though spent with the loss of blood, would do. He laughed merrily, as he added,

"So will this giant, though you have branded him with your mark as indelibly as if you had scored it in hot iron. His cheek will be scarred for life. It was a knuckle-cut."

Steel Cap sighed deeply. He was pale and seemed ill at ease. He had survived the period in life when a sense of triumph rises in the soul at any acknowledgement of prowess, especially when this contemplated nothing higher than a proof of muscular power, aided by pugilistic art.

The conversation between these two remarkable men took place in the chamber of Steel Cap, to which he had retired as soon as he had seen the wounded men cared for properly in another apartment. Here he lay, half reclined on the devain, his hand clasping his head. He murmured rather than spoke,

"Have the poor fellows cared for—I—I—where's Geraldine?"

His voice became faint. The keen-eyed priest fixed his glance upon him, and instantly touched a bell. At this moment, Steel Cap subsided suddenly backward, and said faintly,

"Caraccioli! Come to me! I have been overtasked. It is more than two months since—Ah! It comes! Quick, Caraccioli, quick!"

And, thus speaking, he fell backward, with a piercing cry, falling from the devain to the floor, and striking his head, which was now drawn forcibly to one side, heavily as he fell.

For a moment, his body and limbs were rigid; then the legs were spasmodically drawn up; his eyes rolled rapidly to and fro; violent convulsion of the limbs and distortion of the visage succeeded, the hands were tightly clenched, his tongue partly bitten through by the sudden spasmodic closing of the teeth, protruded from his mouth, while a bloodied foam issued from his lips.

"I feared it!" said Caraccioli. "This excitement, the evident effort tonight. But—."

He did not simply soliloquize; was not idle, and seemed very well to know what to do. At the first call of the sufferer, he had hurried towards him, but not soon enough to prevent his fall. He repeated the bell-call—hastily loosened all the clothes about the throat of his patient; threw open doublet and vest, so as most fully to lay bare the neck, displaying all the upper part of the broad, manly chest; the veins of the neck being literally corded, and swollen almost to bursting; undid and flung off the cap of steel, and then discovered the secret occasion of his wearing such a head piece. The removal of the cap revealed a small silver plate, which, being removed also, discovered what now showed itself to be a ghastly wound of the skull, leaving a semicircular and stellated aperture, as large as a dollar coin.

By this time, Brereton, Clym, and an old woman, had made their appearance in the chamber, all showing great concern and anxiety.

"Water!" cried the priest; and, the goblet brought him, he dashed it freely into the face of the unconscious sufferer; then gently laying his head back, upon the floor, he opened his mouth, and inserted a roll of his hand-kerchief between his teeth. This done, he took from his vest a small phial, in which glowed a ruby coloured liquid, and, with great painstaking, he poured a few drops of this liquid between the teeth, which slowly found its way down the throat of his patient.

Steel Cap gave a low moan; threw himself over heavily on his side, half opened his eyes, and then relapsed into insensibility. There he lay, quite still, breathing heavily, and from time to time sighing deeply. And, as he thus lay, Caraccioli watched him with the anxious watch of a parent over his best-beloved. At length he seemed relieved: Caraccioli rose from his watch.

"He will do now, Clym! The worst is passed. But he has had a hard trial. You, sirrah, have periled your master's life tonight, as well as your own! But I will not reproach you now. He will recover. He will soon be himself again. But—see Jeanette"—to the old woman—"that his couch is immediately made ready. We must get him to bed before he regains his consciousness. Be quiet, and you Clym and Brereton, be prepared to lift him; tenderly as you love your lives. *His* life is worth a thousand of your common man."

And while Jeanette is busied in obeying these orders, and the two serving men waiting to carry out theirs, we may mention, *par parenthese,* that, many years before, Steel Cap had received a terrible blow on the side of the head from the pike of an Algerine corsair on the coast of Barbary. He had carried the corsair by boarding, and, in leaping down upon her quarters, cutlass in hand, had received the stroke, which had crushed in the skull, and felled him to the deck. His men had made short work with the crew of the corsair, especially as they believed the wound of their captain to be mortal. His surgeon, with but little hope of saving his life, had yet proceeded, *secundum artem,* after the practice of that day, to trephine the fracture, and had removed the fragments of bone which were driven in upon the brain. The convalescence had been critical and slow; but, thanks to great nerve and an iron constitution, the patient had ultimately recovered, with no other evil results from the injury than just such as have occurred tonight—the repetition of such convulsions as we have seen, at distant and irregular intervals, which might be precipitated by extraordinary mental excitements, or by as extraordinary physical struggles. The rude surgery of that period did not readily seize their cause, which was the depression of the inner table of bone, at one angle of the seat of injury; and, indeed, Nature herself was busied in remedying this by slowly levelling it away. The intervals between these attacks of Steel Cap grew more and more lengthened, untill now they seemed only to be brought about by the most extreme agitation of the frame or the nervous system. The silver plate was worn for the protection of the wounded part, while the steel cap, which was carefully lined, contributed additional security to the wearer, whose life, as we may conjecture, from what we have seen, had been and still was, exposed to great vicissitudes and as great dangers.

"Jeanette," said Caracciolì, "you must watch with him now, while we watch at the entrance. Clym, you must go after your mistress. The hour is late. It nears the morning. She probably waits for you now. You, Brereton, and myself, will keep watch at the gate. He must not be disturbed. There must be no visitors tonight. We must be armed. We may have such as we do not care to see. This night's work is not yet over. We must see what comes of it! Get your weapons in readiness, Brereton! See that they are in order. I shall arm myself. Clym, where is your lantern?"

"I know where to find it, father."

"Then away! See to your mistress; say nothing of what has happened. But, should she ask, say that your master is very sick. But say nothing unless she asks you. Remember that! Clym was dismissed. Brereton put himself in proper time as a sentinel; and in a few moments, Caraccioli was also in armour—a strong man, cool, composed, self reliant; a dagger at his side, and a petronel in his grasp, and, thus caparisoned, after particular instructions to Jeanette to call him, if required for Steel Cap, he left that personage in the charge of the old Scotch woman, and took his station with Brereton at the entrance of the castle.

CHAPTER 8
Madame Le Vasseur's Evening

Madame Le Vasseur was a clever little French woman; very short, very lively, very unattractive to the eye, yet very popular. She was decidedly clever—very shrewd, and the very woman for her husband. He was a myth, a mystery, a nobody, in the marital sense, and never in the way! He was fashioned somewhat in the mould of that cool, philosophical husband, in the Beppo of Lord Byron, and his habits were not unlike those of his prototype. He could be absent from home for long periods, yet Madame Le Vasseur was never distraught! She had her confidence in him. She knew he would come at last to comfort her; and he did come, always at the proper season.

He found his markets and his profits from the pirates, yet he was no pirate himself. All his transactions were booked, in black and white, and with fair customers. He could have carried his books into the Admiralty with safety, even while his customers were hanging at the yard-arm, and been absolved from all connection with them. He was a man of art; he was dexterous; he was a good accountant, and, by his own arithmetic, was never in any man's danger. He was prudent. And Madame Le Vasseur was like unto him. She was a fashionable woman, it is true; she gave grand parties, but she made her parties subservient to trade. She delighted in music; and her music was always made compensative; she delighted to see the young peoples *very* happy; and they usually paid for the happiness which she could bestow.

Madame Le Vasseur had a business at Nassau. Her friends and her visitors were her customers. She had goods for sale, but only as a favor to her friends. Her husband never returned from a voyage without bringing her a good supply. Nobody asked where they came from. It was enough that she had them for sale—and that they were good—but only for her *friends.* She had many friends, and they were all *dear.* Her friends were all those who attended her *soirees,* her evening dances; her masquerade balls; her thousand pleasant little *reunions,* designed to made the time pass pleasantly upon "dis very desolate island," as she was pleased to phrase it.

Among her particular friends was the Lady Geraldine—she had no other name—nobody asked, or cared, for any other. It was enough that she *was* a lady, the wife of the mysterious Steel Cap; that she had no mysteries herself, and was fond of dress, fond of show, of merriment, and fond of the excitements of society.

Madame Le Vasseur knew the Lady Geraldine like a book. Such was *her* opinion. The Lady Geraldine heard her say so, and laughed merrily. Madame Le Vasseur did not know the Lady Geraldine at all; but the latter never sought to disabuse her of the notion. That lady is as perfect a mystery as her husband; but she was the frankest body in all speaking society.

Madame Le Vasseur knew and acknowledged that the Lady was a "leetle bit strange"—was singular—had her own way generally, and did not seem to be governed by ordinary laws of prudence. The Lady Geraldine was fond of dancing—was fond of music—was fond of society—and laughed aloud, like an amazon. She also sang—like a seraph! But it was always like a seraph in a pretty passion.

The Lady Geraldine was equally popular and provoking. She had a habit of saying sarcastic things, even to the parties that seemed to please her best. She was quick of tongue—ready of repartee—fearless, and never to be taken by surprise. The Lady Geraldine was very liberal. She was a good customer. She liked an article, and took it. The price was an after-consideration. The Lady Geraldine paid punctually and the money was good. The Lady Geraldine was a piquant charm to the circles of Madame Le Vasseur, and Madame Le Vasseur was the most obsequious of all the friends that the Lady Geraldine had on the island.

The party on the present occasion was distinguished. It was astonishing that such a party should be assembled in a region so desolate. There were at least an hundred persons present—male and female, very nearly equally divided. The gentlemen—so called—were all *distingue,* if fine clothes, of very various fashions, could make them so. Many of them appeared as naval or military men. There were Spanish and English, French, and Italian costumes. There was variety enough in costume, for a fancy ball—as in fact it was.

The ladies were also well caparisoned. There were fine feathers, and pearls, and even diamonds. The Lady Geraldine wore pearls, in copious profusion, in hair and about arms and neck; which would not have discredited a presentation at the court of Charles the First. Nor was she alone. There were rival beauties as showy in their jewelry at this reception of Madame Le Vasseur, who would have put Nell Gwynne, herself, out of countenance. Briefly, variety was in the ascendant, and Nassau had no reason to be ashamed of her display at the court of Madame Le Vasseur. Everybody tried to do his or her part, for the parties of the Madame were the most select upon the island.

And there *were* persons present, who *had* done honour to the courts of Europe. There were wild scape-graces of nobility, not yet tamed or subdued by discredit at home. There were some who inherited large titles—in expectancy. There were adventurers who had enjoyed pleasant experience at court, and who were yet young enough to anticipate more. There were men who had known the sweets of power; and there were bold privateers, not calling themselves pirates, who bore commissions of the state, which might be forged, or be bought with money, from varied secretaries and governors, if not of the Crown itself! Briefly, there was no little pride, stateliness, pretension, courtesy and grace, in this strange reunion of discordant elements, among the banks of the Bahamas archipelago.

The Lady Geraldine shone, resplendent, the observed of all observers. She was exquisitely attired; richly, but not without grace and a certain propriety, consistent with her magnificent beauty. Her fine masculine figure, her well set head, with the admirable *posé* of Cleopatra; her ease of manner, her elegance, all compelled instant acknowledgement; and, though many pretty women were present, there were none to contest her claims to universal admiration. Even Envy grew silent as it gazed.

Very soon, the Captain Ferrand and Lieutenant Leonard, her special swains, were at her feet—figuratively at least. There was no physical demonstration of their homage to this degree. Captain Ferrand was a dashing Frenchman, who commanded the successful armies, called the Barracouta. He was a corsair, but he ranked as a gentleman. He was a graceful gallant; and a wonderful dancer. His *pirouettes* were admirable. He could cut a pigeon-wing to the height of the ceiling, and the delight of a whole assembly. He wore a large, well whiskered visage; was rather broad and burly of make; he was not handsome of feature, or fine of form—was rather stout, indeed, and short, not well built, and had the appearance of the greatest physical vigour. He was, in fact, a strong, muscular, bold and impudent fellow.

Lieutenant Leonard was as much unlike him as day to night. He was tall and slender; was not much of a dancer; but was death on sentiment! He spoke of moon and stars perpetually. It is quite probable that Captain Ferrand had never seen either—certainly, he had never expounded any unnecessary vision or thought in their contemplation; and had but little faith in either. But these two, the very antipodes of each other, were the most particular in their devotion to the Lady Geraldine.

The professions of these two gentlemen were well known upon the island, yet occasioned no disquiet or remark. There will be a condition of things in every community which is yet held to be in violation of society, which will yet occasion no disturbance to society. Society is always indulgent to those who minister to its appetites and tastes.

It was so at Nassau. It was well understood that these persons were pirates; but, here, at the house of Madame Le Vasseur, they were received as gentlemen; and by the way, there were much more tenacious of their behaviour as gentlemen, though just from the high seas, as pirates, than many who are yet fully acknowledged as to the manner born—born in the very purple legitimate integrals of high fashion.

It is not difficult to account for this. They were on their good behaviour. Besides, at the ball of Madame Le Vasseur they were doing nothing in professional account. They were quite content to sink the profession for the nonce—when there was no profit to be made by it—in the enjoyment of amusements, and companionships, which their profession did not furnish, and which were yet very agreeable, *pour passer le temps.*

The principle of "high life below stairs" is one of emulation—as we see the servants of nobility putting on the fine airs, as well as the fine clothes, and donning the very names of their masters—a subject which has made so large a constituent in the material of the middle-period comedy of England. So we can readily comprehend the sort of principle, or vanity, which would prompt our pirates, on shore, and associated with parties who *had* been accustomed to good companionship, if not aristocracy in the well-mannered society of Europe, endeavouring, each after his capacity, to emulate what was considered among such circles, the perfection of good breeding. The savage put off his savage habits for a season, and passed into the antagonist role of the fopling and dandy. Captain Ferrand subdued his whiskers, for a while, and left his cutlass on board ship, to attend the parties of Madame Le Vasseur. He wore now an elegant rapier, silver mounted, which he had beguiled, in a close embrace, from the keeping of a Spanish don.

Lieutenant Leonard, naturally inclined to be the courtier, was always similarly appointed, even aboard ship, and in the heat of action; for the fellow *could* fight, and was no milk-sop, though effeminate of air and nuance. He always took care to weapon himself handsomely, even though at the loss of some little power of harm; and his ruffles, at the neck and wrist, were always beautifully white, and regularly crimped by the irons of the *blanchisseuse.* It was perhaps enough for such as he that he should, among the European refugees of Nassau, be enabled to engage in picquet, or euchre, or whist, with the cast-off scion of a noble English house; and these, poor and destitute, certainly living in obscurity and by their wits, were well content to find society even in the fellowship of those, who, at the close of the next voyage, might end a bloody career in a strangling noose at Tyburn or Havana.

Enough—Madame Le Vasseur, considerate of her guests, had provided cards, and even dice for their amusement and profit. There were rooms, aside from the spacious hall given to the dancers, in that old castellated stone mansion of hers, which were assigned to parties who preferred to gather around a table, and brood over their cards, duly considerate of the stakes in Spanish gold, or English shillings, which you might see spread, more or less profusely, on this or that table. Aged gentlemen, and ancient ladies might be seen at these tables equally profound in their meditations and earnest in their games. This practice, too, was one of the small sources of profit to our thrifty hostess. She, herself, engaged in the conflicts of skill, or craft, with the willingness of a Frenchwoman. She was an adept in cards, and her profits, from this source, though not to be named in connection with those from the traffic in fine stuff, were yet not beneath her consideration.

We will suppose the dancing to have begun, with the proper spirit—the tables of the gamesters to have been set, and the seats duly occupied. Merrily did the music sound from the grand saloon, which was gaudily decorated, to the echoes of the many and quickly-twinkling feet. The Lady Geraldine and Captain Ferrand had the floor as partners, objects of admiration to all the room. Her Ladyship was in a wild humour, surpassed herself as a dancer, and every other woman in the room as a beauty. And when she changed her partners, and surrendered herself to the companionship, in the dance, of Lieutenant Leonard, there was no alteration in her exhibition, unless from one degree to the other; rising, finally, to the superlative, which at length exhorted from the company, at the close, a spontaneous burst of admiration. Her magnificent form queened it most triumphantly, as sweeping across the floor flushed with excitement, she subsided with indescribable ease and grace upon the sofa, and found the ecstatic Captain Ferrand on one side, and Lieutenant Leonard on the other, both eloquent with their tributes of applause and admiration.

But these were by no means suffered to monopolize her, and, without showing it, she was especially careful that they should not. It was only necessary to address a glance or smile to the Count Cesario to draw him to her side. The famous political exile of Spain, Pedro Gomez, was equally devoted—so long as the lady pleased that he should linger at her shoulder.

Captain Ferrand spoke to her in French. She answered him in that language as glibly and freely as any Parisian. The Count Cesario was pleased to test her in Italian, and her Tuscan, in reply, was rather better than his, as he knew nothing but the language while she was conversant with its literature. The Señor Don Pedro Gomez bantered her in Spanish about the thousand Dramas of Lope de Vega, and her flexible tongue gave forth its responses in the sonorous language of Castile; and when the venerable Bishop of Psalter, an exile from England, under a shrewd suspicion of forgery and the abduction of another man's wife, ventured to tax her resources in Latin, she answered him with an apt later epigram from Martial, which applied directly to his case, and sent him off in confusion.

And all this was done quietly, with out effort or ostentation. She was even more subdued in manner than usual, though still bright and sparkling; her eager temperament, lively fancy, and long continued association with a superior convention, still irrepressibly teeming forth, somewhat in spite of a reluctant will. The animation of her nature was not to be kept down, however much she might try to modify its expression. But, if her tongue was under some degree of watch, her eyes were licensed rovers; and the play of expression in the mobile lines of her face, and the beautiful significance of emotion in her mouth, were full of the most lively utterances, the meaning of which was not quite so evident to her companions. It was only by a sort of instinct that the obtuse nature of Captain Ferrand caught the idea that there was *michin malico* in her glance; and the import of some of her replies to him, in French, was wholly lost to him except as so many puzzles. There was a singular blending of lure with sarcasm in much that she said, as if this mood was to beguile, in order the more certainly to wound. Ferrand was mystified and confessed himself bewildered. With a petty oath, such as that society of Nassau was prepared to tolerate, he said, still in French,

"The Lady Geraldine is a mocker! Positively you laugh at me! Is't not so?"

"And why not? You will admit that the subject is sufficiently laughable."

"And yet, my Lady, I flatter myself—."

"Oh! Pray don't. You will need medicine after it."

"By ___, my Lady, you are a desperate quiz! You laugh at everybody."

"Alas, no, Monsieur Ferrand—it is pure sentiment. Every smile of mine is a very sad memory, and when I laugh, believe me, it is grimace! What have I to do with either?"

"Ah! You are sad! You are unhappy! I was sure of it. There is a certain something in your face, at times, that tells me you are unhappy. I see! This all owing to your Blue Beard!"

"My what?" With a sharp ringing tone and a keen concentrated glance that shot into his very eyes.

"To your Blue Beard of a husband of course, who will not let himself be known to other people. He is a don, a pacha, a sultan, they tell me, who carries his head in the clouds! The wonder is that he lets Fatima visit Madame Le Vasseur. It is my happiness, however, that he does so."

The keen eyes of Geraldine were looking lightnings, but a quiet smile played upon the lips, as she replied:

"His fatima lets herself do much which, possibly, her Blue Beard does not exactly approve. But what would he have, or you have, in this dreary desert place? I must laugh, you know, Monsieur Ferrand even if I laugh at my neighbours; must dance, though my *vis a vis* may wear a cloven hoof. Ah!"—looking down at the feet of her companion, as if in inquiry—"Ah! Monsieur, *yours* are even now endangering my train."

"Diable!" he exclaimed, recoiling a pace. "Hoofs, Madame," and he thrust out his well-turned and small feet triumphantly, as if to challenge examination. He was prouder of his feet than of his face. They had afforded him, as a dancer, some of his most grateful triumphs. His own eyes examined them, and he was satisfied; and a pleasant smile mantling the face of the Lady Geraldine made him aware of the absurdity of his vanity, and with some ingeniousness, he exclaimed,

"By____! Madame, you might cure me of some of my sins, if you would only take me in hands."

"Monsieur Ferrand, beware of seeking a remedy for them. It were fatal to the patient. To rid you of your sins would be to deprive you of all your possessions."

"Sacre! You are hard upon me tonight, my lady. But you do not mean it. Your wit must keep itself bright, no matter who furnishes the foil. But you are right. There are some sins with which I would not part"—here he stooped to her ear, and in a whisper concluded his sentence thus—"especially if the Lady Fatima would share them with me! Could she now be persuaded to go into the Blue Chamber!"

He paused; and looked into her eyes with a sinister smiling, in which a lurking doubt might yet be seen. There was a vivid flush that rapidly spread over the face of the lady, as warm and rich as that which the setting sun flings over his own curtains ere he sinks beneath the sea. For a moment she was silent; then looking him full in the face, she said,

"So, Captain Ferrand, you are curious about the Blue Chamber. And you are curious about the Blue Beard? You would know the one, and would persuade me to enter the other? I do not see why your curiosity should not be gratified: but people are very apt to pay for such gratifications; and the penalties are sometimes beyond the capacity of those who seek."

"Ah! Madame, you charm me. You encourage me! You stimulate my courage! You provoke me to heroism! What is there that I would not encounter for your sake! Believe me, my dear lady"—this also in a whisper—"I am the man for such a fatima, to storm the castle of any Blue Beard! May I have the honour to see you home tonight?"

A slight but sinister smile played upon the lips of the Lady; then she laughed merrily as she replied,

"And why not, Monsieur? To be sure! I shall be pleased to have such an heroic escort! We sometimes need chivalry here to arrest audacity."

All this was spoken in French. It is not to be supposed that the dialogue was suffered to proceed consecutively without occasional interruptions from other parties. Lieutenant Leonard, who understood not a syllable of French, was completely thrown out, and he was impatient of the scene in which he did not share. He offered frequent interruptions, which were met by Captain Ferrand with a scowl, and by the Lady with a good humored smile. The *empressments* of both parties to this conversation was particularly annoying to the Lieutenant. It augured, as he thought, an understanding between them which was more intimate than grateful to him, and he burst out finally into an ejaculation which brought down upon him a scornful sneer of Ferrand, and a good humoured smile from Geraldine, who seemed thoroughly to enjoy this rather equivocal sort of play.

"May I be utterly exterminated, dear Lady Geraldine, if I do not learn this confounded French lingo, if it is only for the pleasure I shall have in talking with you in a language which nobody but ourselves shall understand."

A shrug of Captain Ferrand's shoulders; who said loudly enough for all the room to hear,

"Be sure that you get the Parisian accent, Leonard; and while you are about it, take some lessons for the meñuet. Your dancing is not exactly the mode, I can assure you."

And the Captain thrust out his nice little feet, for the public admiration.

"I am not of the opinion, Captain Ferrand, that the hearts of ladies are to be won by the shape or size of a man's foot, nor do I see that to skip high, and bounce wide, is the greatest beauty of manhood."

"Skip high! Bounce wide! *Ma foi!* What does the young man mean? Tare—Mr. Leonard, I am not please with this language."

"Nor I with yours, Captain Ferrand," replied the other with spirit.

"Ah! You are not please? Eh! Bien! We shall have pleasure to give you more pleasure, when you please, in some other parts of speech."

"Very good, sir! Lady Geraldine, shall I be so happy to assist you to the harpsichord. The ladies, Madame Le Vasseur assures me, are all eager to hear you in that beautiful ballad of 'The Ocean Rock' which you sang the other night. I am deputed by the ladies—I am commanded—to entreat your music."

Madame Le Vassuer came forward. The Lady Geraldine rose. Lieutenant Leonard offered his arm; Captain Ferrand thrust himself between; scowling defiance on one side, yet laboring to look Sir Lancelot on the other. But the Lady noticed neither; looked at neither; but apparently with a sense of relief, or escape, took the arm of Madame Le Vasseur, and made her way without reserve or hesitation to the instrument. She played and sang the song required; the Count Cesario, the Spanish Don, the Archbishop, and a crowd besides, gathering around her, and going into different degrees of ecstatics.

Lieutenant Leonard succeeded in getting particularly nigh, and when she retired from the instrument, he was close beside her, and engaged her attention in conversation for a while. With him she spoke in English; and curious to say, he had that to utter in courtly English, which Captain Ferrand had spoken in Parisian French! He, too, would like to see the Pasha, the Sultan, the Blue Beard, who held the pretty Fatima in bonds which both parties assumed her perfect willingness to break.

And she smiled graciously upon him. He too offered to see her home; and she gave him a cordial assurance that he should have that felicity. And the Italian Count Cesario, and the Spanish Don Pedro Gomez, all severally concurred in soliciting the same privilege; and to all their prayers unknown to each other the

Lady granted the desired promise. And the several parties congratulated themselves at last on being able to accomplish two objects which before had seemed very difficult of gratification; namely, to visit the interior of Blue Beard's castle, and to make the acquaintance of the Pasha himself.

Steel Cap, though almost daily a visitor at the King's Image, yet held himself aloof from all communication with its guests. He could not of course exhibit this stately reserve when receiving guests introduced by his wife into his own castle. Each believing himself the one especially preferred guest, they were all equally delighted.

Supper was announced! Enough of suppers! People will eat! They are the same animals all the world over, and we do not find that they change their habits much when they run beyond the seas, or that there is much novelty in any of the performances, whatever the company, at the discussion of the creature comforts. Let it suffice that Madame Le Vasseur, like all Frenchwomen, was a good cook herself, or employed the talents of one who could boast a Parisian training; that the arts of the French cuisine were such as to adapt themselves readily to the *materiel* peculiar to the Bahamas; that sea fowl, and sea-muscles, the limpet, the conch, the barracouta and other fish, including the turtle, were in abundance and served up in every style; that there was no lack of dainty dishes, rich viands, and exquisite fruits; that the cordials circulated freely among the ladies, while the gentlemen made free with the rum punch of a liquor which, in those days, had its reputation even in Europe, for the concoction of this then favorite beverage, the taste for which has not yet utterly died out from the palates of men.

The party, especially the masculine portion of it, naturally warmed up under frequent potations. In this province they threw off much of the previous constraint which followed from the desire to appear fine and fashionable. They gradually began to exhibit the more natural traits of temper and of training which belonged to the profession; and the occasional oath became more frequent, and the passionate ejaculation, and the offensive phrase, until the quarrel began to brew in this or that chamber, while loud uproar came from rooms of those, who, retiring from the supper table, had resumed their cards and dice.

The ladies, warned by previous experiences of what might reasonably be feared under such circumstances, began their preparations for departure. Lights were called—servants summoned by name in loud cries by the porter at the door. Soon a hundred torches and an occasional lantern flamed around the house; and when the Lady Geraldine rose to take her departure, the signal for a general break up soon followed.

The Captain Ferrand and Lieutenant Leonard were both in readiness. They had neither of them left the Lady's elbow from the moment when she rose from the supper table. One occupied the right, the other the left, of her chair, taking places just in the rear and stooping to her ear alternatively and how she smiled upon them severally; with so rich a grace, and so pleasant a manner, so well calculated to beguile conceit into confidence, and defraud with delusive fancies the self persuading vanity! The gallants were not such keen scrutinizers of ladies eyes as to suspect the insidious meanings that might be embodied in a smile. It must be admitted that both gallants, Captain and Lieutenant, were somewhat obtuse in such astrologies. They belonged to the stern, silent, half savage, half hero characters in Byron's pirates, who "knew not how to whine, and sigh, / But only to obtain, or die!" And so the occult sign in the orbs of the Lady Geraldine had no significance in their eyes. They saw but the dazzling brightness which beguiles the child in the glance of the serpent, nor dreamed of the deadly fang, that the brightness of eye contributed only to conceal.

When she rose, each at her elbow they both proffered her an arm.

"Tare, Lieutenant Leonard," said Captain Ferrand, "dis honour is for me, Tare, tonight."

"Pardon me, Captain Ferrand, but I have the advantage. I have the honour, with permission of Lady Geraldine, to serve her with my arm."

"Sacre! We shall see dat!" and Ferrand rudely pushed between the Lieutenant and the Lady. Leonard repelled him—resisted! Swords were instantly drawn over the very head of the Lady. And while all was uproar in the room, and parties rushing forward with loud outcries, her calm of face, action, manner were wonderful, and suddenly compelled the astonishment of all the lookers on. The smile upon her beautiful countenance had deepened into scorn; and as she looked unmoved, and continued singularly silent, one might suppose her reflection to have been somewhat of this sort, though not to be spoken in words:

"What matter if these brutes cut each others' throats! It is as good a way of disposing of such cattle as any other—perhaps the best for themselves, as saving them from a more ungrateful and ungraceful mode of death!"

Could a mere glance of the eye, or curl of the mouth, action or attitude say this much, such must have been held the utterance of hers! But, even as the swords crossed, clinked together and flashed in air, the Lady stretched out her right arm, as if between them, and said,

"Coolly, gentlemen, respect my nerves! You shall have my full permission to carve each other at another time! But I have promised you both that you shall see me home tonight. I promised neither of you my arm, and neither shall have it, since it is evident you prefer your own arms; and do not fancy that I have limited myself to your small attendance. The Count Cesario will also be of my escort; and the noble Grande Don Pedro Gomez; and here is our excellent Bishop of Psalter, who is only too happy to show that the gallant is not totally lost in the priest; and, with all these, noble, and distinguished and graceful, and gallant, do you suppose that I am to be narrowed down in my promise to the attendance of a mere captain and lieutenant! Fie upon this presumption gentlemen! Is my escort ready?"

A score of voices were quick to answer. There was an outcry! And the lady made her way to the entrance, and out into the court, amidst the flash of flambeaus. Clym of Rydon being at hand, with his lantern, and, properly rebuked, Capt. Ferrand and Lieutenant Leonard, being made to give way to the venerable Bishop of Psalter, and to the great political exile, Don Pedro Gomez; and to the gallant gay Count Cesario—in brief a dozen at least of worshipers, all of them in some way distinguished in Nassau above the multitude. And with this escort she passed through the admiring circle, now crowded about the entrance smiling grandly as she went, whilethe music followed, and merry voices broke forth in song, as the several parties began to scatter, here and there, in as many different directions.

Chapter 9

Madame Le Vasseur was in despair at the departure of her visitors—and was very glad to get rid of them. She wrung the hands of her favorites at parting—almost wept her farewells and adieus—and the parting gone, thanked God that all was over! But the clever little Frenchwoman had not spent her night or money unprofitably. Her parties paid.

Still, if her petty despair was only stimulated, she was yet somewhat puzzled in her diagnosis of a certain case. The Lady Geraldine, whom she fancied she knew so well, had contrived somehow that night to confuse her judgment. Certainly the conduct of the fine lady had been strangely contradictory. Madame Le Vasseur was not so obtuse, indeed, as Ferrand and Leonard, and could see false lights hung out in those eyes of the Lady Geraldine which might well puzzle the most experienced mariners. She was conscious of a contradictory something in their expression, with which she was not satisfied. And she was resolved not to be puzzled. She was not willing to confess that her sagacity in decyphering character could possibly be baffled, and her pride was concerned in this case, if not her interest, for *entre nous,* she was in the private councils of Captain Ferrand,

and found her profit in it. She relied rather upon the Captain's audacity than upon his tactics, and, without any self disparagement, the excellent captain had no small faith in the Frenchwoman's capacity for stratagem. It was necessary that Madame Le Vasseur should recover some lost stitches in her net work; should find some lost clues in her study of Lady Geraldine's heart or temper—felt herself puzzled the more she mused over the matter, and was vexed to think that a Celt could be a problem to a Gaul. Such nevertheless was the case, and the subject of most mortifying reflection.

"Ferrand," quoth she, "does not understand the Lady Geraldine, and neither in fault do I—tonight. She is wrong here. Something's wrong."

And she tapped her own head significantly.

"She's touched in the upper story, or she means mischief. And even when she means mischief only, it yet works like madness in a woman's brain. There was something in her eyes, tonight, in her voice, in all that she said, looked and did, that puzzles me—distracts me. She looked at me suspiciously more than once. I caught her eyes upon me with a sharp, wicked gaze, that means something. Has she found out anything. Has Ferrand blurted out anything, in his rude headlong way? He'd stand a better chance, if he had less impudence."

And so Madame Le Vasseur worried herself with conjectures that led her to no conclusions.

On a sudden a door opened; a slight footfall was heard, and the next moment, a small, wiry, awkward person entered the room, habited in something like a blouse of gray. His face was mean, catlike and cautious in expression, sharp and vigilant. This was Monsieur Le Vasseur, the lady's husband.

He sat down, and so did the Lady. There were no embraces between them, no kisses, not even the shaking of hands. Yet he had been absent several months, none knew where, or how employed.

"Well?" said the Lady.

"Yes, well enough."

"Good time this time?"

"Yes—very. Teche, you know, is here."

"What that beast, Blackbeard."

"Yes!"

"And is he likely to give us trouble this time?"

"Hardly; he's off again."

"Ah! Indeed, and why so soon."

"He picked up a lugger, who reports a galleon, loaded with plate, just setting out from Vera Cruz. I came with him, this trip."

"How came that?"

"Oh! We're friends now. I helped him in a little matter. He brought my bales, and was civil enough to land 'em before leaving."

"And he's gone!"

"To hell, I hope! I never wish to see him again."

"Amen!" said the Lady devoutly.

"Are all your guests off."

"All."

"Good! The porter will be here within the hour. We must store all away in the vaults before daylight. We shall not open this cargo for a week or two."

"Ah! Why? There's demand—and plenty of money! Ferrand is here, you know; and Hornsby, with a new vessel—."

"Yes, we will wait awhile."

"And Leonard has temporary command of the *Night Hawk.*"

"Where's Harris?"

"Half dead—stabbed through and through by Purvis, his cook. They killed Purvis on the spot."

"Well."

But we need not pursue these details, which were all discussed between the parties in this cool, dry, unexpressive manner, as if mere things of course, in the ordinary way of business. The husband called for brandy, which was set before him, and he drank but sparingly. Then looking more earnestly at the woman than he had yet done, he said,

"You have been trafficking with Ferrand?"

"Yes; a little. Well!"

"It is not well! I warned you that you were not to do anything which might bring us into trouble with Steel Cap."

"And why not?"

"It is not for you to ask. It is not for me to tell. When I say to you hands off, it must be hands off. You are to keep your hands off Steel Cap, as you value your life and my own. Why will you meddle with this thing. You know what Ferrand's after. You little know what he will find."

"But who, after all, is Steel Cap?"

"Are you well off, woman, where you are? Keep so! Do you know enough of business to make money. Don't learn any other business. Enough: the day you are caught meddling with Steel Cap, your business is done for—you are done for—and I shall find it difficult to find another proper woman to put in your place. You must please the Lady Geraldine in any way, without troubling yourself to please Captain Ferrand. Mark me, his time's nearly up."

"Mon Dieu! Monsieur Le Vasseur you terrify me. What do you know?"

"What I shall not tell you, for sure. Are you getting to be a magpie. Why should you chatter? Look you, our business is large enough, and profitable enough. Eh? It's not—say."

"Yes! Well; but—."

"Comment! How but? Have you not said enough. Hark! It is the porter's keys—get in and send back the slide."

Both parties left the room, to meet together in a vaulted chamber hewn out of the limestone rock, several feet, or yards, beneath the foundation of the house. Very cunning, indeed, was the construction of this vault, and very curious the mode of entrance. But we need no description of them now. The bales were safely stored before daylight. Monsieur Le Vasseur, gathering up a large sum of money which his wife had collected, disappeared as suddenly as he came. But few in the island had been made aware of his coming, and the mode of his departure was unknown to his own wife. Like Macbeth, he kept his chuck ignorant of some of his performances, having, we may suppose, a due regard to her conscience, which he did not choose to burden, more than he could help, with his sins, or his secrets!

Madame Le Vasseur took his departure very coolly. But she had her soliloquies about his policy.

"Le Vasseur," quoth she "is such a coward! Why should he fear this Steel Cap? What is the secret between them. Does Geraldine know it? Ah! If she knows, how is it that I do not know. Something's gone wrong. I must find out. Besides, I must keep faith with Ferrand. Must!"

She was mistaken in more respects than one. Le Vasseur was no coward, but a very firm and resolute man—a most decided will, in a small if not a feeble frame. But he shrank from brutality and from blood. He had cunning of nature, not cruelty. He lived upon the pirates, but loathed them nevertheless. Even while his wife spoke of him as a coward, she feared him. She was rather uneasy in respect to what he said about Ferrand and Steel Cap; but by dint of repeated assurances to herself that he was quite too timid to be as fully successful as he might be, and certainly too much so, to be properly a restraint upon herself, she resolved to follow her own notions in the path upon which she had entered, with a caveat for her own use, to have a full explanation with her husband, whenever he should again return. Meanwhile, deeds were to be done; and of these she had her misgivings, especially when she remembered what Le Vasseur had said of Ferrand's time being nearly up. It troubled her as she remembered that Le Vasseur had the most remarkable prescience, and that his predictions almost certainly came true. But her involvements made her a little more obtuse than usual, and like a good wife she remembered that husbands were mere mortals, like the rest of men, and could not be expected to know everything. So she resolved to dismiss all anxieties from her mind, while continuing her practice, endeavouring to shape events to her own, and the desires of her present ally, the persuasive Captain Ferrand.

Meanwhile, the Lady Geraldine with her select escort of dons and counts, bishops and captains, proceeded accompanied by a hundred torches, with music of flute, and bugle, violin and clarinet in the advance, made her way in the direction of Blue Beard's castle. Her escort was not limited to the small party which had received her invitation. Somehow, it had got noised abroad at Madame Le Vasseur's, before the breaking up of the party, that the castle of Steel Cap, that mysterious abode of the mysterious Bashaw, was to be laid bare that night for inspection. Nothing of the kind had been pledged, as we happen to know, but it was quite enough that such was the rumour; and society was slightly unconventional and so free in Nassau, and people were very curious, and accordingly, a goodly number of cavaliers, and not a few of the ladies were found following our party, at a modest distance, resolved to take advantage of any opportunities which might occur for the gratification of their unusual desires. The music, the crowd, the open air—the torches waving, the occasional shout or cry—all contributed to the increase of that excitement which the wine and cordials and the Jamaica punch of Madame Le Vasseur had supposedly begun; and the result was something of that affair which in recent periods we have learned to distinguish as the charivari! Wild ballads were sung, wild shoutings filled the air, the young men ran and bounded, wilted and fell; blows were exchanged and weapons drawn, and an occasional execration from unlicensed lips so too certainly betrayed the occupation of the individual so recently on his good behaviour.

Meanwhile, however, the immediate escort of the Lady Geraldine kept close attendance upon her step.

Explanatory Notes

Note: the first number refers to the page in the current volume. The second and third numbers refer to the manuscript page and the line on that page.

Page **34**; ms. page 3, lines 5–9: "Cape Cotoche . . . years!"—the northernmost point on the Yucatan peninsula, Cape Catoche, also the site of the first European landing in modern-day Mexico. Simms is referring to Mayan ruins, some of which are visible from the coast, believed then to be much older than later archeology would determine.

Page **35**; ms. page 3, line 15: "basserest"—low table, from the French, *basse,* or low.

Page **35**; ms. page 5, lines 20–24: "Guanahani . . . Columbus . . ."—Simms's words reflect what was known at the time about Columbus's first sighting and landing in the New World, but the exact island has been the subject of debate for centuries. Guanahani is the name that natives gave to the island Columbus called San Salvadore, one of the islands of the Lucayan Archipelago, though his description matches more than one island. Cat Island was long believed to be Guanahani until an abstract of Columbus's diary was published in 1875–76.

Page **36**; ms. page 7, line 3: "abaca" (*Musa textilis*)—a kind of banana plant, commonly called Manila hemp in Simms's day, cultivated for its fiber.

Page **36**; ms. page 7, line 13: "New Providence"—the most densely populated island in the Bahamas today and site of the capital city, Nassau. As Simms indicates, it was first under Spanish control, named by a sixteenth-century governor who credited his survival of a shipwreck to divine providence.

Page **36**; ms. page 7, lines 20–21: "The Brothers of the Coast"—a loose coalition of buccaneers, often commissioned privateers, active in the Caribbean, the Atlantic, and the Gulf of Mexico primarily from the late seventeenth through early eighteenth centuries. Based in Port Royal and Tortuga, Brethren (as the term was commonly translated) ships were noted for their democratic rule, codified as a code or custom, which so appealed to sailors who encountered them that they often joined the pirates. Henry Morgan is one of the most famous Brethren. In the words of historian Jon Latimer, "By combining the freebooting traditions of European mercenary soldiers with those of oppressed sailors, the brethren of the coast became a sanctuary for all manner of outcasts—social misfits, military deserters, runaway slaves and indentured servants, those escaping debts and other responsibilities—to create a myth of independence embodying the very ideals of liberty, equality and fraternity that would destroy the *ancien régime* little more than a century later." Jon Latimer, *Buccaneers of the Caribbean: How Piracy Forged an Empire* (Cambridge, Mass.: Harvard University Press, 2009), 76. For more, see his chapter 4.

Page **36**; ms. page 8, lines 16–17: "the Vikings, the Sea-Dragons of the Northmen" —three terms considered synonymous in Simms's day, although sea dragon also applied to Viking longboats, with their elaborately carved prows, and to the decorative motif that adorned their flags and shields.

Page **37**; ms. page 9, line 24–page 10, line 2: "deeds of derring-do"—daring action or feats, usually driven by desperate courage. A common phrase in Sir Walter Scott novels, its meaning is based on a chain of linguistic misunderstandings and errors; for more, see the Oxford English Dictionary.

Page **37**; ms. page 10, lines 4–5: "There is no peace beyond the line . . ."—Elizabethan privateers were famous for their unswerving commitment to raiding Spanish vessels, and this motto, symbolizing that commitment, was emblazoned on the flags of both Sir Francis Drake (1540–1596) and Sir Henry Morgan (1635–1688). Historians later debated exactly which line the phrase referred to; Garrett Mattingly documented that it should have been "lines," a reference to the "lines of amity" agreed to verbally by the French and Spanish diplomats who negotiated the 1559 Peace of Cateau-Cambrésis. The treaty was in force on the European side of the Tropic of Cancer and the prime meridian, passing through Ferro in the Canary Islands; to the west and south, it had no force, a belated agreement with what was already a well-established practice. Garrett Mattingly, "No Peace Beyond What Line?" *Transactions of the Royal Historical Society,* 5th ser., 13 (1963): 145–62.

Page **37**; ms. page 10, line 23: tapia—rammed or pressed earth, often incorporating plant fiber or matter; a common sixteenth-century construction material.

Page **37**; ms. page 11, line 25: attainted—tainted; corrupted.

Page **38**; ms. page 13, line 6: buccaneer—from the Caribbean Arawak word *buccan,* a wood-framed device for smoking meat, which was the common local practice for preserving it. French hunters who settled Hispaniola called it *boucane* and became known as *boucanier;* this was anglicized as buccaneer. The term became synonymous with piracy when the *boucanier,* driven from the island by the Spanish around 1630, settled in Tortuga, inaugurating an age of piracy made famous by Alexandre Exquemelin's 1684 book, *The Buccaneers of America,* which also cemented the term's association with piracy in the public imagination.

Page **38**; ms. page 13, line 6: the French corsair (from the French *corsaire*)—French privateers commissioned by the king with a letter of marque to plunder rival shipping. Seized cargos were auctioned, with a portion retained by the privateer and crew and a portion reserved for the king.

Page **38**; ms. page 13, line 7: the Spanish or Portuguese picaroon—from the Spanish *picaron,* or rogue: pirate.

Page **38**; ms. page 13, line 8: the Dutch *Flibustier—boucanier* who became known for piracy. The name may be a derivation of the English "freebooter" and the Dutch *vrijbuiter,* or one who plunders freely; also possibly derived from the English "flyboat," the translation of the Dutch *fluyt,* a single-decked, square-rigged, shallow-draft craft that could be crewed by a few sailors.

Page **39**; ms. page 13, line 17: Pot houses—taverns.

Page **40**; ms. page 14, lines 13–15: "Spanish milled dollar"—the English term (ca. 1581) for the Spanish *real de a ocho,* or eight-real coin, made of silver and minted on a coin press. Manufactured from 1732–1826, the coins were called "milled" because they were made from coin blanks (*planchets*) produced with a milling machine. The coin could be physically divided into eight pieces, thus the name "pieces of eight," and their consistent weight and size made them an international currency.

Page **40**; ms. page 16, line 27: Birserker—Norse warriors famed for their battle rage, an almost trancelike fury that became the basis of the English word *berserk.* The name derives from their habit of wearing a wolf pelt as a kind of shirt or robe.

Page **38**; ms. page 16.5, line 24: "He was nothing but a Spaniard"—a common sentiment among English pirates, who often retained a privateer's loyalty to their home country's politics and refrained from attacking English shipping unless absolutely necessary, but offered no such clemency to Spanish ships.

Page **42**; ms. page 17, line 18: "clean-limbed"—well-proportioned or shapely.

Page **42**; ms. page 20, line 11: shy—an attempt to damage by sarcasm or verbal attack.

Page **42**; ms. page 20, line 21: corslet—a piece of body armor, usually consisting of a breastplate and back piece.

Page **45**; ms. page 28, line 18: calipash and calipee—turtle flesh.

Page **45**; ms. page 29, line 19: *par coutere* (French)—"after the custom"

Page **45**; ms. page 29, line 27: The cavalli—or crevalle jack, *Caranx hippos* (also known as the common jack, black-tailed trevally, couvalli jack, black cavalli, and yellow cavalli), a common marine fish found throughout the Atlantic, prized as a game fish as well as a mainstay of modern commercial fisheries.

Page **48**; ms. page 25, line 14: John Bull (also page **000**; ms. page 90, line 22)—the literary embodiment of British imperialism and subject of the political allegory, *The History of John Bull* (1712), once thought to be the work of Jonathan Swift and now attributed to Queen Anne's physician, John Arbuthnot.

Page **50**; ms. page 41, line 28: gripe—grip; grasp.

Page **50**; ms. page 41, line 29: *couteau de chape*—(French) a large knife; chape is the metal mounting or trim of a scabbard.

Page **51**; ms. page 44, L7–8: *selon les regles*—(French) following the rules of fashion.

Page **52**; ms. page 47, L15–16: Eugene Aram (1704–1759)—an English schoolteacher and philologist whose work established the connections between the Celtic language and European languages as well as disproved the then-accepted linguistic connection between Greek and Latin. Later convicted of murder, Aram was immortalized in Thomas Hood's ballad "The Dream of Eugene Aram" and Bulwer-Lytton's 1832 novel *Eugene Aram.*

Page **53**; ms. page 50, line 9: Zenobia (240–ca. 274)—a queen of the Palmyrene Empire in Roman Syria, famous for leading a revolt against the Roman Empire.

Page **53**; ms. page 50, lines 15–16: Mary Stuart—Mary I of Scotland, more commonly known as Mary, Queen of Scots (1542–1587). The only surviving legitimate child of James V of Scotland, she is known for her turbulent life and eventual eighteen-year imprisonment and execution by her cousin Elizabeth I of England.

Page **53**; ms. page 52, lines 10–11: Charles the First (1600–1649)—king of England, king of Scotland, and king of Ireland from 1625 until his execution in 1649. His controversial reign was defined by religious and political struggles, chiefly with Parliament, which ultimately led to his imprisonment and execution. After his death he was treated as a popular martyr and canonized during the reign of his son, Charles II, as a saint of the Anglican Communion.

Page **55**; ms. page 55, line 26: Platos and Sidneys—Plato's *Republic* (ca. 380 B.C.) and Sir Philip Sidney's *A Defense of Poesy* and *The Countess of Pembroke's Arcadia* present visions of idealized societies, though their utopian character has been the subject of modern scholarly debate.

Page **55**; ms. page 57, lines 7–8: Geraldine—indicating an Irish dynasty, one of the most celebrated families of Ireland, also known as the FitzGeralds. Elizabeth FitzGerald (1527–1589) was known as the "Fair Geraldine."

Page **58**; ms. page 65, lines 27–28: "The person is historical, Caraccioli *had* been an Italian Priest"—the first chapter of volume 2 of Charles Johnson's *Life of the*

Pyrates is devoted to James Misson, a fictitious French pirate whose friendship and collaboration with a defrocked Italian priest Caraccioli founded the utopian pirate haven of Libertalia on Madagascar. The pseudonymous author of the *Life of the Pyrates* claimed that the chapter and part of its successor, on Thomas Tew, were based on documentary sources, a claim substantially true of some chapters in the book but not of these chapters. The inclusion of trial transcripts and other documentary sources would have helped to mislead Simms. While Misson is entirely fictitious, there are several historical figures named Caraccioli; though none matches this description precisely, the heretical doctrines Simms's character espouses are historically accurate.

Page **59**; ms. page 65, lines 30–31: "French philosophy of a subsequent period"—probably Jacobinism, the French revolutionary movement known for its constitutionalist view of human rights and opposition to the Church and responsible for the Reign of Terror during the French Revolution.

Page **59**; ms. page 65, lines 33–35: "of a modern German school, which equally undergoes the ban of the Christian church"—probably communism. Marx and Engels's *The Communistic Manifesto* (1848), commissioned by the Communist League, provides a view of history as defined by class struggle and describes how capitalist society would be replaced by socialism and eventually communism; its advocacy of atheism incurred the wrath of the Church. Simms could have read the German edition but may have had access to an English translation.

Page **61**; ms. page 72, line 6: "read these letters to Misson"—Simms is remembering the claim made in volume 2 of Johnson's *The History of the Pyrates* that this chapter, devoted to a fictitious French pirate named James Misson, was based on "a French Manuscript, in which he himself gives a Detail of his Actions" (Schonhorn, ed., *A General History of the Pyrates,* 1972, 383). The book's authorship and textual history is complex. For decades scholars believed its pseudonymous author was Daniel Defoe; later scholarship debunked that attribution and now tends to credit its publisher, Nathaniel Mist, for its authorship. Mist is a significant figure in eighteenth-century British literary and political studies, a publisher whose Jacobite sympathies incurred the wrath of the authorities on several occasions and explains the often sympathetic treatment accorded many of the pirates in the book. Historians credit it as the most historically significant book on piracy, a complicated blend of fact and fiction responsible for many of the popular myths about pirates. Misson's behavior as a pirate captain is idealized, and the entire chapter may be an allegory disguising a Jacobite political critique, but some aspects of Misson's conduct, for example, the democratic nature of his captaincy and its multinational appeal, have historical roots.

Page **63**; ms. page 79, line 6: petronels—a sixteenth- or seventeenth-century firearm, from the French *petrinel* or *poitrinal,* so named for its firing position, placed against the chest, or its mode of transport, slung across the chest. It featured either a matchlock or wheellock firing mechanism.

Page **65**; ms. page 82, line 21: Cheapside—a London street famed for its jewelers' and mercers' (silk and fine fabrics) stores.

Page **65**; ms. page 82, lines 24–25: "What says the 'Postle? Milk for babes, meat for grown people"—a paraphrase of 1 Corinthians 3:2: "I have fed you with milk, and not with meat: for hitherto ye were not able *to bear it,* neither yet now are ye able." The phrase was made popular by William Boles's 1731 book, *Milk for Babes, Meat for Strong Men, and Wine for Petitioners. Being a comical, sarcastical, theological account of a late election at Bagdad, for Cailiff of that city. Faithfully translated from the Arabick . . . By . . . Alexander the Copper-Smith* (Cork: George Harrison, 1731).

Page **65**; ms. page 84, lines 27–28: "One stupid moment motionless he stood"—a line from the 1730 masterpiece *The Seasons* by Scottish poet James Thomson (1700–1748). One of Simms's oft-used quotations.

Page **67**; ms. page 88, line 17: Himmel—(German) Heaven.

Page **69**; ms. page 97, line 5: Horatii and Curiatii—in Roman legend, male triplets who represented Rome in a battle against Alba, which was represented by the Curiatii, also triplets. After two of the Horatii had been killed, the remaining brother defeated the Curiatii. When the sister of the Horatii bemoaned the death of the Curiati who had been her lover, her brother killed her. Condemned to death, he was spared when he appealed to the people. To do penance, he was led, veiled, under a yoke. The battle of the Horatii is depicted in a neoclassical painting by Jacques-Louis David.

Page **70**; ms. page 98, lines 6–7: "You play with a knife like a Malay"—indicating Malaysian martial arts famous for knife and other edged-weapon combat. *Silat,* the collective word for indigenous martial arts originating in Indonesia, includes edged-weapon combat and is practiced in Malaysia, southern Thailand, Singapore, Vietnam, Brunei, and the Philippines. It includes hundreds of different styles tending to focus on strikes, joint manipulation, throws, bladed weaponry, or various combinations.

Page **70**; ms. page 99, line 15: cock of St. Peter—reference to the Gospel of Mark, in which Jesus told Peter that "before the cock crow twice, thou shalt deny me thrice" (Mark 14:30).

Page **71**; ms. page 101, line 18: *hors de combat* (French)—"outside of the fight," or unable to fight or perform, militarily.

Page **72**; ms. page 103, lines 28–29: "tied and hung . . . for the carrion birds"—reference to those convicted of piracy, who were often hanged and their bodies suspended in chains, exposed to the elements, and preyed on by crows and insects.

Page **73**; ms. page 105, line 18: hurdle-short for hurdle-bed; a kind of litter, usually for the transport of those wounded in battle.

Page **74**; ms. page 108, lines 5–6: Honour among thieves—a popular maxim recorded as early as 1622 and common by Simms's time (see, for example, Jeremy Bentham, *Principles of the Civil Code,* for a chapter by that title).

Page **74**; ms. page 108, line 11: 'peach—short for impeach, to make a charge against or accuse of treason or high crime, usually against the state.

Page **74**; ms. page 108, lines 16–17: "I'll dance in the air, without shoes or stockings"—that is, he will be hanged from the gallows.

Page **74**; ms. page 108, line 18: King's evidence—evidence provided against associates, usually in exchange for clemency or immunity from prosecution.

Page **74**; ms. page 108, line 19: Old Bailey—the main criminal court in England, named for the street in central London where it is located.

Page **75**; ms. page 112, line 12: fig tree—reference to Genesis 3:7, in which Adam and Eve sewed fig leaves into garments after the Fall, when they realized they were naked.

Page **76**; ms. page 115, lines 18–19: chirurgeon—surgeon (archaic).

Page **78**; ms. page 121, line 15: *par parenthese* (French)—incidentally.

Page **78**; ms. page 121, lines 18–19: Algerine corsair—pirates operating out of Algiers.

Page **78**; ms. page 121, lines 19–20: Coast of Barbary—a European term denoting the Northern African coastal region associated with the Berber people, noted for its piracy during the sixteenth and seventeenth centuries.

Page **78**; ms. page 122, line 12: *secundum artem*—"according to the art;" according to the accepted practice of a profession or trade.

Page **78**; ms. page 122, line 14: trephine (French)—using a cylindrical saw of the same name to trepan, or remove a portion of the skull, usually to relieve pressure on the brain.

Page **79**; ms. page 126, line 10: Mme. Le Vasseur—this name may have been based on Olivier Levasseur (ca. 1688–1730), a pirate nicknamed La Buse or La Bouche (The Buzzard) for the speed and ruthlessness with which he always attacked his enemies.

Page **79**; ms. page 126, line 15: Beppo—the eponymous character in Lord Byron's *Beppo: A Venetian Story* (1817), a lengthy poem written in Venice that tells the story of a Venetian lady whose husband, Giuseppe, or Beppo for short, is lost at sea. After three years, in accordance with Venetian custom, she takes on a *Cavalier*

Servente. At the Ventian Carnival, she encounters a Turk who turns out to be her husband; he explains that he was captured and enslaved, then set free by pirates, whom he joined. Now, with the spoils of his piracy, he returns to civilization to be rebaptized and reclaim his wife, which he does, becoming friends with the cavalier. Its satiric digressions, Italian poetic conventions, and commentary on Italian and English mores mark it as an important precursor to *Don Juan.*

Page **81**; ms. page 131, lines 20–21: "The Lady Geraldine wore pearls . . . a presentation at the court of Charles the First"—under Charles I the court repudiated the excesses and scandals of the Jacobean court and became known for its decorum and ceremony, celebrating the monarchy and symbolized by its embrace of the masque.

Page **81**; ms. page 131, line 24: Nell Gwynne (1650–1687)—the long-time mistress of Charles II of England, she was a folk heroine, nicknamed "Pretty Witty Nell" by Samuel Pepys.

Page **81**; ms. page 132, line 10: scape-grace—scoundrel, rascal; an idle, mischievous person.

Page **81**; ms. page 133, line 12: *posé* (French)—the attitude of a person or position of the body.

Page **81**; ms. page 134, line 9: pigeon-wing—a showy dance step supposedly imitating the movement of pigeons that involved leaping into the air and striking the legs together. The term is broadly synonymous with the graceful execution of intricate dance steps.

Page **82**; ms. page 136, line 10: "to the manor born"—from *Hamlet,* act 1, scene 4: "And to the manner born," or predisposed to the practice.

Page **82**; ms. page 136, line 23: *pour passer le temps* (French)—to pass the time.

Page **82**; ms. page 137, lines 2–3: "high life below stairs"—John Collett's 1763 novel of the same name, a satire about servants in their quarters imitating the dress and behavior of their masters.

Page **83**; ms. page 138, line 15: *blanchisseuse* (French)—laundress.

Page **83**; ms. page 138, line 26: Tyburn—an English village that served for centuries as the place where London criminals, traitors, and martyrs were executed.

Page **84**; ms. page 143, lines 6–7: *michin malico*—mischief. Simms quotes this phrase, from *Hamlet,* act 3, scene 2, in several of his works; see, for example, *The Forayers* (2003), 137, and *The Cassique of Kiawah* (1859), 106.

Page **85**; ms. page 144, line 9: Blue Beard—the namesake of a folk story about a man who marries a beautiful young woman, Fatima. He leaves her the keys to his castle, telling her not to enter one room. Unable to resist, she opens it and finds the corpses of six previous wives, narrowly avoiding their fate through the timely intervention of her brothers, who kill him. Classed as a tale of punished curiosity, the story was first recorded by Charles Perrault; his French folktale served as the source for the English version. The story is linked to Giles de Laval, a marshal of France executed in 1440 for debaucheries and murders.

Page **85**; ms. page 144, line 15: pacha—variant spelling of pasha, a provincial governor or other high official of the Ottoman Empire or modern Egyptian kingdom.

Page **87**; ms. page 149, lines 24–255: *Ma foi* (French)—my faith.

Page **88**; ms. page 153, line 22: *matériel* (French)—the material part of a thing.

Page **89**; ms. page 155, lines 16–17: knew not how to whine, and sigh, / But only to obtain, or die!"—Byron's couplet, rendered slightly differently, either from faulty memory or to fit the context. Byron's couplet reads: "'Tis true I could not whine nor sigh, / I knew but to obtain or die." Byron, *The Giaour, A Turkish Tale* (Philadelphia, Moses Thomas, 1816), 93.

Page **89**; ms. page 156, line 26: Tare (French)—crazy; unsound mentally (slang).

Page **91**; ms. page 165, line 5: Teche—Edward Teche, aka Teach or Thatch. The pirate Blackbeard.

Page **93**; ms. page 169, line 8: chuck—a colloquial, familiar term of endearment, applied to husbands, wives, children, and close companions.

“Never a Whit Wiser, Never a Whit Less Human”

Simms’s Postwar Conversation with the Devil

DAVID W. NEWTON

“Sir Will O’ Wisp or the Irish Baronet; A Tale of Its Own Day” was written during the last years of Simms’s life and remained unfinished at the time of his death in June of 1870. The original manuscript is part of the Charles Carroll Simms Collection at the South Caroliniana Library, University of South Carolina. Consisting of 187 handwritten pages and approximately 18,140 words, the manuscript is written on uniform stationary-size paper, a rare occurrence during the postwar years, when circumstances often forced Simms to write on scraps of paper or on the reverse side of stationery he had used previously for drafts of manuscripts. At the time of his death, Simms had completed a draft of six chapters, ranging in length from 17 to 49 manuscript pages. Any description of how Simms composed the manuscript or the timeframe for its composition is at best conjectural. Simms most likely wrote the draft during a continuous period of time rather than writing sections of the manuscript intermittently. The manuscript does not contain any major editorial emendations nor are there large sections that are heavily edited. Most of the editorial emendations focus on word choice, replacing one word for another that is more appropriate for the context. Simms’s emendations seem to be made in the process of writing rather than upon returning to edit the manuscript at a later time. The manuscripts illuminates Simms’s creative process and offers evidence of how he reconsidered words and quickly interlined them in the midst of writing. If manuscripts can be said to possess such qualities, Simms’s writing exhibits a creative energy, moving forward with little looking back, with a prescient confidence about where the story is headed. This only compounds the mystery of why Simms abandoned the story somewhere near the end of chapter 6. The reasons may have been related to his declining health or to financial pressures to finish other works that had better prospects for publication. There is also the possibility that Simms simply had arrived at a crossroads with the story and was uncertain how to proceed.

The chapters that Simms did complete offer insights into the story's evolving narrative scope and overall purpose. Chapter 1, titled "My Familiar," introduces the narrator of the story, Richard Silex, a writer whose literary achievements are unappreciated by the citizens of Mongrelia, the fictional town where he resides. He calls his narrative a confession and reveals that recently he has come into possession of a "familiar . . . a domestic demon—one of those active, adroit, and intelligent spirits, who, at times, under special laws of attraction, sympathy, animal or intellectual magnetism attract themselves to the fortunes of men for their special comfort and edification . . ." (3). Silex observes that his first encounter with the demon did not occur in the way that ancient authorities had described. There was no smoke, no flames, none of the ominous signs that so often herald the arrival of demons. Instead, while working alone at his writing desk late one evening, Silex unexpectedly hears a loud sneeze and discovers a well-appointed gentleman standing behind him. Silex is troubled because the demon does not appear with "appendages of horns and hoof" (6). To the contrary his appearance is urbane and sophisticated:

> His face was a good one but by no means remarkable. Such a face I have often seen. It was rather Gallican in contour and general expression but had some of the Irishman in it—the rich dark red of his complexion and a certain dash of frankness and impulse which won directly upon your confidence. . . . There was, besides, a somewhat satirical cast in his general expression, showing a slight disposition to sneer at much and laugh at many things in society, a something reminding you of Mephistopheles, which was in contrast with the otherwise benevolent expression in general. The figure was excellent, I should say perfect—symmetrical, beautifully developed, tall, stately, well set and muscular. (6–7)

In chapter 2, "Purely Psychological," the stranger introduces himself as "Will O' the Wisp" (199). Although he is a demon, he assures Silex that he intends no harm and seeks nothing more than to be employed in his service. Silex expresses his doubts about the demon's intentions, so Sir Will promptly responds by sitting down at Silex's writing desk, exclaiming that life is not to be spent fretting over such toils (135). He then proceeds to write responses to all of Silex's correspondents in the blink of an eye, "the pen rather coursing over the paper than resting upon it" (12). Silex is secretly delighted and exclaims, "What a boon for an author could his fingers keep such equal pace with his thoughts" (13). Equally astonishing, Silex observes that Sir Will "not only divined what I would myself have written, but prepared answers, admirably adopted cases, upon which my mind had as yet arrived at no decision" (13). While Silex envies this considerable display of talent, he believes that through bargain, deception, or both that Sir Will seeks ownership of his soul. Sir Will is genuinely offended by the accusation, and he promptly informs Silex that devils are no longer in the business of harvesting souls: "But, my dear Mr. Silex, all that thing has gone entirely of fashion. We have more souls on hand than we know what to do with. They are positively rotting on our hands. We wouldn't be bothered or burdened with an increase on any terms, and in truth we think of abolishing the old establishment entirely, under the counsel of our excellent Brother Beecher, who with a throng and others of his kinship have pretty much taken the business out of our hands" (17). Simms directed his satire here toward Henry Ward Beecher and others from the North who supported abolition and other social reform movements during and after the Civil War. In contrast Sir Will insists that his purpose is to relieve Silex of "old superstitions" and to guide him toward a new truth (207).

As chapter 3, "Signed, Sealed, and Delivered," begins, Sir Will has departed, and Silex falls into a dreamlike reverie where he receives a vision of "ethereal loveliness" in which "all languor and all love, pervaded my whole frame" (20). It is a transcendent vision that Silex describes in imaginative poetic detail. When he finally awakens, he finds Sir Will sitting beside him. Silex asks if this vision were real or simply an ephemeral dream, a product of his own human imagination. Sir Will assures him, "It was no delusion. If you could comprehend the thing which you call the soul, you would see that it was quite as real as anything that you beheld with your eyes in your daily intercourse with men" (22). He proceeds to explain to Silex that with the proper development of the spiritual, of the artistic imagination, the "promise of vision expands" (22). Unfortunately, in most people, the pursuit of material things diminishes the spiritual capacity of the soul. Sir Will confesses to Silex that he desires "to lift you into nobler stature and confer upon you some of the bright domains not of this earth but which yet exist within its atmosphere" (24). Silex remains skeptical, however, believing that the demon will "steep me for a season in bliss, only to steep me for another season in sulphur" (24). Sir Will assures him this is not the case and offers Silex a deal. All he requires in compensation for his services is anything that Silex casts away, especially his clothing. After further assurances from Sir Will that Silex will not have to sign any documents in blood, a contract magically appears that both man and demon sign. As the chapter closes, Sir Will informs Silex that on the following day he will appear in public to the citizens of Mongrelia as Sir Will O' Wisp, an Irish baronet, a famous nobleman and dignitary visiting their city.

Chapter 4, "A Screed of the Spiritual," is the longest chapter in the manuscript. Alone in his study, Silex reads in amusement the many announcements in the local newspapers describing the arrival of the famous Irish baronet at the Spread Eagle Hotel when he is again surprised by Sir Will's unexpected appearance. Sir Will reports that the baronet has already received calls from many of the town's highest elected officials and most prominent socialites, seeking his influence and association. Rumors are rampant about the purpose of the baronet's visit, and there is widespread speculation that he is a representative of the Fenians, an organization dedicated to Irish independence. Sir Will is amused by the shallow, superficial behavior of the town's citizens and says to Silex, "In spiritual respects your race has sunk several degrees below their ancestors. You surely must have suspected this before. The evidence is potent to all your really philosophical minds" (33). While Silex is hurt by these criticisms, Sir Will states that devils always speak the truth. The two men then engage in a lengthy discussion of mesmerism and spiritualists, since Silex is eager to know if such activities truly are communications with the spiritual realm. Sir Will assures him that they are genuine; however, Silex is not persuaded since "men do not seem to have grown wiser or better since their revelations" (40). Sir Will agrees, but states that the fault lies not with the revelation but with human nature, which, despite all of the advances over the centuries in human civilization, never has been fundamentally altered. According to Sir Will, human beings "have become more learned, more scientific, more cunning, calculating, and circumspect but never a whit wiser—never a whit less human—still an anomalous blending of the angel and the beast. And the beast almost invariably swallows up the angel" (40). This harsh assessment of the human condition upsets Silex. As the chapter concludes, Sir Will assures him that despite this grim reality the artistic pursuit of the spiritual still has great value, since anything "which appeals to the soul and inspires the spiritual activity is better for you than a life which regards only the baser instincts of appetite" (43).

Chapter 5, "Draughts of Persephone-Platonic," the shortest chapter in the manuscript, opens with Sir Will in his role as domestic familiar, preparing dinner for his master. Silex comments on the exquisite features of the wine, one unfamiliar to him, which Sir Will calls "Persephone-Platonic" (44). Wine, Sir Will effuses, "is the necessary element of genius, inspiring the poet with fresh songs, the philosopher with the clues to discovery, the orator with the golden figures of rhetoric, and the warrior with grand conceptions of conquest and the plans of battle" (45). For Silex the wine possesses spiritual properties, and he exclaims to Sir Will, "I am sure that I float upon a new element, and that I behold swans swimming around me on a placid sea, while music from an invisible source soothes my senses with a dream of ecstasy, in the glow of which Love puts on a new aspect of charm and all life seems to resolve itself into Love" (45). When Silex awakens from his reverie, he suddenly remembers that Sir Will has appointments at the Spread Eagle Hotel where he is staying. To Silex's astonishment, Sir Will shows him through a vision that he is already at the hotel, having created an "eidolon," a double of himself, to meet his guests (46). After a brief discussion of the literary arts, Sir Will departs for the hotel followed in short measure by Silex.

In the sixth and final chapter, "First Reception," the narrative departs from the lengthy, private philosophical dialogues between Silex and Sir Will that anchored the earlier chapters. Instead, the story moves into the public arena and takes aim at the diminished role of the artist in a world where materialistic values no longer permit the development of spiritual "susceptibilities." While Simms used historical and cultural references throughout the narrative to situate the story within the social landscape of postwar America, these factual references are blended with fictitious names and places—Counsellor Gregorius Gander, Billabop Baggs, Captain Puritan Standish, Mongrelia, and the Spread Eagle Hotel, for example—that reinforce the narrative's increasing shift toward an allegorical social satire. As Silex enters the baronet's suite, he discovers that it is filled with visitors from the town, including the mayor, who is surprised to learn of the friendship between the baronet and Silex. Sir Will praises Silex's talents as a writer, but the mayor is unimpressed, exclaiming, "Well I have heard that he makes verses and conundrums and things of that sort, but nobody thinks anything of him here" (54). The debate that ensues contrasts the useful arts with the fine arts and concludes with the mayor extolling the virtues of Mongrelia's nobility, men who, unlike Silex the writer, provide a useful social function: "We have, here, Sir, as noble an aristocracy as any in the world, Sir. I say it proudly, Sir William, that even in your country, no more accomplished gentlemen could be found. The best blood, Sir, of the best families of Europe courses through our veins!" (56). The chapter concludes with the arrival of representatives from several women's societies who seek an audience with the baronet.

While the sixth chapter is significantly developed—the third longest in the manuscript—there is no evidence to suggest whether or not Simms intended to expand it further. Although the emphasis on social satire would in all likelihood continue, an emerging partnership between Silex and Sir Will against the citizens of Mongrelia also begins to emerge in chapter 6. One can imagine Sir Will's devising an elaborate plan to exact revenge against the town for its neglect of Silex and the imaginative arts; Silex would no doubt relish his secret knowledge of this devilish work. Demons, however, are a notoriously unpredictable lot, so how Silex's bargain with the devil ultimately is resolved can only be imagined. What seems certain is that Sir Will, in one manner or another, would play a central role in orchestrating the events that follow.

Although "Sir Will O' Wisp" was written during the postwar years, its origins can be traced to one of Simms's earliest short stories, "Jack-O'-Lantern: A New-Light Story," published in the *Southern Literary Messenger* in May 1838.* The clues to this unlikely connection are embedded in the manuscript of "Sir Will O' Wisp," which contains three printed columns that Simms cut from a copy of the published version of "Jack-O'-Lantern" and pasted into the manuscript of "Sir Will O' Wisp."† Simms copied the remaining sections of "Jack-O'-Lantern" into the manuscript by hand. Some of these sections were copied verbatim from the original story, but in other sections Simms significantly altered the original, both deleting material and adding new descriptive details and events. The three printed insertions also include editorial emendations in Simms's handwriting. On the first column where the name "Jack-O'-Lantern" appears, Simms edited out the name and inserted the following note in the margin: "But to be more aristocratic and less queer in society you will be Will O' the Wisp, in place of Jack-O'-Lantern" ("Sir Will" Manuscript 27). "Jack-O'-Lantern" is a brief, unfinished fragment, approximately seven printed columns, totaling 3,595 words, considerably shorter than the more extensively developed postwar version that became "Sir Will O' Wisp." While Simms developed the story further in "Sir Will O' Wisp," adding additional chapters and more extensive narrative details, the original story fragment—often word for word—is embedded in the first three chapters of the postwar narrative. "Jack-O'-Lantern" is not among Simms's well-known short stories. Beyond its inclusion in some early bibliographical descriptions of Simms's fiction, there are no references to this early story in either of the two major biographies of Simms, written by

*The published text of "Jack-O'-Lantern: A New-Light Story" from the *Southern Literary Messenger* appears in the appendix of this volume.

†The printed columns appear on pages 27, 77, and 81 of the manuscript of "Sir Will O' Wisp."

William Peterfield Trent and John Caldwell Guilds, respectively, or in the major scholarship on his published fiction. Despite these omissions, Simms obviously held the story—or at least the concept behind it—in high regard, committing time and creative energy to its development during the difficult final years of his life when his health and financial exigencies offered limited opportunities for such work.

Further evidence of Simms's appreciation for the literary potential of "Jack-O'-Lantern" can be found in a letter that he wrote to James Lawson, one of his closest friends and literary associates in the Northeast. Written while Simms was in Charleston, South Carolina, and dated July 20, 1839, the letter reads in part, "I wish you could look over the numbers of his magazine* that you have in possession, and find one containing a chapter under the title of 'Jack-O'-Lantern'—the article is mine, and I wish to continue it, making a story, of political, commercial and moral satire. Show the article to Wetmore,† and between you let me know what you think of it as an introduction. My own opinion is that it possesses considerable spirit and is well written. Keep the thing secret, for White was especially pledged to my anonymous [*sic*], and if the plan is continued it will be prudent that the author should remain unknown" (*Letters* 1:151). The story was published anonymously under the pseudonym "Eyes-In-Glass." Simms frequently published works under pseudonyms, but James Kibler has noted that this is the only documented instance of Simms's using this particular pseudonym (*Pseudonymous* 51). Simms's comments in his letter to Lawson suggest that he believed the work's philosophical content would require an anonymous authorship. The story is subtitled "Chapter I," indicating that Simms planned other serial installments of it in the *Southern Literary Messenger* or elsewhere. However, Simms included an asterisk after "Chapter I" and offered this warning: "And, possibly, chapter last, since I cannot be certain that the taste of the reader will so highly approve of my devil as my own does. Time will show. I will bind myself to no conditions. If the mood suits me . . . and the 'Messenger'—there will be more words to this argument. The public shall be made wiser, if they have the wit to desire it. I shall be happy to serve and enlighten them, but I will not throw pearls away upon—those who do not know how to wear them" ("Jack-O'-Lantern" 336).

*Thomas Willis White was editor of the *Southern Literary Messenger,* beginning in 1834.

†Prosper Montgomery Wetmore (1798–1876) was a business associate of James Lawson from New York and a literary associate and friend of Simms.

"Jack-O'-Lantern" was written during a time of extraordinary creative activity by Simms in the late 1830s, when he was also finishing work on *The History of South Carolina, The Damsel of Darien,* and *Border Beagles* (*Letters* 1:51). However, there is no evidence that Simms ever wrote drafts or published any subsequent chapters of this early story fragment before he began work on "Sir Will O' Wisp" after the war. While the "Jack-O'-Lantern" fragment is embedded within "Sir Will O' Wisp," the story that Simms returned to decades later is situated in the postwar era and includes references to the Freedmen's Bureau, the Battle of Bull Run, and Sherman's march through the South. The revisions that Simms made to the original story as he wrote "Sir Will O' Wisp" suggest that a different story was emerging. Although "Jack-O'-Lantern" is about a writer's dalliance with the devil, its tone overall is comic and lighthearted. "Sir Will O' Wisp" has its own comic sensibilities but not the playfulness of the original. One can see specific sections in the manuscript where Simms edited out details from the original story to create this new effect. Even Silex and Sir Will were altered to reflect this change in sensibilities. To some extent the editorial changes reflect the movement from the brash confidence of a young writer to the more measured, world wise, and weary perspective of a writer articulating a different vision. Rather than looking backward to the 1830s, "Sir Will O' Wisp" offers Simms's uncompromising vision of the world that the Civil War had wrought.

By naming his gentleman demon Will O' Wisp, Simms connected his story to familiar folklore traditions and to some well-established literary antecedents. The term *will-o'-the-wisp* has its origins in the folklore of the British Isles. *The Oxford English Dictionary* suggests that will-o'-the-wisp originally was among the most widely used names for *ignis fatuus* (Latin for "foolish fire").* From the perspective of modern science, *ignis fatuus* and its associated names usually referred to a natural phenomenon commonly called swamp gas that would appear as phosphorescent lights hovering above marshes, swamps, or peat bogs. While science has not fully resolved the mystery of how such floating lights are created, they appear in folklore throughout Europe and the United States, including the American South. The word *wisp,* or *whisk*, refers to hay or straw that is bundled together and set on fire to create light.

*See also Jabez Allies, *The Ignis Fatuus, or Will-O'-the-Wisp and the Fairies* (1846). Allies was a British naturalist and one of the first writers to chronicle the history of folklore in England and the British Isles in the nineteenth century.

In folklore the will-o'-the-wisp usually is personified as a mischievous or even a malevolent spirit that leads unwary travelers astray with flickering lights. Its figurative connotations extend to persons, things, or ideas that can be deceptive or misleading. The term first appears in print in England during the early seventeenth century, but its origins in folklore are undoubtedly much earlier.* In *An Encyclopedia of Fairies: Hobgoblins, Brownies, Bogies, and Other Supernatural Creatures,* Katherine Briggs has listed many different British regional variations for the same phenomenon, among them Copse- (or Corpse) Candle, Spunkies, Puck—familiar from Shakespeare's *A Midsummer Night's Dream*—Hobby-Lantern, and the more familiar Jack-O'-Lantern (231). Other names can be found throughout the British Isles and in folklore traditions throughout Europe. The literary origins of the synonymous term *jack-o'-lantern*—which Simms used as the original name for his devil—can be traced to the same century as will-o'-the-wisp.† An early reference can be found in Shakespeare's *The Tempest* where Stephano says to Caliban, "Monster, your fairy, which you say is a harmless fairy, has done little better than played the jack with us" (act 4, scene 1, lines 196–97). In American literature one of the earliest references to the jack-o'-lantern is found in "The Great Carbuncle," by Nathaniel Hawthorne, published in 1837, only a year before the publication of Simms's short story. While the jack-o'-lantern's association with Halloween makes it the more recognizable name in the United States, the will-o'-the-wisp also appears in contemporary American popular culture.‡

In the margins of the postwar manuscript, Simms noted that his decision to change the name of his title character from Jack-O'-Lantern to Will O' Wisp was prompted by his desire to find a more aristocratic name. However, Simms

** The Oxford English Dictionary* attributes one of the earliest written references to will-o'-the-wisp to English dramatist John Day (1566–1628) in *Law-trickes* (1608): "I haue playd Will with the wispe with my brother and haue led him vp and downe the maze of good fellowship." The *OED* attributes one of the earliest recorded references to will-o'-the-wisp in American literature to Henry Wadsworth Longfellow, in his prose romance "Hyperion" (1839): "His imagination is continually lantern-led by some will-with-a-whisp in the shape of a lady's stomacher" (303).

† *The Oxford English Dictionary* attributes one of the earliest written references to both jack-o'-lantern and will-o'-the-wisp in the same work to naturalist John Ray (1627–1705) in *Observations Topographical, Moral, & Physiological* (1673): "Those reputed Meteors . . . known in England by the conceited names of Jack with a Lanthorn, and Will with a Wisp" (410).

‡For a contemporary example of the appearance of the will-o'-the-wisp in American popular culture, see Disney Pixar's *Brave* (2010), an animated film set in ancient Scotland.

may have been contemplating other ways that the new name fit the development of his devil in the new story. In *The Fairies in English Tradition and Literature,* Katherine Briggs has described associations between the will-o'-the-wisps and the demonic, recounting one local legend of a man who outwits the Devil and is condemned to wander the countryside (52). In another version of the same folktale from Shropshire, England, "Will the Smith, after being given a second spell of life by St. Peter, spent it in such wickedness that he was debarred from Heaven and Hell. The most the Devil would do for him was to give him a piece of burning pit coal to warm himself, with which he flickers over boggy ground to allure poor wanderers to their deaths" (Briggs, *Encyclopedia of Fairies* 231). In some traditions the coal is placed in a turnip or a large gourd, such as a pumpkin, giving rise to the jack-o'-lantern.

By adopting the name Will O' Wisp, Simms also associates his devil with two important literary precursors, John Milton and Johann Wolfgang von Goethe, whose poems about seductive devils provide a frame of reference for understanding Simms's own unique literary creation. While Milton did not use the term will-o'-the-wisp, his description of Satan's seductive temptation of Eve draws upon the same *ignis fatuus* tradition that Simms employed in his story. Satan is described as

> Kindl'd through agitation to a Flame,
> Which oft, they say, some evil Spirit attends
> Hovering and blazing with delusive Light,
> Misleads th' amaz'd Night-wanderer from his way (*Paradise Lost* 9:637–40)*

Furthermore Simms began both "Jack-O'-Lantern" and "Sir Will O' Wisp" with the same epigraph from Goethe's *Faust,* and he inserted into the postwar story other references to Goethe's epic poem. Silex, for example, insists that he "employed no incantations such as Faust uses for raising Mephistopheles" in summoning his own demon (3–4). In English translations a will-o'-the-wisp provides the light that guides Faust and Mephistopheles up the summit of Brocken Mountain, where a coven of witches are gathering. Mephistopheles announces to Faust,

> Allow me to summon the will-o'-the-wisp!
> I see one there who's burning merrily.

*A similar description of the will-o'-the-wisp, an "evil thing that walks by night, / In fog or fire, by lake or moorish fen" (432–33) can be found in Milton's *Comus*. Simms admired Milton and frequently cited his writing in his own works (Brennan, *Poet's Holy Craft* 46–47).

> Hey there, my friend! May I ask you to join us?
> Why blaze away to no good purpose?
> Be kind enough to light us up that slope! (*Faust* 3855–59)

Milton used the folklore tradition of the *ignis fatuus* to imagine Satan's demonic seduction of Eve, leading her astray into temptation, and Goethe imagined the will-o'-the-wisp in the service of his master, Mephistopheles, lighting the way toward Faust's damnation. While Simms's devil seems decidedly less menacing, these folklore traditions and literary antecedents created undercurrents that inform Silex's own anxieties throughout the story and shape how he interprets Sir Will's intentions. The folktale of a malevolent spirit who leads travelers astray also offered Simms a potent metaphor for understanding his own personal circumstances and the spiritual condition of the nation in the aftermath of the Civil War.

Simms was fascinated by spiritualism throughout much of his adult life, and "Sir Will O' Wisp" reflects his continuing interest in the subject. In a letter dated May 4, 1856, to Justus Starr Redfield, one of Simms's most important literary associates from the North,* Simms acknowledged that "Spiritualism as a philosophy is in more complete accordance with my own speculations, felt & pursued for 30 years, than any other system" (*Letters* 3:431). In a letter to his friend James Henry Hammond, from December of that same year, Simms recounted his own encounter with two mediums during a trip to New York. Justus Redfield had introduced Simms to Charles Partridge, a renowned proponent of spiritualism and editor of the *Spiritual Telegraph,* who in turn had arranged a meeting between Simms and a local medium, a man Simms identified only as Pittee (*Letters* 3:476). Simms described the experience at length in his letter to Hammond, but two aspects of his account warrant consideration here. Pittee was a talking medium, someone who channels only one spirit, in his case, a deceased Irishman named Collins. Simms recalled that Pittee when in his trance spoke in an Irish brogue, "just as we might suppose an Irish spirit, from the lower orders, would be apt to talk with the bog still sticking to his brogans, and the flavour of the poteen still bubbling up under the tongue" (*Letters* 3:477). The resonance with Simms's invention of Sir Will, the Irish baronet, is striking here. Simms later described his meeting with George Redman, a well-known medium and spiritualist writer who told Simms that he sensed the presence of Simms's second daughter, Mary Derrille Simms, who died of scarlet fever in 1842 (*Letters* 3:477).

*Redfield's publishing house in New York published the reissued, authoritative editions of Simms's novels.

Through the medium she reportedly told her father that she was his "constant attendant and guardian." Simms was "greatly surprised and excited by the whole affair" (*Letters* 3:481–82). He concluded his letter to Hammond by observing, "The truth is, I desired to believe, there was something to me inexpressibly sweet & precious in communing with my absent child and that I still do not surrender myself to the faith that I have done so, must be taken in proof of my sterner sense of what is due to evidence and historical & moral authenticity" (*Letters* 3:483).

We see here Simms wrestling with the possibility of a spiritual "familiar" who watched over and protected him. However, less than a decade later Simms imagined an entirely different possibility in the devastating aftermath of the deaths of two other children and an accidental fire that destroyed his home at Woodlands. Once again writing to his friend Hammond, on April 10, 1862, Simms confessed, "We, my dear Hammond, who have speculated so often in spiritualism, have arrived at certain conclusions in favour of the Hebrew notion of Demonology. At all events, both of us have had personal experience which inclines us to believe that there are certain persons who seem to be perpetually pursued by some angry Fate, which haunts his steps. . . . I am still as bitterly pursued as ever, & can now only await patiently and in expectation for other strokes, each perhaps more heavy & more deadly than the last" (*Letters* 4:402). Simms's intimate, haunting confession paints a dark image of a writer who felt hunted and pursued by a demonic presence, an "angry Fate." Although Silex and Sir Will appear to share a more collaborative partnership, this darker sensibility certainly underlies Silex's apprehensions about Sir Will in the story.

Simms's interest in spiritualism was not isolated to biographical experiences alone. His prose works and poems describe similar supernatural events that include ghosts and otherworldly spirits such as will-o'-the-wisps. One of the earliest is found in the poem "Love, Desire, and Enjoyment," published in *Early Lays* in 1827. It describes two "self-will'd" children pursuing an elusive will-o'-the-wisp (26–30). Other references to will-o'-the-wisps as fairies and even familiar attendants appear in three early short stories written by Simms: "A Dream of the Earth" (1833), "A Fairy Tale," (1833), and "Sweet William, A Tale of Faerie" (1837).* The "slender and graceful—symmetrically perfect" features of the will-o'-the-wisp in "Sweet William" echo the description of Sir Will O' Wisp ("Sweet

*"A Dream of Earth" was published in *The Book of My Lady: A Melange.* "Sweet William: A Tale of Faerie" was published in *Martin Faber, The Story of a Criminal; and Other Tales.* See Guilds, "William Gilmore Simms and the Cosmopolitan," for evidence of Simms's authorship of "A Fairy Tale"

William" 168). Other references to the will-o'-the-wisp are figurative, including one in Simms's Revolutionary War biography of Francis Marion that describes the elusive Swamp Fox as "a very 'will o' the wisp' in military affairs, almost as difficult to find, at times, by his own followers, as by the enemy" (*Life of Marion* 146). Simms also used the term figuratively in the postwar novel *Joscelyn* to describe "the madness which comes from vanity . . . a thing of ever-varying caprice, to be easily diverted from its object (*Joscelyn* 120).

While these examples provide evidence of Simms's familiarity with the folklore and literary traditions associated with the will-o'-the-wisp, other evidence further points to Simms's own personal identification with his postwar devil. In "Sir Will O' Wisp," there is a curious symbiosis between Silex, the unappreciated writer who gives voice to Simms's philosophical perspectives and social anxieties as an author, and the devilish Irish baronet whom he calls his familiar. In a letter written from Woodlands, dated December 27, 1839, a year after the publication of "Jack-O'-Lantern," Simms was once again writing to his friend James Lawson, this time about a caustic review of *The Damsel of Darien,* published in the *Knickerbocker* the previous month. The review reads in part: "Simms had failed to please those who read merely to beguile an evening hour, or instruct those who wished to improve their minds. The author's very depth of thought and power of reasoning, *will-o'-the-wisp-like,* entice him from his purpose. . . . With all his power of description, his knowledge of human character, and his felicity of expression, Mr. Simms is often careless, and occasionally affected" (*Letters* 1:457).

Given the postwar story's emphasis on a neglected writer who forges an alliance with a demon named Sir Will O' Wisp, this criticism casts Simms's use of the name in a new light. The criticism bothered Simms enough that he noted it in his letter to Lawson, and it is unlikely that he would have forgotten it when he returned to the story decades later and decided to give his demon the same name. The story also addresses two facets of Simms's writing that the early review specifically criticizes: the "depth of thought and power of reasoning" presented in the philosophical debates between Silex and Sir Will and the usefulness of writers such as Silex for an audience that reads "merely to beguile an evening hour." As a struggling, unappreciated writer, Silex parallels Simms's marginalized social position after the war, and Silex's philosophical perspectives and social criticisms reflect many of Simms's own. This relationship between Silex and Simms, however, is complicated by Sir Will, who also serves as an authorial presence for Simms in the story. Many of the philosophical positions Sir Will articulates belong to Simms as well, even when they are presented in response to Silex's own statements and questions. In his conversation with the mayor of Mongrelia, it is Sir Will who responds to the charge that artistic works have no useful value. In such moments, the review's criticism of Simms as "*will-o'-the-wisp-like,*" frivolously bewildering readers and leading them astray, assumes a deeper resonance.

Sir Will is more than a voice for Simms's philosophical positions in the story, however; he is the author of events, designing plots, moving and manipulating characters to achieve his own purposes, which remain unknown. His active, creative presence is in stark contrast to Silex, who remains a passive observer of events throughout the story, a writer sitting alone in his isolated study. Together the two characters articulate Simms's own position as a writer unable to exert control over the personal and professional circumstances he faces. As such, Sir Will is a doppelgänger, a spectral double of Silex, and Simms as well, a symbol of their desire for autonomy, creative agency, and mastery over people and events. He is what every writer probably desires most, the written word as an organic, creative force, capable of giving shape to the material world. This was especially true for Simms. In his biography of Simms, Guilds has observed that "Simms felt a need, almost an obsession, to be in charge and his unusual verbal facility made it possible for him, by effective speaking and writing, to take control of situations, through his ability to explain, interpret, clarify, or make plausible to others, who looked to him for leadership. At times, this compulsiveness led to the manipulation of the thoughts and actions of others around him" (*Literary Life* 332).

What Guilds has referred to in his biography as Simms's "will to write" is a manifestation of the "will-o'-the-wisp," the creative power and agency of the artist (*Literary Life* 304). Sadly, in "Sir Will O' Wisp" no synthesis emerges from this dialectic between Silex and Sir Will. Their dialogues provide no final closure; the events that Sir Will sets in motion do not lead to any final resolution. Instead the story alternates between philosophical speculation and an emerging social satire that is at moments comic and keenly perceptive, and, at other times, bitter and demeaning. It is through this fragmented lens, Simms's assessment of his own status as a writer emerges.

That Simms's vision of the human condition would become increasingly pessimistic near the end of his life should come as no surprise. Simms aspired for most of his life to become acknowledged as a national writer; through his active participation in the Young America movement, he sought to create along with writers from across the nation a national literature that would be commensurate with the emerging, progressive vitality of the new nation. By the time of his death in 1870, however, Simms was a marginal literary figure at best, tied to the disgraced and defeated region he had so passionately defended. Even his status as the major figure in the development of southern letters would be eclipsed by Mark Twain and William Faulkner, creators of a more acceptable narrative aesthetic for what southern literature eventually would become. Twain, born when Simms was just beginning his career as a writer, was also a southerner by birth but spent much of his life outside the region. His novel *Adventures of Huckleberry Finn* not only expanded the literary possibilities of a distinct vernacular voice but also offered a devastating critique of the same southern slave society that Simms so often defended. When Twain died in 1910—forty years after Simms—he was a revered literary figure and an international celebrity, the creator of what many still regard today as an authentic American literature.

Beyond their regional roots, there is little that would seem to link together the professional careers of Simms and Twain as writers. However, near the end of their lives, both writers suffered humiliating public losses and painful private tragedies—including crippling financial failures and the deaths of children—and began to write works that combined philosophical speculation with satirical social commentary. Unfinished at their deaths, these works were more pessimistic about human nature and the value of human civilization than anything either had previously written. Both writers also chose to structure their works around mysterious figures with supernatural abilities whose ultimate motivations remained obscure. Twain's work, referred to by scholars as *No. 44, The Mysterious Stranger,* has a complicated publication history, created in part by the existence of different versions of the story that Twain left unfinished and by an edition that was radically altered by editors and published not long after Twain's death.* Twain's story involves a mysterious young man with supernatural powers, enigmatically named "44," who unexpectedly appears in the Austrian village of Eseldorf in 1490 and befriends a young printer's apprentice named August Feldner. Other versions of the story are set in the United States and feature a character who calls himself Satan. Through the conversations between 44 and August, Twain intertwined scathing social commentary with philosophical speculation on organized religion, human nature, and the solipsistic nature of reality, resulting in a work that bears many similarities to Simms's "Sir Will O' Wisp."

*See Kahn, *Mark Twain's Mysterious Stranger: A Study of the Manuscript Texts* (1978) and Csicsila and Rohman, *Centenary Reflections on Mark Twain's No. 44, The Mysterious Stranger* (2009).

While Simms placed considerable faith in the possibilities of social progress, his works across many decades contain realistic conceptions of evil as both intractably individual and social. Many of his best known novels and stories contain grim portrayals of perverse crimes and unspeakable violence. Murder, war, and the destruction of innocent life all played central roles in Simms's fiction; society is in a continual struggle against the corrupting influences of power and ambition. Still, Simms's realism always was balanced by a fundamental belief in the essential goodness and decency of people and, equally important—crucially important—a belief in human progress, that any particular social horror or personal tragedy is always measured against the fundamental conviction that people and society will progress and improve. For every villain in Simms's fiction—and there are many who seem far more demonic than Sir Will—there are heroes and heroines both aristocratic and ordinary who work to balance the scales of justice and offer hope for a future where such virtues prevail.

Twain never fully shared Simms's optimism about human nature or the potential for social progress. As *Adventures of Huckleberry Finn* painfully illustrates, innocence and virtue, if they exist at all, are mostly the province of children and dangerous traits when found in adults. Numerous other works by Twain offer the same vision. Human society is artificial, superficial, and deadly dangerous, a collective evil that more often than not eclipses what little goodness humans as individuals might possess. By the time Twain turned to writing *The Mysterious Stranger,* his sense of despair was even darker, descending into a radical questioning of reality itself. As the novel concludes, 44 shares these "truths" with the astonished August: "It is true, that which I have revealed to you; there is no God, no universe, no human race, no earthly life, no heaven, no hell. It is all a dream—a grotesque and foolish dream. Nothing exists but you. And you are but a thought—a vagrant thought, a useless thought, a homeless thought, wandering forlorn among the empty eternities!" (*Mysterious* 187). For Twain the painful nature of reality—physical suffering, the loss of loved ones, unmitigated evil, and eventual death—gave way to a solipsistic dream, a nightmare that obscured everything else.

It is fascinating to see how close Simms came to embracing Twain's final vision in "Sir Will O' Wisp." Simms's devil—one side of his double-voiced perspective in the story—insists that human nature is degraded almost beyond repair. In one critical exchange, Sir Will explains to Silex, "We can believe in individuals as in the case of Job but not in the race; for though many may be called, there are precious few chosen. Certainly, under no form of inspiration have they grown either wiser or better. They have become more learned, more scientific, more cunning, calculating, and circumspect but never a whit wiser—never a whit less human—still an anomalous blending of the angel and the beast. And the beast almost invariably swallows up the angel" (126–28). While Sir Will holds out some hope for individuals, he denies any possibility of human progress. Humans have become more educated, more rational, and less prone to superstition over the centuries, but they never have overcome their base, materialistic instincts. And their bestial desires more often than not efface their higher sensibilities. The rest of the story bears this out. Aside from Simms's portrayal of Silex, his own alter ego, the story is devoid of individuals with any redemptive potential. The town of Mongrelia is filled with nothing more than what Sir Will calls "aristocratic and fashionable people," pretentious, comic figures, utterly vain, superficial, and materialistic in their orientation to life.

Simms's decision to name the setting of his story Mongrelia sheds further light on his vision of this modern, postwar reality. The word *mongrel* is derived from the Middle English word *ymong,* meaning mixture, and, earlier still, the Old English word *gemong,* meaning crowd. The modern-day English preposition *among* comes from this same lexical root. Since the fifteenth century, *mongrel* has been used to describe the intermixing of plants or to describe animals, like dogs, that are not pure bred. The word *mutt* is the more commonly used term in the United States today. When applied to people and cultures, however, the term *mongrel* is decidedly more negative and often has been used in reference to individuals of mixed ethnic ancestry or to the social and cultural intermixing of different ethnic groups. It is difficult not to read this term in the context of the postwar South during Reconstruction, an era when social relationships between the races were changing dramatically. Simms, for example, frequently expressed frustration in his letters about the mismanagement and inefficiencies of new institutions in the South, such as the Freedmen's Bureau.* Sadly, "Sir Will O' Wisp" too often descends into racially derogatory satire that undermines the story's nobler efforts to affirm the spiritual susceptibilities that Sir Will offers to show Silex.

*Simms first mentioned the Freedmen's Bureau in two letters to his son William Gilmore Simms Jr. in March 1868 (*Letters* 5:118, 123) and later in May of the same year in a letter to Major William John Gayer, a lawyer in Charleston (*Letters* 5:128), although agents from the bureau had been present at Woodlands as early as the fall of 1865. In each letter Simms lamented the ineffectiveness of the bureau in providing provisions to farms in the Barnwell District, where his plantation, Woodlands, was located. See Singleton, "William Gilmore Simms, Woodlands, and the Freedmen's Bureau" (1996) and Abbott, *The Freedmen's Bureau in South Carolina, 1865–1872* (1972).

This tension in the story between the drive toward satire and the desire for a higher spiritual perspective exemplifies what was at stake in the aftermath of the war: the fragile balance within human nature between "the angel and the beast" (43). Human nature, according to Sir Will, is in essence a mongrel-like intermixing of higher, noble aspirations and base, instinctual desires. While individuals may aspire to this higher purity and achieve it, the human race as a whole never can. No amount of civilizing progress can remediate this essential condition. However, in Mongrelia individuals—including the aristocracy—no longer aspire to the higher values associated with art and culture; they have become merely fashionable, motivated by the desire for power and the acquisition of material things. In this context Mongrelia refers to a loss of the higher spiritual and aesthetic sensibilities that are an essential part of human identity. The consequences of this effacement include not just an erasure of the spiritual but a radical reorientation of society itself, which is no longer enriched by the presence of these vital spiritual realities. In this context, to be mongrel is to be bestial, without any sustaining connection to the spiritual.

"Sir Will O' Wisp" certainly is not the only work that Simms wrote to articulate this tragic vision. In "Sonnet—The Age of Gold," he lamented that

> Cash is conqueror,
> Wins hearts as soon as empires—puts his foot
> Upon the best affections, and will spur
> His way to eloquence, when Faith stands mute . . . (*Selected Poetry* 132)*

In the introduction to Simms's lecture series *Poetry and the Practical,* a work that explores the spiritual and pragmatic purposes of art, James Kibler has observed, "Simms continually cautioned his fellow man against materialism and the forsaking of imagination and creativity for the limiting pursuit of what passes for 'wealth'" (xxii). This insight has an illuminating corollary in "Sir Will O' Wisp." When Sir Will meets the mayor of Mongrelia late in the story, he praises the artistic works that Silex has produced and asks the mayor, "Can it be that you have never heard of his 'Lamia,' his 'Endymion,' his 'Aglaus,' his 'AEnone,' and all those several fine and beautiful translations from the Greek which contributed so large a part of my intellectual treasure in the wilds of my mountain home?" (57) The mayor admits that he has not and instead stresses the importance of

*In his explanatory notes to *The Selected Poetry of William Gilmore Simms,* Kibler has noted that "Sonnet—The Age of Gold" was first published in the *Southern Literary Messenger* in 1844 (Simms, *Selected Poetry* 362).

material "art" that has utilitarian value alone. Kibler has observed that Simms described the same dilemma in his lecture series *Poetry and the Practical:* "When societies exchange their rightful legacy for material utility . . . the road becomes a dead end that produces no meaningful great art" (xxxii). In the aftermath of the war, these dire conditions had only escalated in the United States. In a letter written to William J. Widdleton, dated June 29, 1868, Simms criticized the "worthless publications put forth by some of your neighbours, and seeming to sell" and lamented "the present desultory & superficial condition of the public mind" (*Letters* 5:141).

"Sir Will O' Wisp" asks readers to consider if art, the artist, or even the artistic imagination can survive in a such a diminished world. As an artist, Silex is portrayed by Simms as a genuinely decent man, confined to his cloistered study, reduced to writing letters to patrons who cannot appreciate his artistic talent and who see his usefulness in only the most pragmatic ways, his genius applied to the task of writing popular works that will appeal to the "superficial condition of the public mind" (*Letters* 5:141). The name *Silex* further illuminates his experience. The word's historical connotations allude to a hardened rock, such as flint, or to once-hardened minerals that have been finely ground into a silicate and then used as filler in paint and other substances. Silex hides much from both his readers and his devilish inquisitor; after all, his soul is literally at stake, if not from the demonic Sir Will then from the world around him. But when his honesty does emerge, it becomes painfully clear why Silex is an apt name. He is Simms, the artist, a susceptible soul ground down by life, hardened in ways that would seem to deny him the one thing that he desires most as an artist: imagination, insight, a higher perspective that aspires to see the connection between all things. This was no melodramatic fiction for Simms in the postwar years. The first lines of his poem "Sonnet—Exhaustion," published in 1867, evoke the same sensibility:

> I am so weary, wounded, scant of breath,
> So dispossessed of hope. So comfortless,
> That sometimes in the dread of this duress,
> I half persuade myself to fly to death.*
> (*Selected Poetry* 254)

*In his explanatory notes to *The Selected Poetry of William Gilmore Simms,* Kibler has noted that "Sonnet—Exhaustion" was published twice, first in the *Charleston Courier* on April 5, 1867, and then several months later in the *Southern Opinion* on October 12, 1867 (Simms, *Selected Poetry* 394).

The desire to escape this painful reality, the artistic drive to envision another, better world through dreaming and imagination figures prominently in "Sir Will O' Wisp." The story includes several dream sequences in which Silex is transported by Sir Will into a spiritual realm where he experiences what can only be described as the transcendent contemplation of the beautiful. Silex describes his first dream-vision in this way:

> A dreamy sense, all languor and all love, pervaded my whole frame, and . . . I beheld floating clouds of amber and purple chasing each other, as it were, slowly around my ceiling. The ceiling, after awhile, ceased to be piquant or apparent. The walls had fallen outward, and a boundless prospect of ethereal loveliness spread itself before mine eyes. . . .
>
> And in this dreaming condition and magical atmosphere, I had a vision of fair ones, that glided by me, a troop of hundreds, each more lustrous of eye than the preceding, each more and more voluptuous of charm, that gazed down upon me as they flitted by, looking with languishing and loving glances, deep down into my eyes, as if they would drag up my heart from its deep recesses and make them happy with all its pulsations. And swiftly did the heart throb and pulsate to all of joy. . . . (141)

This is only a portion of the extended dream-vision that Silex struggles to capture in words. It is an extraordinary moment, strange its fusion of exotic imagery and erotic undertones, an attempt through language to unite the material with the immaterial. Sir Will says on several occasions that he wishes only to heighten further Silex's susceptibilities to these higher realms of perception. While Silex remains suspicious of Sir Will's motives, the visions he receives are not illusions. As he explains, "There are some dreams which are realities—realities of the soul—to which Imagination and Fancy minister under conditions which relax all Common Laws. And, as it were, tear away all those barriers of the flesh, which, desiring the mortal life, usually circumscribe the grander faculties of humanity and which ordinarily lie latent, to be developed only after death" (141).

For Simms, Silex's dream-visions were not, unlike those employed by Twain, a solipsistic escape from the soul-crushing pain of material reality. They represent a higher reality, one that art always aspires toward, and one that Simms, even in his most despairing moments, refused to surrender to the ravages of his dying body, to his devastated homeland, or to a nation that he feared no longer believed in the value of the artistic imagination. Silex's conviction of this truth is echoed by Sir Will, who assures him, "It was no delusion. If you could comprehend the thing which you call the soul, you would see that it was quite as real as anything that you beheld with your eyes in your daily intercourse with men" (142). Still, Sir Will also cautions, "If the desires of the mind be gross, the sensibilities perish, and the body itself loses of its beauty. As the soul sinks, the body grows more and more animal" (142).

This is a beautiful sentiment, powerful in its evocation of a higher vision, and it is consistent with Simms's sensibilities throughout his life. To the very end, Simms struggled to hold on to these higher susceptibilities, always aware of how the materialism of the world threatens to extinguish this vision, this higher ordering. "Sir Will O' Wisp" is further evidence of this continuing tension and of Simms's own struggle to maintain this imaginative vision as the chapters of his own life drew to a close. As the story moves toward its unfinished conclusion, this transcendent vision is continually threatened by the emerging social satire that begins to dominate the plot. In contrast to the higher susceptibilities that Silex experiences, the satire represents a descent into the bestial, bitter anger, the desire to hurt and wound others. And this is where Simms suspended the progress of his story, at the crossroads between these two paths, one higher and one lower, the angel and the beast.

Regrettably, we will never know what happens to Silex the artist or to the citizens of Mongrelia or even to the devilish Sir Will. Such conclusions must be left to our own creative imaginations. However, it is likely that an ending to "Sir Will O' Wisp" actually exists, if one only knows where to look. In May of 1870, just weeks before his death, Simms delivered what would be his final lecture before the Charleston Agricultural and Horticultural Association. In his biography of Simms, Guilds has observed that "the afflicted writer literally rose from his sickbed to write . . . perhaps the most moving address of his career" (*Literary Life* 319). *The Sense of the Beautiful* is a profoundly spiritual, poetic speech and a powerful testament to Simms's enduring vision at the close of his life. The speech reverberates—at times, almost word for word—with ideas that Simms included in "Sir Will O' Wisp." In his vision of the human condition, Simms—ever the romantic, ever the realist—remained unchanged: "This little word in itself, which we call 'man,' is possessed from his very birth by two powers which seem to contend for his possession. The one is immortal, an angel; the other wholly mortal, an animal. The antagonism between them never ceases till the mortal shall put on immortality. The animal is one to make fierce battle. He possesses very terrible powers; eager appetites, fiery passions, lowly instincts. . . . These are very terrible attributes. How shall the angel subdue this animal?" (*Sense of the Beautiful* 3–4). This question occupies the very crossroads where "Sir Will O' Wisp" ended and could go no further. Yet, here in Simms's final speech, there is a movement forward, a clear answer, a sense of resolution, one that echoes and affirms Silex's own dream-vision and Sir Will's promise to cultivate in the artist the highest of spiritual susceptibilities. In his speech, Simms affirmed, "For it is only when you can receive and cherish this sense of the beautiful in your bosom that you can subdue the animal. . . . It is this sense which develops all the soul's activity. It endows the soul with the eyes to see, the heart to feel, and all the subordinate senses to enjoy the marvellous beauty in this beautiful world which comes to us freshly, with every dawning, directly from the hands of God" (6).

Just as in Simms's post war story, the sense of the beautiful, this higher susceptibility, comes while under "the dominion of a spell of reverie," a dream, as "your thought wanders back over long tracts of time" and "you recall sacred memories" (*Sense of the Beautiful* 18). Gone is the satire—the "fiery passions, lowly instincts"—that had come increasingly to dominate the plot of "Sir Will O' Wisp," replaced by intimations of transcendent beauty that call the artist and his audience to a higher purpose. "Sir Will O' Wisp" plays a role in reaching this final vision, however, for the only true and certain measure of the vision's authenticity is the depth of struggle, hardship, and suffering that proceeds it. Simms willingness to wrestle with the private and public demons that pursued him during the final years of his life makes "Sir Will O' Wisp" a tale worth reading.

Works Cited

Abbott, Martin. *The Freedmen's Bureau in South Carolina, 1865–1872.* Chapel Hill: University of North Carolina Press, 1972.

Allies, Jabez. *The Ignis Fatuus, or Will-O'-the-Wisp and the Fairies.* London: Simpkin, Marshall, and Company, 1846.

Brave. Dirs. Mark Andrews, Brenda Chapman, and Steve Purcell. Disney Pixar, 2012. DVD.

Brennan, Matthew C. *The Poet's Holy Craft: William Gilmore Simms and Romantic Verse Tradition.* Columbia: University of South Carolina Press, 2010.

Briggs, Katherine M. *An Encyclopedia of Fairies: Hobgoblins, Brownies, Bogies, and Other Supernatural Creatures.* New York: Pantheon Books, 1976.

———. *The Fairies in English Tradition and Literature.* Chicago: University of Chicago Press, 1967.

Csicsila, Joseph, and Chad Rohman. *Centenary Reflections on Mark Twain's No. 44, The Mysterious Stranger.* Columbia: University of Missouri Press, 2009.

Day, John. *Law Tricks, or Who Would Have Thought It.* 1608. Reprinted, Cambridge: Oxford University Press, 1850.

Goethe, Johann Wolfgang von. *Faust I and II.* Ed. and trans. Stuart Atkins. Princeton: Princeton University Press, 1984.

Guilds, John Caldwell. Introduction. In John Caldwell Guilds, ed., *Stories and Tales. The Writings of William Gilmore Simms.* Centennial Edition. Vol. 5. Introductions, explanatory notes, and texts established by John Caldwell Guilds. Columbia: University of South Carolina Press, 1974. xi–xxiv.

———. *Simms: A Literary Life.* Fayetteville: University of Arkansas Press, 1992.

———. "William Gilmore Simms and the *Cosmopolitan,*" *Georgia Historical Quarterly* 41 (March 1957): 31–41.

Hawthorne, Nathaniel. "The Great Carbuncle." *Twice Told Tales* (1837). In Fredson Bowers et al., eds., *The Centenary Edition of the Works of Nathaniel Hawthorne.* Vol. 9. Columbus: Ohio State University Press, 1974. 149–65.

Kahn, Sholom J. *Mark Twain's Mysterious Stranger: A Study of the Manuscript Texts.* Columbia: University of Missouri Press, 1978.

Kibler, James Everett, Jr. Introduction. In William Gilmore Simms, *Poetry and the Practical.* Ed. James Everett Kibler, Jr. Fayetteville: University of Arkansas Press, 1996. xi–xlvii.

———. *Pseudonymous Publications of William Gilmore Simms.* Athens: University of Georgia Press, 1976.

Longfellow, Henry Wadsworth. *Hyperion: A Romance.* 2 Vols. New York: Samuel Colman, 1839.

Milton, John. "Comus." In Merritt Y. Hughes, ed., *Complete Poems and Major Prose.* Indianapolis: Odyssey Press, 1957. 89–114.

———. *Paradise Lost.* In Merritt Y. Hughes, ed., *Complete Poems and Major Prose.* Indianapolis: Odyssey Press, 1957. 211–469.

Ray, John. *Observations Topographical, Moral, & Physiological Made in a Journey through Part of the Low-Countries, Germany, Italy, and France.* London: Royal Society, 1673.

Review. *The Damsel of Darien. Knickerbocker* 14 (November 1839): 457–58.

Simms, William Gilmore. *Border Beagles; A Tale of Mississippi.* Two Vols. Philadelphia: Carey and Hart, 1840.

———. *The Damsel of Darien.* 2 vols. Philadelphia: Lea and Blanchard, 1839.

———. "A Dream of the Earth." *The Book of My Lady: A Melange.* Philadelphia: Key & Biddle, 1833. 13–37.

———. "A Fairy Tale." *The Cosmopolitan: An Occasional.* Vol. 1. Charleston: William Estill, Publisher, 1833: 100–17.

———. *The History of South Carolina, from Its First European Discovery to Its Erection into a Republic.* Charleston: S. Babcock & Company. 1840.

———. "Jack-O'-Lantern: A New-Light Story." By Eyes-In-Glass. Chapter I. *Southern Literary Messenger* 4.5 (May 1838): 336–39.

———. *Joscelyn; A Tale of the Revolution.* 1867. In *The Writings of William Gilmore Simms. Centennial Edition.* Vol. 16. Introduction and explanatory notes by Stephen Meats. Text established by Keen Butterworth. Columbia: University of South Carolina Press, 1975.

———. *The Letters of William Gilmore Simms.* Ed. Mary C. Simms Oliphant et al. 6 vols. Columbia: University of South Carolina Press, 1952–82.

———. *The Life of Francis Marion.* New York: Henry G. Langley, 1844.

———. "Love, Desire, and Enjoyment." *Early Lays.* Charleston. A.E. Miller, 1827.

———. *Poetry and the Practical.* Ed. James Everett Kibler, Jr. Fayetteville: University of Arkansas Press, 1996.

———. *Selected Poems of William Gilmore Simms.* Ed. James Everett Kibler, Jr. Athens: University of Georgia Press, 1990.

———. *The Sense of the Beautiful.* Address before the Charleston County Agricultural and Horticultural Association, May 3, 1870. Charleston: Walker, Evans & Cogswell, 1870.

———. "Sir Will O' Wisp or the Irish Baronet; A Tale of Its Own Day." Charles Carroll Simms Collection, South Caroliniana Library, University of South Carolina.

———. "Sweet William, A Tale of Faerie." *Martin Faber, the Story of a Criminal; and Other Tales.* Vol. 1. New York: Harper & Brothers, 1837. 161–210.

Singleton, Robert R. "William Gilmore Simms, Woodlands, and the Freedmen's Bureau." *Mississippi Quarterly* 50.1 (December 1996): 19–36.

Trent, William Peterfield. *William Gilmore Simms.* Boston: Houghton Mifflin, 1892.

Twain, Mark. *No. 44, The Mysterious Stranger: Being an Ancient Tale Found in a Jug, and Freely Translated from the Jug.* The Mark Twain Library. Foreword and notes by John S. Tuckey. Berkeley: University of California Press, 1982.

Sir Will O' Wisp or the Irish Baronet; A Tale of Its Own Day

"Time travels in divers paces with divers persons. I'll tell you who Time ambles withal, who Time trots withal; who Time gallops withal and who he stands still withal."

WILLIAM SHAKESPEARE, *As You Like It*

Manager. You know that upon German stage everyone tries what one he likes. Therefore, spare me neither machinery nor scenery upon this occasion. I put everything at your disposal. Use the greater and the lesser light of heaven. You are free to squander the stars. There is no lack of fire and water, red lights and blue, rocks and cascade, birds and beasts. So you shall spread out in this narrow booth the whole circle of creation and travel with considerate speed from Heaven, and through the world, and finally to Hell.

JOHANN WOLFGANG VON GOETHE, *The Faust*

CHAPTER I
My Familiar

It is scarcely the best social policy to begin the work of confession on one's first entry into the world, where, now-a-days, if men confess to any sins at all, they are such only as are sufficiently equivocal to pass for virtues; but, as my aim is a moral one, and my hope the reformation of this very infirmity among mankind, I know no better mode of beginning than to put myself *rectus in curia,* and make a clean break of it before I claim any further hearing. And so—to the work of confession.

Stare not therefore, ye rigidly pious, whether Charlatan or Christian—frown not, ye saints of the congregation and holy men of the tabernacle—wring not your hands, ye godly dames whose mission it is to help unto grace and gravy the infinite number of cleverish and good looking young novitiates who are possessed of the spirit and lack all other possessions—when I honestly declare unto ye that, like Saul and Socrates of old, and the witch of Endor, John Faustus, Michael Scott, Machiavelli, and very possibly, the Rev. Edward Irving, I have my familiar—my domestic demon—one of those active, adroit, and intelligent spirits, who, at times, under special laws of attraction, sympathy, animal or intellectual magnetism attract themselves to the fortunes of men for their special comfort and edification; bringing them tidings from remote spheres; shrewd suggestions of the future, blended with not always pleasant recollections of the past giving them counsel which, through time, may yet not be judicious; reporting the daily news, and affording him such occasional peeps into the secrets of society as are refreshingly fragrant in the ears of the *blasé.* In brief, my demon is one who does for me my divining, my *clair-voyancing* and *discovery,* with little or no trouble to myself. He sits beside me and whispers in my ear; or he goes before me and indicates my way; serves me in a thousand ways which shall be nameless; and all from sheer love and sympathy. He is my slave of the Lamp and the Ring, and costs me not a shilling for his keeping.

How I became familiar with my familiar is, dearly beloved, without making myself too familiar, none of your business. By what laws of attraction or sympathy I should have been chosen, by himself, as his Lord and Master cannot be said, even though I should myself be possessed of a knowledge of the mysterious laws which govern the subject. That there are laws, growing out of human susceptibilities, and the degrees of advances which individual men may reach, by which they are put naturally *en rapport* with supernatural agencies, is beyond all question. The fact is apparent from a thousand histories, all of which are as worthy of confidence as Bancroft's *United States,* a Puritan chronicle, or the report of a Freedmen's Bureau in this our Mongrelia.

In acquiring my demon, I persuade myself that I was quite as innocent as Socrates. He came to me, suffice it to know, not as visitors from the nether regions are usually supposed to come, reeking with fumes of sulphur and smelling of recent bituminous fires. There was no flourish of trumpets warning me of any approach; nor did I detect either at his coming or his departure any of that pleasant musical twang with which the old writers of psychology usually described the exits and the entrances of infernal spirits. Never was an apparition more innocent or less imposing, though, by the way, there was something peculiar in it. Nor was I at all conscious or apprehensive of his presence. I certainly employed no incantations, such as Faust uses for raising Mephistopheles. I described no circle, uttered no invocation, appealed to no medium, and though I had Dr. Dee in my library, I took no lessons from a work which, from its dense stupidity, was quite conclusive to me that the lying Doctor, if he had any intimacy with the devil, derived no intellectual advantages from the association. So far as I can say my whole intercourse with the demonic world has been confined to the devil of the printing office, and his presence has been too frequently a subject of annoyance to make me at all desirous of extending my knowledge among the fraternity.

Unsought, undesired, unsolicited, unprayed for, my familiar suddenly stood before me. Nay, I err. He came behind me—such was the unobtrusive modesty of his first approach; and my devil made his presence first known to me not by sight but by sound. But that was no vulgar sound, though frequent enough since Maccaboy first became popular as a nasal titillator. The way of it was this: My snuffbox—a capacious one—a Scottish mull, supposed to have been once the property of George Buchanan of famous memory, lay open upon my table. I had just drawn from its capacious vault a generous thumb and finger full of the aromatic dust, applying it to my own nostrils. Use had made the organ somewhat obtuse. Custom had staled their sensibility and lessened the proactive in the tobacco, and with a feeble effort to sneeze, I snapt my fingers in the air, shaking from them what of the powder they had withheld from my proboscis.

Very remarkable was the result which followed. If my own nose was incapable of any demonstrative effort at a sneeze, what was my surprise, if not consternation, to hear immediately behind me one of the most enviable of all nasal acknowledgements. Such a sneeze, so vastly superior to any that I had ever produced—that I had ever heard from any nose before—that I felt, as by an infallible instinct that it was not a sneeze of humanity; and I clearly comprehended the action of my Maccaboy upon the sternutatory organs of an infernal.

"Ha! tshe–tshe–tshe–tshe–tshe—Ha! Ha! tshe!"

Such was the report. Such was the conclusive testimony then involuntarily given to the pungent merits of my Maccaboy, the excellence of which I had begun to question.

It was with a feeling not unlike a terror that I turned to confront the strange proboscis that was capable of such eloquent utterance. A moment's glance, while it put me more at my ease, seemed to tell me everything. On looking at him, I felt, all of a sudden, that he was no stranger. We had certainly met before; but as I readily divined his true nature, in the same instant, the unpleasant conviction was forced upon me that I had been no better than I should be. One is very apt to meet the devil in the best circles, and to become familiar with him as a gentleman without discovering one of his secrets as a devil. In old times one had better security in the inevitable appendages of horns and hoof; but, since Cuvier, seeing him in this costume, denounced him as granivorous, not able to devour men, and so (*on dit*) kicked him out of his laboratory, the demoniacs have adapted their habits much more closely to those of science and society.

Well, my demon—there he stood, confronting me with the most unobtrusive presence in the world, a smile on his countenance, which was still flushed, however, by his sneezing performance, and as mild and benignant a blue eye fastened upon my own, as ever lightened up beneath the forehead of a philanthropist. His face was a good one but by no means remarkable. Such a face I have often seen. It was rather Gallican in contour and general expression, but had some of the Irishman in it—the rich dark red of his complexion, and a certain dash of frankness and impulse which won directly upon your confidence. He had the dark hair also, and a beautiful moustache of the same colour, well waxed and pointed, *a la Napoleon,* and a neatly cut Grecian nose and chin; the former being of Roman dimensions however, which sufficiently accounted for the magnitude of his sneezing capacity. There was, besides, a somewhat satirical cast in his general expression, showing a slight disposition to sneer at much, and laugh at many things in society; a something reminding you of Mephistopheles, which was in contrast with the otherwise benevolent expression in general. The figure was excellent, I should say perfect—symmetrical, beautifully developed, tall, stately, well set and muscular, well rounded too, but with no tendency to obesity. His costume, *salon les regles,* was imitable, simple, neat, dark of colour, and evidently made by an inspired tailor, such as might call on Brummel for his *imprimatur.* Not to seem extravagant in my eulogy, I content myself with saying that I have seen the editor of a ladies magazine a far worse looking fellow, and infinitely less of the gentleman.

Enough of description. I had risen and stood facing him. I was at a loss what to say, and pointing to the door, I said—

"Pardon me, Sir, but pray how did you get in? I had locked my door in order to prevent intrusion."

"Very true," he replied, "but you forgot to close the keyhole!"

Here was an answer which told me much in a sentence, but contributed, as you may suppose, somewhat further to my disquiet. But with that divine instinct which we have never denied to the devil, while denying him all other virtues, he readily discerned my annoyance, and saw that I was dashed by his intrusion. With that facility of speech and felicity of manners which has made the devil a proverbial gentleman, he proceeded in a brief speech or two to put me more at ease; taking care in what he said not to ascribe my discomposure to any other cause than the natural irritability of an author, when disturbed in his devotions at his desk.

"Pardon me, my dear Sir. I should have recollected that you belong to that class—the *genus irritabile vatum*—the approach to whom requires the nicest courtesy, and the most conciliatory address. I have been precipital; but should not have been so, had it not been for your Maccaboy, which by irritating my nostrils baffled all the efforts of my tongue. It operated a greater surprise upon me than my presence does upon you. It is a vile nostrum, which the delicacy of my olfactories could never endure; and let me counsel you that it will destroy in time all of the delicate sensibilities of yours. Once more, pardon me that I intrude. I see that you are busy. Pray resume your labours. They are of a nature to require your most intent regards, and to call into requisition all the finest tastes of your nature."

How the devil did he guess what I was doing. I was busily engaged, in secret, preparing for the press a collection of the most fashionable negro melodies, such as Jim Crow, Coal Black Rose, Clare De Kitchen, and other pieces of like moral, religious, national, and practical interest, with an elaborate philosophical and psychological inquiry into the susceptibility of the negro for the higher arts of statesmanship, poetry, and philosophy, to say nothing of science, with copious appendices of illustrative notes, such as would become a work of such magnitude and value; and the whole labor and conception were to be kept secret until I was fully prepared to burst upon the world with the book complete! And yet this stranger—this demon—looking so little demonic—seemed to know all about it.

I looked at him still confused. He smiled pleasantly and said gently, laying his hand upon mine,

"Pray resume your seat, my friend, and proceed in your labours. I can wait upon you."

"Friend!" was my involuntary ejaculation. Were we really on such intimate relations already?

"And why not, my dear Mr. Silex. All friendships must have a beginning, and I doubt nothing of the grateful in ours, if we begin rightly; so please make yourself at home, which is the only sure process by which to make your guest at home."

He drew a chair for himself as he said these words, with the air of a man of the world, resolute to take his ease at his word, and doing it so naturally and gracefully that no landlord ever thinks proper to take umbrage. I followed his example, seated myself, and looked to him in silence.

"Suffer me," he said, "to make one request. Will it please you to shut down the lid of your mull, and place it in your escritoire. The tobacco is quite too potent for my nerves."

The devil talk of nerves, thought I; but I complied with his request. When he made it, he put on the very happiest airs of the exquisite, trained in the very best schools of Parisian fashion in the days of Louis the Sixteenth. Throwing one leg over the other, I discovered the nicest fitting boots, and no sign of the hoof. His coat was a beautiful fitting frock which amply covered the tail of the beast if he wore any such appendage.

CHAPTER 2
Purely Psychological

There we sat for a few seconds surveying each other in silence. His coolness, complacency, and ease of manner had the effect of restoring my own. I acquired courage as I looked at him, and recollected that he was an intruder. Was not this my room, my chamber, my study, my sanctum. The reflection brought back all my firmness, especially as I saw nothing in the countenance of my visitor which could affright or should offend. Nay, there was nothing sinister or insidious in the pleasant smile with which he regarded me. Speaking a little formally, I said at length—

"Beg pardon, Sir, but you will find it tedious perhaps, waiting upon my humours or my labours. May I be honoured at once with the purpose of your visit?"

"Nay, my dear Mr. Silex, it will not be tedious, either to watch your labours, or endure your humours. I am the most flexible of friends. As for my business, that is not so easily told. As, however, I perceive that you already know me—"

Here I expressed a little reluctance, and prayed for more direct information.

"I cannot deny," was my response, "that I have a shrewd grasp, but—." There I paused.

"Your guess, my dear Mr. Silex, is as good as an instinct. I should be a poor devil, if meaning to make myself known to a party, I had left him to acquire his knowledge by the process of guessing. No! No! Sir! Where one desires to make himself, and the other hath the capacity for understanding, your instincts are quite as good as mine, and there needs no formality between persons already acquainted."

"How?—"

"Of that hereafter. I can explain all to your satisfaction in due season."

"But your name, Sir, if you please?"

"My dear Mr. Silex, your own favorite Shakespeare has some sarcasm about the waste of unnecessary words, or choice about them, in naming even the subjects of our delight and pleasure. Besides, there is something less than civil, certainly something less than social, in calling folks continually by their title of dignity. I freely confess to you a willingness to dispense with mine. It weighs like a slate garment very heavily upon me at times. I am, like many of the princes of old, and some of the officers of penal justice in modern times, infinitely more fond of a snug disguise, and a good humoured *nom de guerre,* than of the solemn ceremonial which follows upon and announces the presence of superior attributes. At present, sir, as I see you still somewhat at a loss, you will do me the favor to recognize me under one of my many names—the most innocent and least imposing, perhaps, among them—and whenever you may deem it necessary to call me by a name at all, which I trust will not be often the case, to know me as Will O' the Wisp. I shall certainly be willing to give you all the light I carry, should you require it. Will O' the Wisp is a common acquaintance, and nobody should be seriously alarmed or annoyed at his presence. You, I know, who are a poet and philosopher, will readily show yourself above all idle superstitious fancies; and you will soon find, upon doing so, that if I have few virtues, I have many uses; and my more imposing names of sovereignty thrown out of the account, there can be no objection to the employment of my services."

"Your services, Sir William?" I exclaimed with some wonder, in the sudden commotion of my thoughts, not exactly knowing what to make of this sort of introduction—"Your services!"

"Ay, my services," he replied, "I propose to serve you, because I see that you need my help, and because I have somehow taken a liking to you. You smile, but I am above jest in this. I am serious. In my friendship for you I have sought you out, and I am resolved to become your friend, companion, assistant, anything, whether you will or no! You want an amanuensis, and considering the color of the work on which I see you busy, perhaps I am the very person of all the world whom you should soonest choose. But I insist not on this. Take me in what capacity you please. I am an actor of all work, as the comedians call themselves. I can be a boon companion, a grave counsellor, a curious penman, and a dapper valet. Make me what you please, with a will, and rely on me to be the thing which you most desire. I will take no refusal; you must employ me."

So liberal an offer—so graciously made—was not to be rejected idly. Still, it required some deliberation. I had some doubts—shall I call them apprehensions—inherited from the teachings and traditions of childhood. He saw me hesitate and threw in certain additional suggestions.

"My library" said he, "is large, various, ample, for all your purposes. Indeed, next to that of my cousin, Belial, it is the very best in our dominion. I can bring you any volume you please, especially of the literature of New England. It is a favorite literature with us; indeed, we not only furnish the work of the authorities, but employ most of the writers. They have long since adopted our creed which denies anything to faith and, overthrowing their old idols, setting themselves up in their place. Setting self esteem against authority has given us the dominion of the world! You are sometimes at a loss for the proper authorities and I shall be glad to furnish them."

Still I hesitated. I was not prepared to substitute the Yankee Brogue for the English language, and only kept Webster's dictionary to look up its vulgarisms. Besides, there was my literary moral, which had its scruples; and to draw my authorities from proverbially lying Chronicles was a little too much at first even for this devil. He had betrayed the cloven hoof in showing how the devil had obtained dominion of the world through this very process. He read my thoughts, changed his tactics, and gave me a beautiful discourse, leading me from metaphysics to the consideration of the tastes, the sentiments and through these to psychology; and I confess I thought him very fine. At the close, he said,

"But my dear friend, this subject is tedious. Life is not to be consumed in argument even though that argument shall involve all the philosophies. *Dum vivimus vivamus.* We do not live, unless we recognize play as a part of employment, and quite as essential to existence. Why fret over your toils. Give yourself respite. Let me help you. Your correspondence seems quite extensive. Let me give you a taste of my quality in assisting you in your answers. Here, I see that your correspondents are of every description. You have letters from critics, historians, divines, widows, old maids, and young ones. What a medley. It must addle your brain to answer any three of these at a single sitting. But you shall see how I will dispose of them."

And speaking thus, he without ado turned over a pile, and without caring to read the several letters which he undertook to answer, he at once proceeded to write, writing like flash, the pen rather coursing over the paper than resting upon it. What a grand devilish faculty it was which he possessed!

And, even as he wrote he flung me his replies. I was amazed. Nothing could be more suitably said in any instance. He had finished a dozen before I had got through reading one.

"Wonderful!" I exclaimed. "What a boon for an author could his fingers keep such equal pace with his thoughts."

He laughed and wrote on. And I read with increasing amazement at every letter. He not only divined what I would myself have written, but prepared answers, admirably "adapted to cases," upon which my mind had as yet arrived at no decision. He furnished the necessary suggestion. To certain magazine publishers who had obtained my articles, and had dishonoured my drafts, he threatened exposure in the *Herald* and other universal organs. To others who were meditating how to escape payment, he hinted at certain partnership secrets, the exposure of which involved a catastrophe.

To a politician, aiming at an office, wanting support and certain speeches at certain gatherings, and giving occasional dinners which were significant of as much courteousness as pretension, he wrote a brief but comprehensive essay upon the arts of cuisine, laying great stress upon the quality of the dinner as the essential of the politician. He cancelled the employment of a certain celebrated cook, concluding with an acceptance of the invitation, promising only a proper bill of fare, and that my wine for the current month of warm weather should be *Lachryma Christi.*

To a lady of fashion, a showy widow, who held herself at thirty-five to still be a marketable commodity, and whose card and note for the next *soiree* was rather a summons than a solicitation, he pleaded a rule to accept no invitations for Friday, but expressed a profound regret that pleasure should need to give way to law. He complimented her at the same time upon the felicity of her style and the *recherché* fold of her envelope, the tints of which he said fancifully seemed to be woven out of the colors of the rainbow.

"Never," said he to me, "accept a woman's invitation, the tone of which argues her certainty that you will come. Disappoint her. In dealing with a widow, be sure always that you do not let her off too easily, or yourself too cheaply."

To the editor of a weekly magazine, who, like the maggot that feeds upon the brains of the elk, continued to draw upon those of young masters and misses for his material and to requite them in puffs, he recommended the transformation of his magazine into a sort of foundling hospitality, providing soup every day. This in the nature of a satirical essay so distinguished that the editor alone, of all his circle, could not perceive the satire. To a tailor soliciting customers, and proffering long credit, he sent the pattern of a new style of coat for the summer to which no pockets need be attached.

Seeing him take up certain other letters, I was about to interpose and prevent his perusal of them, but he promptly anticipated my movement, and handing them to me, said—

"These you will probably prefer to answer yourself."

"What! you know their contents."

"Perfectly! I could suggest the proper answers also, but they would hardly suit you, in your present mood of mind, and I prefer that you should acquire some of your lessons through your own experiences."

I was conscious of a suffusion of the cheek, but took the letters and locked them in my escritoire. He smiled pleasantly, but said nothing. It was necessary that I should express my thanks for what he had done.

"Oh! No thanks, my dear Mr. Silex—all this is nothing. I shall do better things for you as we grow together, and as you shall develope your several needs and wishes."

"Really, Sir Will, I am very grateful for your services, and your friendly interest in my affairs. You are, indeed, a most valuable acquisition. I know not how I shall ever requite you."

"Requite me, Mr. Silex. I ask for no requital. Love's labours are his own pleasures; and the pleasure of serving you is quite enough reward for me."

"Indeed! This character is not always or often accorded to the gentlemen of your House. You are generally supposed to be somewhat exacting for your favours—a rigid exacting for all your dues. Among men, the notion is that you do nothing for nothing, but require something more than the ordinary rates of interest. Our factors are now content with 25 to 60 percent. But you require the very soul of the borrower."

"Twenty five to 60 percent is very likely to exact all soul from all who borrow at such rates. But any report has done our household much wrong if it supposes that we make any such executions. We have been always content with something less even than your minimum. Indeed, my dear Sir, nobody has been more misrepresented and more misunderstood than the persons of our household."

Never did injured mortal look more in need of sympathy. I felt myself getting lachrymose.

"What!" I proceeded. "Is your love for me, personally, so great that you are willing, in any case, to do gratuitously those things for which you or your

Superior is understood, in the case of all other men hitherto, to have exacted eternal service, nay, subject to eternal tortures?"

"I really do not understand you, my dear master," was his reply, and he really looked the innocence which he avowed.

"'Pon my soul," I responded, "you are exceedingly dull, Sir Will O' the Wisp, or I have been grievously imposed upon by old wife stories. Is it really possible that you propose to serve me for nothing—to concentrate upon me and for my benefit, those wondrous, various, and subtle talents of which you have just given me such surprising examples? Do you really ask no manner of compensation—nothing in return?"

"Nothing!—what should I ask, what need—that you can give—unless it be that which I really desire—your confidence, your sympathy, your affection?"

"And there is to be no *bond* between us?"

"Bond? With what use—for what purpose? What are you thinking of?"

"Well, in plain language, Sir William, do you not desire to bind me, body and soul, in return for your services? Do you not desire a mortgage of my soul?"

"Ha! Ha! Ha! What excellent nonsense. Truly you have sucked in old wife's stories at the bosom of some Lapland witch. Your body? What should I want with it. I have one of my own and can have as many as I desire, and get a new one every day. Your body is made up of so much fish, flesh and fowl which you get daily from the market. The mutton of yesterday, and the beef of the day before, and the pork steaks of last Saturday, and the fish of the Friday before are all resolved into yourself, and it is only yours, as you have paid for it, and it cannot easily be segregated from the constituent mass which you carry."

"Well, but the soul?"

"That is of even less account in my sight than the body. What should I want with it—what do with it—of what profit to me or my master? What do you know about your soul that you should make so much about it, even if I should propose the bond and mortgage which so much affrights you. You need no bond to give my master or myself a title to it. But, my dear Mr. Silex, all that thing has gone entirely of fashion. We have more souls on hand than we know what to do with. They are positively rotting on our hands. We wouldn't be bothered or burdened with an increase on any terms, and in truth we think of abolishing the old establishment entirely "out", under the counsel of our excellent Brother Beecher, who with a throng and others of his kinship have pretty much taken the business out of our hands. Our Master has sunk very much into lassitude since these brethren work so industriously for us, and Hell, instead of being where it was, in the Old Superstition, in the centre of the earth, is now transferred to its surface; and we, Devils as you call us, have been so completely outdone by the philanthropists of the present generation, in the arts damnable, that we are setting up for a new rôle and aiming at the amicable. In that fact you may discern one of the reasons which prompts me to an alliance with you. All my brethren—all of courtly presence at least—are following my example, and seeking alliances on earth—reviving such bonds and such only, as those of Pylades and Orestes. I shall be your Pylades if you please. In respect to souls, my Orestes, next to the grievous mistake into which you have been led by your pious grandmother, touching the character of our gentry below stairs, is that monstrous error which men in general seem to entertain as to the value of the article you think we trade in. As a general rule nothing can be more insignificant. I have seen ten thousand human souls dancing on a fork of lightning, no thicker than a cambric needle, without one jostling the other. One of the amusements in former times—but rather out of fashion now—was to sit on a summer afternoon, shoot out spears of lightning, and call up some hundred thousand souls for a procession, followed by torrid dances, upon their points. Souls, indeed! The subject is an annoying one, rather, and we will return to it hereafter, when I shall somewhat more enlighten. The ignorance of your race on this topic and the vileness and stupidity of its conceptions as to us and our realm and our objects may be found in the conceptions of your dramatic artists, in the spectacle, "The Black Crook," which has embodied the highest notions of your people on these grand topics. Here all Hell is evoked and thundered at, and one of our Princes brought up, throne and all, to treat with a miserable, miserly old wretch, crooked, deformed, dirty and utterly despicable in every way; a wretch whose daily life proves his non-possession of a soul; and this poor pitiful sort of life of his, he can only prolong by entrapping a silly youngster, whom a pretty young witch would beguile to her own and our purposes in half the time. One word more before leaving this subject for the present. Souls, my dear friend, are special endowments. Not one in a hundred possesses the commodity, as you might see every day for yourself. Souls are chosen, and assigned to certain temples, or shrines or cases, which you call bodies. Some of your churches really teach this truth, when they speak of the elect, but without knowing how to comprehend it. The thing would be easy if they could only conceive of the Election having been made at the original endowment."

"You bewilder me. All this is very new to me."

"Precisely. The first step to knowledge among men is mostly to unlearn. We must first rid your mind of old Superstitions, before we can inoculate you with new truth. And your studies under my direction will contemplate this necessity.

Still I propose to bring you on rapidly, as, indeed, is very much the way with us below. We have experts for masters always and rarely fail to find a susceptible quickness in our pupils."

"My dear Sir William," said I—"you have given me so much food for reflection, so much provocation to thought, and so excited me that I need a sedative, and I think that you will permit me to take a single pinch of Maccaboy and light a cigar immediately after."

"Surely, but in that case I will leave the room till you have puffed away your doubt and cares together."

"Not so, my dear Sir, if my use of tobacco is to drive you out, I must forego it."

"By no means," he replied promptly—"I shall amuse myself, be sure, by looking into the street, where I can always see a dance of souls of all dimensions, following in the wake of a hand organ, which ought invariably to proceed all of your processions which contemplate human liberty, the advance of civilization, public education, the charities, and all popular conventions. *Au Revoir.*"

In an instant he was gone. How, when, whither, is not to be said. The door was still closed. I tried the key. The bolt was shot. My mind was all in a whirl, and I had to resort to my mull of Maccaboy.

CHAPTER 3
Signed, Sealed, and Delivered

My Maccaboy never seemed so deliciously to titillate my nostrils as now. The sternutatory explosion which followed seemed a beautiful and very pronounced echo of that—tshe—tshe—tshe—tshe—tshe—aschew—which it had exported erstwhile from the nose of my demonic acquaintance—and very decidedly superior to any demonstration which my own nose had been making for a season or more. The snuff seemed to have a better flavour, and when I lighted my cigar, an exquisite, though very delicate odour, seemed to diffuse itself through the chamber, something quite different from the usual cigaratic aroma. I breathed, indeed, a delicious atmosphere, and gradually sunk into one of those reveries in which the fancy becomes oriental and carries one into oriental gardens. Those of Harun al-Rashid rose up before me; and anon, before my eyes, swam thousands of

> "Those gay creatures of the Elements,
> that in the colours of the rainbow live,
> and play in the plighted clouds."

A dreamy sense, all languor and all love, pervaded my whole frame, and with half shut eyes, realizing all the visions that made the charm of the *dolce far niente,* as described in the delightful retreats of Thomson's "Castle of Indolence," I beheld floating clouds of amber and purple chasing each other, as it were, slowly around my ceiling. The ceiling, after awhile, ceased to be piquant or apparent. The walls had fallen outward, and a boundless prospect of ethereal loveliness spread itself before mine eyes. I was under a spell, especially, as these sights were at length succeeded by sounds, sweet, soft, musical as the lute of Apollo, that appeared to arise from innumerable wind harps, touched by the most gentle breezes from the South.

And in this dreamy condition and magical atmosphere, I had a vision of fair ones, that glided by me, a troop of hundreds, each more lustrous of eye than the preceding, each more and more voluptuous of charm, that gazed down upon me as they flitted by, looking with languishing and loving glances, deep down into my eyes, as if they would drag up my heart from its deep recesses, and make them happy with all its pulsations. And swiftly did the heart throb and pulsate to all of joy, at every glance, especially when one, last of all, came to gaze and linger above me; one in whose every lineament I found glow and animation—one whose very lineament I knew—the tall, pale woman, graceful and white as the lily, with eyes deep of meaning yet bright as the mountain lake, set in the heart of loveliest hills of beauty, who had long since won me as a watcher of her steps and a worshipper of her feet.

There are some dreams which are realities—realities of the soul, to which Imagination and Fancy minister under conditions which relax all Common Laws and, as it were, tear away all those barriers of the flesh, which, desiring the mortal life, usually circumscribe the grander faculties of humanity and which ordinarily lie latent, to be developed only after death.

I dreamed, but certainly, I did not sleep. I saw all these things. I was helpless to do more than see. I could feel too, but had no power of action. I could not return the pressure of the beautiful lips which were laid on mind. I felt myself sighing that I could not speak, and the tears gathered in my eyes at the enjoyment of a rapture that I could not declare in language.

And the music rose into deeper and more earnest tones, and the procession passed from sight and I then became conscious that one was sitting beside me, and in the speaking smile upon his lips, I could see that it was to his magical powers that I owed this majestical sweet vision, and drank from such indefinable founts of rapture.

I was still languid from the deliciousness of my dream. I said to him—

"I have slept."

"No."

"I have surely dreamed."

"No! You have seen. You were in a trance and had a vision."

"You too beheld."

"I cannot help but see. I create."

"And I owe this exquisite delusion to you."

"It was no delusion. If you could comprehend the thing which you call the soul, you would see that it was quite as real as anything that you beheld with your eyes in your daily intercourse with men."

"But I saw scores of beautiful women, none of whom—save one—did I know."

"True; but this has often happened to you in your dreams. They are not the less real because you do not know them. They are yet to be known. It is in the growth of the susceptibilities that the promise of vision expands; and the blended forms of susceptibilities and sensibilities enlarge the province of enjoyment. One of your poets writes—'Who drinks beer, thinks beer.' If the desires of the mind be gross, the sensibilities perish, and the body itself loses of its beauty. As the soul sinks, the body grows more and more animal. The woman may have a celestial beauty today, but, if the animal shall preponderate, in her tastes and appetite, you find her coarse tomorrow. This is a common experience. Your vision has been simply in degree with your susceptibilities. Could you rise a degree higher, you would reach a very heaven of discovery, which would amaze as much as it would delight you, as far above anything that you have felt, seen, known or dreamed, as Heaven is above earth. It is because of your susceptibilities that I have sought you out, and seek to serve you."

"And it is to you then, that I owe the exquisite delight of this hour."

"Hour! It has not been five minutes. Your cigar is yet unextinguished; pray empty it, for it annoys me."

"Yet, it seems to me more delicious than any tobacco I have ever enjoyed."

"Your mull is newly filled as you will see. Smell of it. Do not smoke."

"Again, my good Sir William, I owe all this to you."

"Let me beg of you not to employ this name unless we meet in company. It is my *nom de societé.* I am a person whose mission as well as tastes calls him into society, and I must have some ordinary title by which to be known to the vulgar and fashionable. I shall be fashionable here. Your community will run after Lord and Baronet. I have therefore made a selection. My name, in his Imperial Majesty's is quite of another sort. Tomorrow, you will find that of Sir Will O' Wisp on the record at the Spread Eagle Hotel. Perhaps you can guess the consequence. I shall have five hundred Republicans calling upon me and leaving their cards;

some three score will seek to carry me home with them, and, unless I take my precautions in season, they will divide my luggage among them, take it off, and each will insist that where my chattels are there should my heart be also. But I shall remain at the Spread Eagle. It is a famous name in these parts, where they are all Loyalists, liberty loving, but rather given to lying and stealing. Pardon me, but it is my necessity to speak the truth. I am afraid that I can make no favorable report of your virtues as a people when I return home."

I laughed—rather chaffed however, at our Spread Eagle reputation in foreign lands. Then, I said, trying to bring him back to a subject which he seemed a little anxious to evade.

"But, my good fellow, tell me. You have seen what I have seen within this hour. You have said so. Now, do I not owe all this delicious and majestical vision to your agency."

"Surely, I did not think it needed that I should tell you so in words. To present you with such shows, as shall appeal to your susceptibilities and warm your sensibilities will be my duty while I serve you. Through these I trust to lift you into nobler stature, and confer upon you some of the bright domains, not of this earth, but which yet exist within its atmosphere. I trust you were pleased with what was shown you."

"Pleased! Delighted—ravished. I swam in a very sea of rapture. But—what's to pay? That subject comes up again, and I find it not easy to divest myself of what you describe as an old superstitition of the nursery. I still fear, I confess, that you are driving some little bargain after my soul; that you are a cunning solicitor—a greedy stock broker in souls; and that you steep me for a season in bliss, only to steep me for another season in sulphur."

"Pshaw! What nonsense. I tell you that we poor devils are in search of human sympathy, and that, therefore, we seek out alliances with those who have sensibilities to sympathize with us, and such susceptibilities, as and under proper training, will arise to the full appreciation of ours."

"But—"

"But—if nothing less will satisfy you than a bargain of some sort or other, then I will take compensation for my services. You shall give me your cast off clothing, your old coats and trousers, boots, shoes, slippers, and briefly everything that you will to cast away. The moment that you will to cast anything away, no matter what, that thing shall become mine. I especially insist upon your trousers; and should you ever become a married man, then you shall throw in your wife's frocks and petticoats the moment she shows dissatisfaction with them. There you have my terms. Keep your soul, and do what you please with it, but remember, you are bound for your own breeches, and should you marry, your wife's petticoats and whatever else she and you may please to discard. Whatever you or she shall be pleased to discard shall become instantly mine, by a law of moral gravitation. Are you satisfied with these terms?"

"A bargain," I exclaimed, delighted with the humor of the fellow, not less than his generosity. "Breeches and petticoats! You shall have them all! Why, Sir William, you are the very pink of liberality, and I rejoice at your coming. Pray resume your seat, and let us talk over this matter, that it may be the better understood between us. There may be something covert and equivocal in it, after all. You gentleman of the wisp and lantern are apt to hang out false lights for the temptation of the unwary, and I am resolved to see that you have no occult signification in what you say, before I sign this agreement. It may be my soul, after all, that you are driving at, in aiming at my breeches. I know many men whose souls never go beyond their breeches, and though I trust that mine is not of this sort, yet I would take every precaution against involvements. I will have legal advice first in this business."

"You are right, my dear sir," he replied promptly, "take what precaution you please, and be satisfied before you take a single step in this matter. I have no disposition to deceive you—indeed, I am not a proficient in the arts of falsehood. I know many a lawyer who would put me to the blush for incompetence, and might, if lying were a prime requisite in my dominions, usurp their sovereignty. Even if your soul were in your breeches, there would be little danger of its loss; all you have need to do is shake them well before giving them to me, and unless it be a very sleepy or very adhesive soul, it is physically impossible that it should stick there long after the shaking."

"But the instrument, itself! How would you have it drawn up? Possibly you may desire that it should be written with my blood; if you do, I must tell you—"

His immoderate laughter silenced me.

"How much" quoth he, "have you to unlearn! You have been among the Germans, I see, and have studied in the pages of the several Doctors—Dee, Faust, and Matthew—to say nothing of a thousand other witch doctors from the days of her of Endor. Bonds written in blood! What a diabolical fancy, and, pardon me if I say it, rather a dirty one. I pray you, my dear Sir to look upon me as one possessing a tolerable taste and rather delicate stomach. These blood-pudding imaginations are my abomination. I must improve your taste, I see, if only to commend you adequately to my own. Leave the drawing up of the instrument to me. It shall bind me rather than you. Keep your blood and soul to yourself. I would not rob you of a particle of either. Indeed, it is my interest that you should be possessed of both in perfection. Enough that I am to have your discarded wardrobe—your breeches will content me. And mark me, you must not forget the petticoats of Mrs. Silex when she shall show herself disposed to cast them away."

"You shall have them all," I answered cheerfully.

The deed, a simple instrument, was drawn out in the twinkling of an eye, the contract signed and delivered, and copies taken by both. As men of honour, we needed no witnesses. Nothing could well exceed the delight of my new servant at the completion of the negotiations, and his installation into office as my actor of all work. His joy broke out in tumultuous expressions, the moment the papers were completed.

"I congratulate myself, my dear Mr. Silex, as well as you, on our mutual acquisitions. There is nothing so distressing as being out of place. I have been trying for sometime to employ a master of my own heart, and my rapture is now excessive at having found him."

"A double-edged compliment," I muttered to myself, with a slight shiver. He beheld and divined the sensation.

"Ay, I see," he cried playfully, "you are still unassured. You do not conjecture my value yet. But let me convince you. Say, what shall I do for you? It is proper that I commence duties forthwith. Let me know them. I am ready now. I have no trunks to remove. My wardrobe is already here. As for my bedding, I want none. A chink in the chimney will yield me a sufficient sleeping space, and your saving in candles, alone, will be no small item. You only have to set me above the chimney-piece when you want a light, and I will burn at both ends to please you. In food I am moderate. A fricasseed frog is the utmost that my stomach will bear, and in wine I am a single bottle man. In supplies I am a prime commissariat, and you would find me valuable for this quality, even if my consumption were greater than it is. To speak with due modesty, you will find me a wondrous acquisition and will soon begin to wonder how you ever did without me before."

"I nothing doubt it, Sir William."

"Plain Will, if you please when we are alone together. Sir William only for visitors and state occasions, when we meet in company. We shall meet in company, perhaps frequently, and it will be our mutual policy to know as little of each other as possible. Between us, and at our own fireside, familiarity will do, and plain "Will," Sir, more agreeable to my ear than any titular distinction.

At the Spread Eagle I shall ostensibly remain, as Sir William O' Wisp, the Irish Baronet. I shall deliver my letters tomorrow to all your aristocratic and fashionable people. I have provided all necessary credentials, and have in memory all the Irish Chronicles, from the very hour, when St. Patrick first fixed his eye on the snakes of the country making them skedaddle almost as fast as the Yankees at Bull Run."

"A dangerous topic, Will, involving *Scandalum Magnatum,* fornication, and the seven deadly abominations."

"And now, Sir, your supper hour is at hand. Will you suffer me to give you a taste of my quality in the preparation of your coffee."

"At your pleasure, Will."

"With your pleasure, Sir, I will endeavour to do something more, in providing such a repast as I was wont to serve up to my friends, and enjoy in Italy, some five hundred years ago. I must tell you I once kept house and a wife in that delicious country, about that period."

"Is it possible?"

"I will tell you of that story tomorrow. You will find it all written in Machiavelli. He was an old friend of mine, and we had many a bowl together. He knew something of my history himself, and I supplied the particulars in which he was deficient. Altogether a very pleasant history. Did you ever read Machiavelli?"

"Never."

"Then I will tell you the story at our next meeting. You will find it equally informative and refreshing. But now, for supper."

"If you please, Will."

He was gone, as usual, without my seeing how he went. I confess I had some qualms of stomach, to say nothing of conscience, as I thought of that proverb which warns us against all beverages, however pleasant, of the Devil's brewing. But, even while I thought this, the coffee urn was hissing upon the table. There was a salver too of delicious cates and cakes such as I never tasted in my life before. How made, where made, and of what made, I never knew; I can only say that I never knew what delicious eating was until that moment; and never was the sublime in the coffee berry so exquisitely by the arts of the *Connoisseur.* What a miracle of a servitor had I found! I calculated the daily savings, out of the funds of a penny—a denier, and the bowels within me were exceedingly rejoiced. Why, as a cook alone, Will deserved the whole wardrobe, not leaving to my wife petticoat or skirt. But, as we get on together, we shall see that the very least of his merits lay in his excellence as a cook.

CHAPTER 4
A Screed of the Spiritual

I was hardly prepared for the prompt and efficient proceedings of Sir William Wisp, when, in the papers next morning, I saw his arrival at the Spread Eagle announced in all the newspapers with a terrible blowing of the Ram's Horn, enough to bring down all the walls in our Jericho. "We are most happy," said the Editor of the *Loyal Screamer,* "to announce the arrival in this city of the distinguished Irish Baronet, Sir William O' Wisp, so well known in all the great literary and scientific circles of Great Britain and the rest of the world. He arrived yesterday in the beautiful steamer, the *Kickappoo Lighter,* commanded by that most efficient of all Sea Captains, Puritan Standish, Esq. He has taken up his quarters at that glorious mansion, decidedly superior to any in the United States, for its wines, viviands, and victuals—the Spread Eagle—so admirably kept by our friend, Billapop Baggs, Esq. Baggs has assigned to Sir William that splendid suite of rooms, three in number, designed for newly married couples and bridal parties; the furnishing of which by our friend Samson _____ is the delight and wonder of all visitors. We trust that our noble guest will find everything in our ancient citizen to afford him equal satisfaction with the splendid quarters which he occupies. He will no doubt be waited upon at an early hour by the public authorities and the chief citizens of this place, and it is quite probable, that the well known acquirements, talents, and accomplishments of our noble visitor will suggest to our authorities the propriety a public reception and a grand dinner to be followed by a ball. It has always been the pride and pleasure of our citizens to recognize genius, talent, virtue, science, and philosophy, especially when they are all so exquisitely blended with accomplishments such as these which do honour to the name of Sir William O' Wisp."

There was much more of this same sort of eloquence. But enough is as good as a feast.

The Eagle Banner had a column to the same effect, followed by a very suggestive paragraph:

> "Of the special objects of this important visitor, nothing is precisely known, but it is shrewdly conjectured that its purpose has reference to the cause of the Fenians. Sir William is known to carry a warm Irish heart in his noble bosom, and his patriotism has undergone no chill in consequence of the temporary reverses of the cause of Fenianism. It is rumoured that several of the Head

Centres have had secret interviews with him since his arrival in this country, and last night he was known to be closeted with several visitors, all unknown, but suspected, until a very late hour. It did not escape public attention also that the Consul of her Britannic Majesty, at this port appeared very restless and uneasy during the afternoon, going to and fro, and lingering for at least two hours, about supper time, in and about the portico of the Spread Eagle."

The Cock of the Walk, the Star of Liberty, and the *Programme of Daily Sensations* each gave its columns to the distinguished stranger, in strains of like eulogy rising through all degrees of comparison each suggesting a different motive for his coming to the country; but all agreeing to congratulate the country on the grateful auguries of future glory which the visit involved.

Pipe in mouth, I was yet reading and smiling over these beautiful examples of Spread Eagle literature, when a sudden and terrific sneeze behind me, assured me of the presence of our Irish Baronet. As soon as he could recover himself from this involuntary demonstration, he said,

"Please put away that pipe. It disturbs my nervous system. My organization, I must repeat, is singularly delicate, as you will readily conceive when you have learned more of the position which I occupy in the dominion of my sovereign. There I am, *par excellance,* the Courtier, and, by the way, it was because of my superior uses in society that I have been employed on my present mission."

I complied with his modest desire, put aside my pipe, squared myself above to comfort him, and motioned him to a chair, which, like a well bred gentleman, he took without delay or hesitation. Laughingly, I pointed to the newspapers.

"I see—" said he—"I have seen them all. You have read them?"

"Every syllable. You have been prompt, my dear Sir William, and I perceive that you are already familiar with the ropes."

"Not I," he replied. "I have had nothing to do with the matter. You owe it all to the bold free inventive genius of your own people. Wonderful people! They save us all trouble in working out our problems and anticipating their own future uses in a realm, where their liberties shall be still larger, if not more elevated. They are prompt enough not to need any prompting." Hardly had my name appeared on the register of the Hotel, before there was a score of visitors sending up their cards. Five editors, seven colonels, two wine merchants, four aldermen followed these, and hung on till midnight. I offered wine, but they all preferred whiskey, and never having been taught the manufacture of this peculiar beverage, I had to procure it from the hotel. A terrible liquor. I never tasted it before, but through civility drank of it with my guests. The consequence is that I have a touch of headache this morning."

"What! You have a headache?"

"In my human form, I am always more or less liable to the ailments of humanity. It is only by a superior prudence to that of men in general that I can avoid them. Besides, as I have told you, my organization is singularly delicate, and suffers from every grossness. Let me apprise you that there is no deficiency of good taste in our domain, and our food and beverages are of a sort which assimilate with the spiritual rather than with the merely mortal nature. It is only when I put off my humanity now that I can refresh myself with the things I relish."

"But where do you get them?"

"Pooh! from the air, if I please. I have but to will my banquet and it is spread. Your fictions, such as the Arabian Nights, have quite an inkling of the truth in these respects, with the single difference that you are to assume the parties to be of a few degrees more spiritually advanced than the moralists of the present day. In spiritual respects your race has sunk several degrees below their ancestors. You surely must have suspected this before. The evidence is potent to all your really philosophical minds. Why, man, the great majority of your people are simply beasts, like the negro with the disadvantage in comparison with the monkey of being *minus* a tail."

"Faith, you are complementary."

"Pardon me, but it is my necessity always to speak the truth."

"This is not usually held to be the merit of your order."

"That is only because of the ignorance of yours, and those miserable superstitions that you have sucked in from your grandmothers. But, though we always speak the truth, under a penal necessity incident to our nature, we labour under the Curse of Cassandra, who never spoke otherwise, yet was never believed until belief was useless. This will be your danger in your intercourse with me. Have faith, my friend, my master, and you will find our intercourse singularly profitable. It will save you from much loss and harm and help you to many successes."

"We must try, Sir William."

"Do please. For your sake as well as mine. My wardrobe depends on it you know."

"Pshaw! That is mere farce. But, be frank with me. What is the real profit you expect to make out of me? I still have a lurking suspicion that my soul is in danger."

"The last thing you have to fear. There *is* profit to be made out of you; but I can hardly explain to you in words its kind and character. Suffice it that I have need to assimilate as much as possible with some of the more subtle elements which peculiarly belong to humanity."

"And which *you* have not."

"And which *we* have not."

"Ah! And how am I to know, my friend, but that this assimilation means absorption—means that you will suck from me a precious element of my nature, absorbing it into yours, and leaving me sterile. Methinks, that is very like robbing me of my soul."

"By no means. The soul has its own faculty, not only of expansion but diffusion, and the assimilation in question is affinity not absorption. If a danger at all, it will be in your acquiring an affection for me, such as—permit me to say—I already entertain for you. In fact, it was this sympathy, by a divine instinct, as it were, which first moved me to seek you out in preference to any other person."

"Smoothly spoken and unctuous. You have a happy knack of compliment, my friend, and, baiting, if you do for souls. You know what appetizing dainties to put upon your hook. But can you not explain, more clearly to me, this process of assimilation which is to bring about affinity, yet avoid absorption?"

"You could hardly understand me now. But you shall be made to see and to feel, if not to hear. I have processes by which to reach your understanding, which shall be fully exercised in time. For the present my nomenclature would be incomprehensible to you."

"Answer me one question, if you please. Are not your processes somewhat akin to those which are employed by the class of magicians, whom we call mesmerizers, mediums and spiritualists?"

"Hardly. These are *mediums,* my friend—and have no design, and know not what they do. Their powers are secondary, and derive from influences inferior to their own, and of more or less original power."

"They are necessarily demonic."

"Not necessarily! Do you suppose that any Deity would suffer his rival to exercise so great a power, yet refrain, himself, from its use? Do you think that he whom you call and conceive to be *your* God, would suffer mine to possess the exclusive use of a power which exercises so wonderful an influence upon men, nor seek, in like manner to counteract his influence were it not so. Your race would otherwise be wholly at the mercy of ours; your imaginations would be wrought to madness along with your possessions, and you would be the creatures of every miserable caprice of fancy, vainglory, lust and absurdity, that ever was borne upon the winds."

"Then this mesmerism, or spiritualism, is, in truth, something."

"To be sure; and its exercise is in degree with your susceptibility."

"But these mediums lie and contradict each other."

"Precisely; That is a matter which depends wholly upon the sort of power of which the medium is the mouthpiece. There will be no difficulty in comprehending then, unless you suppose such an equality of condition and power, in the spiritual world, as enables each of them to deliver the same oracles. There is as much inequality in knowledge among spirits divine as demonic as exists among mere mortals. They all know more than men, of course, but none of them knows *every*thing, but the *One* in either region."

"But why should either employ a medium in conducting their intercourse with men? It is assumed that something is to be delivered from a spiritual or superior source. Why should not the communication be made directly to the party whom it concerns, just as well as through a third party who has no interest in this matter?"

"It is done in certain instances, but only in accordance with the peculiar susceptibilities of the individual. There are certain laws governing the subject which you could scarcely comprehend. It should be enough that you know that a medium is in most cases an essential."

"But I do not know that such is the fact."

"Indeed! Why should Samuel appear to the witch and not to Saul? Why should Saul apply to the witch if she was not recognized as a medium for such intercourse? In the case of Paul, another Saul, a man of peculiar powers and susceptibilities, the vision came to him, with the voice. To the ears of the crowd above him, who equally beheld the vision with himself, there was no voice. Socrates acknowledges his Demon. Apollonius of Tyana asserted his communication with the spirit world, but said nothing to his medium of intelligence. And there were others. Caesar appears to Brutus, according to your histories, and makes an engagement to meet with him again at Philippi—thus predicting his death."

"*Rari nantes in gurgite vasto.* These are occasional instances in the lapse of a thousand years. It would be but reasonable to discard them as the reality of a diseased imagination—a morbid condition of the stomach—some derangement of the liver—"

"Precisely as your physicians regard them, but these are professionally skeptical, though there is not one of them whom a dream will not scare, as in the case of Richard the Third out of his seven senses. Your great master of dramatic fiction has conceived something of the fact and the law in this matter, when he makes Hamlet receive from a medium, Horatio, a drill sergeant, and some common soldiers, the first information of the ghost, who, though he *shows* himself to them, will not communicate with them. He desires to do so only with his son, but needs to prepare him for the interview, the delicate organization of young Hamlet making it doubtful if he could endure the visitation, unapprised or in the presence of other parties. When the son is thus reconciled through a medium, to the apparition, the father no longer appears to the medium, but to the son in person; and even then, the latter is almost maddened by the spectre and shaken from his propriety. The laws in such cases require certain susceptibilities and a certain capacity for and manner on the part of the recipient. The dull metal is made the agent of the lightening, so diffusing as to disarm it. The medium chosen is usually one of small intellect, a coarse organization, and dull sensibilities. In degree as one's mind is individual, distinct, commanding, with strong will, and coercive intellect, it is reluctant to submit to a foreign power which operates by coercion."

"I conceive something of this, but how is it that these revelations are so infrequent? That you can address only a few solitary instances of such demonic or spiritual influences once or so in a thousand years?"

"I could adduce you a hundred thousand. You have on your records only the few instances in which men either simply acknowledged the supernatural influences or boasted of it. But you know nothing of the thousands who kept silent in their knowledge, who, from pride or fear, or some selfish motive, made no confession, and preferred rather to make profit than to boast. But, why not suppose that the instances, few or many, in which you know, were those only which were called for by the necessity of the case."

"Then there are too many miracles. They were supernatural."

"Not so—they were all under the regular operation of laws, but of laws which operate only under certain conjunctures. They occur, perhaps, like the comets; but may be calculated, just as certainly by the mental astronomer, sufficiently developed in his sensibilities, susceptibilities, aims, and acquisitions, as by him who has made the stars his study may be calculated the return of the comets. You must rise to a certain plane of susceptibility and intelligence before you can gain the requisite vision. What shall we say of him who, at the bottom of the mountain, denies the prospect of him who has gained the summit? When Moses stood upon the mountain and beheld the land which he yet could not reach, he was the Israelites' medium—their eyes—capable of beholding the vast and beautiful empire beyond, even while they strode forward, faint and feeble, like men blindfolded, groping a doubtful way, through the dim valley at his feet."

"But how, if these mediums fail, as they do—die out, as it were, and are heard of no more. Sometimes, they confess their power is gone, altogether, and at other times they speak what is wild, if not false."

"The wild may not always be false. These are revelations which you still study, which you reverence, but which you cannot comprehend or resolve. That the mediums die out, is very true, so have died out all the prophets. They served their turn. They answered for a while the required purposes. They had their uses, and only died out when they had no longer any use."

"But this mesmerism, spiritualism, or whatever else you call it—that seems to have died out also."

"Not so. There are three millions of people in your own country who even now believe in it; though they may do so in secret. The great body of mankind dreads ridicule more than anything besides. They prefer, accordingly to indulge that faith, in secret, which, if expressed might be a subject of vulgar mock and obloquy. But they are even more tenacious of their secret, because it *is* a secret, than if they were to publish it from the house-tops. As for the power dying out in the individual medium, here and there, the fact is so. They had their uses, and accordingly their inspiration. Most of them were clod poles, chosen as such, as sufficiently flexible, undemonstrative in their own minds, to be used as the mere mouthpieces of a superior intelligence. While acting under this inspiration, they acquired importance in society, and were unwilling to give up the vocation when all their capital was withdrawn. They became convicted of falsehood and folly in the end as not content to be mediums, but as intelligences for themselves, carrying on a petty trade, on past credit which they contrived to discredit, in their very first operations."

"One thing more. Supposing that the superior intelligences designed to communicate with man, the difficulty seems to lie in this, that no adequate results have come from their communications. Men do not seem to have grown wiser or better since their revelations. We are not shown any buried treasure. No man seems to be richer. The world at large is not richer. There are no doubt thousands of regions where great treasures lie hidden from sight. It is true that the mediums have endeavoured to indicate such places; but no discovery has followed. It is true that they pretended to be able to cure a thousand secret diseases of the human system; but I have never yet been able to verify a single case of recovery and improvement. We hear of such miserable stuff as the turning of tables, the rapping on floor and wall, the transmission of facts of little or no importance, the playing of instruments by invisible hands, and the untying of knots more intricate than those of Gordius by unseen fingers working in the dark. But of what consequence is this sort of performance, allowing it all to be true, to either the spiritual or human world—how paltry on the part of the one, how utterly unprofitable to the needs of the other."

"To answer you, *seriatim,* is not easy. A part of your answer has been already made when I suggested that the dull medium, his uses exhausted, was still not willing to give up a vocation which he could still work to profit. He endeavoured to supply by trick and impudence the lack of gift and inspiration. I have seen the workings of many of these cattle, and some of them, in my human character, I have exposed, and—bedevilled. They have been proved imposters in the end who might have been inspired in the beginning. You can understand how it is that a clerk whom you have discharged may yet seek employment on your credit. We find among your sacred records that a prophet specially sent to announce the destruction of a city, within a limited time, is found false in his prediction and reproaches his master for being so discredited. You say that men do not seem to grow wiser or better since these revelations. I agree with you. But that is not the fault of the prophet, perhaps. It is in most cases the fault of the men. The great Greek Dramatic poet gives you the case of Cassandra, who always predicted the truth but never found faith among her hearers. Nor must you be suffered to forget what *my* master said to you, speaking of man as a race, when it was accorded to him the power to test the virtue of a single individual in the case of Job. *We* believe in man no more now than we did then. As a race he is detestably dirty, unclean, and mean and worships the old gods Bacchus, Venus, and Mammon just as he did 3000 years ago, though, being a consummate liar, he worships them all when in public under the name of Jehovah. We can believe in individuals as in the case of Job but not in the race; for though many may be called, there are precious few chosen. Certainly, under no form of inspiration have they grown either wiser or better. They have become more learned, more scientific, more cunning, calculating, and circumspect but never a whit wiser—never a whit less human—still an anomalous blending of the angel and the beast. And the beast almost invariably swallows up the angel. But the amazing part of your objections to the new revelations of spiritualism is that which complains that it reveals no buried treasure of the mine or deep. It would be—were I dealing with a vulgar mind—enough to say that coeval with the recent revelations of spiritualisms was the discovery of the vast treasures of California. But this would be a fool's answer or a rouge's, even though it should satisfy the doubts of a thousand inquiries. What has the spiritual world to do with your accumulation of wealth and treasure. Heaven and Earth both know that you possess in perfections already all the arts essential in these discoveries. If you looked at all deeply into the laws of nature, you would see at once that as all the Earth was given into your hands for use and development, the development of your own manhood lay entirely in the development of its secrets; and, just in degree as you exercised your manhood, which involves the idea of wisdom as well as muscle, were you to be rewarded by the material developments of earth and air and water, of the woods and rocks, of the mines, the minerals and metals; of all things material, of all agencies, essential as the pabulum of art, sciences, and intellect in every way. The spiritual world gives you credit for your ability to work in material things—for your capacity to make money—for your eager passion to do so, and would be most unprofitably employed in hearkening to your cry of the daughters of the Horse Leech for more. My excellent cousin, Mammon, has been too long a favorite and devoutly worshipped god among you to have left you in ignorance of the fields which you shall despoil; and, when his processes are found too slow, my second cousin Moloch steps in and shows the way through a path of slaughter of your brethren how you may add to your accumulations by appropriating the accumulations of others. Do you not see that you need new revelations by which to learn how to steal or murder. Is it not possible for you to conceive of a spiritual working by which to correct these tendencies? You claim to have six thousand years of *God,* Jehovah, and nearly two thousand years of Christ, long prior to these new revelations of the spiritualists. But did this knowledge make the race any better as a whole. Read your own records of massacre for the past six thousand years, of spoliation and crime, and ask yourself if there was any period in the world's history in which Mammon and Moloch did not prevail over all other contesting Divinities. Your race is of this earth, earthy. Its natural tendency is downward. It professes to believe, but lies. It avows a faith in the soul's immortality, but lives as if the soul were already damned, and so living it forfeits every poor apology of a soul that it ever had. Now, this spiritualism, if it shall only serve to remind you that you have a soul, is a thing of vital necessity to you. If, by constantly reminding you, it shall keep your soul upon the wing, continually striving to struggle upwards; it will be perhaps the best of all processes for extracting you from the meshes of your own miserable earthly instincts. Here is a use, certainly, of far greater importance than any you have yet named for the benefit of humanity, and for realizing on behalf of your race what was so hopefully conceived of it from the beginning. Be sure of this, that any creed, however erroneous in fact, which appeals to the soul and inspires the spiritual activity is better for you than a life which regards only the baser instincts of appetite—the acquisition of wealth being, in fact, the chief means with most men for the gratification of beauty, instincts, appetites, passions, and a miserable social pride and a more miserable social vanity. You see I speak the truth to you. Serving you now, I cannot help it, though, in doing so, I argue against the best instincts of my eminent cousins, Mammon, Moloch, Venus, Bacchus, and Company."

CHAPTER 5
Draughts of Persephone-Platonic

There was a pause after this in which we took wine, furnished from some hitherto hidden crypt unknown to me, but sufficiently familiar to my companion. It was a wine the flavor of which quite new to my palate was much more delicious than anything I had ever tasted before, although I was admitted to be something of a connoisseur in the juices of the Madeira and other grapes, to say nothing of the Rhine wines and those of the South of France. There was an ethereal something about this new beverage, which especially commanded itself to my taste, and I made a remark to this effect.

"You perceive it then?" said he. "It should possess that etherial in the highest perfection, considering its source. We call it the "Persephone-Platonic." It never produces the vulgar result of intoxication. It appeals rather to the soul than the brain. It warms up all the sensibilities, inspires the affections and sympathies, makes all things genial to mind and eye, and possesses the whole nature with a certain sedative delight, which needs no excitement of the blood. The grapes were grown in the vineyards of my Lady Aunt and Queen, Persephone, herself. The manufacture is due to the immediate art of my eminent uncle, whom you call Bacchus, but whom we generally know among ourselves as Dionysus, or, in more familiar phrase, Uncle Dion, especially when he is seen riding upon his favorite ram. You will allow me to correct a singular mistake which your people make in respect to his attributes. They represent him as a drunkard, when in fact he is the real and first founder of the only Temperance Societies among you that have ever done any good. He encourages the use of wine as promotive of temperance and an antidote to much of the poisons which are to be found in food. He asserts that no wine drinking nation has ever shown a tendency to drunkenness; and that none but the wine-drinking races have ever achieved greatness and trod the heights of fame and glory. Wine, he insists, is the necessary element of genius, inspiring the poet with fresh songs, the philosopher with the clues to discovery, the orator with the golden figures of rhetoric, and the warrior with grand conceptions of conquest and the plans of battle. But all such horrible beverage as your whiskey he holds to be of most pernicious use; disordering the brain, discarding the imagination, and drying up, not only all the proper sources of thought and inspiration, but rendering the brain a mere pulp, leading finally to what is described as *remollient,* which results in the meanest idiocy. But I digress. Enough that you have the best security for health and youth and enjoyment in this wine; you can hardly drink too much of it, though considering the source from which it comes, a little suffices for great results. Do you not feel it already,"

"In heart, head, limbs, blood, bone, muscle, thought, feeling, fancy! I almost dream that I fly. I am sure that I float upon a new element, and that I behold swans swimming around me on a placid sea, while music from an invisible source soothes my senses with a dream of ecstasy, in the glow of which Love puts on a new aspect of charm, and all life seems to resolve itself into Love. Ah! my friend. I ask it with mournful misgivings—what supply of this divine beverage have you brought with you, and between us, how long will this liquor last in our house?"

"I have but a single decanter!"

"Alas! Alas!" I cried, interrupting him—"Such is human happiness ever so short-lived—ever so fleeting. The flower fades from the moment we take it to our bosoms—the cloud swallows the star even as we kneel in worship. *Sic transit gloria mundi!* Alas! Alas!"

"Nay, you despond too readily. Have I not counselled faith as the security for all possessions, even for those which you but dream and scarcely dare to hope. Hearken! Though I have brought with me but a single bottle, it is one of vast resources. It is self-supplying. It no sooner empties than it fills itself. It is only when I *will* otherwise that it fails to do so."

"You give me new life! Let me drink once more of this divine beverage. Ah! thou most benevolent of all bottles, I bless thee that I have come to a knowledge of thy virtues. May it then always be a dweller in this house. Thou shalt have a sacred place in my cupboard, and the milk which thou giveth forth shall have preference over all other beverages on my tongue. Thou art the very heart of Bacchus—"

"By Bacchus, that is the very name which we ourselves have given it. To set forth on our travels anywhere, we always provide ourselves with the Breast of Bacchus, who never withholds the divine liquor from him who sucks from his bosom with a will."

"The *will* be mine forever. And do not thou, O' Will of the Wisp, interfere, at any moment, thy *will,* so that drawing from the Breast of Bacchus, I shall find the fountain dry."

"Never, so long as I remain thy servant."

"Servant. No! Say friend, companion—well beloved! But—Hark!"

The clock over the mantel was trembling under the strokes of 12 midday. It occurred to me that at about this hour the visitors of Sir William Wisp, the Irish Baronet, would be making their calls.

"My dear Sir, it is needful that you leave me now and seek your hotel. At this hour, your visitors will begin to call upon you. You will have a throng. The paragraphs in the morning papers will have done their work, and I pity you when I consider what persons you will have to meet, what balderdash you will have to hear. We are here a whole city of orators. Everybody is eloquent, and the rhetoric will be such as you have hardly ever heard before. It will need that you be present at call."

"Do not fear! And, by the way, I am not a stranger to your sort of oratory. It has an Irish flavour if not an accent and I am prepared for endurance. Several of your chief men are now memorizing the speeches they will devise to make. I know the substance of them all. I shall be present in season. Indeed, I am present even now, through my *eidolon*—my other self."

"Ah! Indeed! And how do you manage that?"

"Very easily." You shall see."

And, with the words, he elevated his head, looked out upon empty space in the middle of the room, and I distinctly saw two little sparklets shoot out from his eyes, carrying a little stream of light with them, fine as a cambric thread, but bright as a sunbeam. In another moment, a perfect *facsimile*—another yet the same Sir Will O' the Wisp occupied the space, and stood confronting me—the same perfect and symmetrical figure, noble air, and beautiful face—admirably true to the original. There they stood—the two—for a moment, as like as the two Dromios; when Sir William waving his hand, in the next moment, the simulacrum was gone.

"You shall see" said Sir William, "that I shall not be found wanting at the Hotel. Look!"

Again he waved his hand, and before me rose the whole interior of the splendid rooms assigned to the Baronets in the Spread Eagle Hotel, and in the centre of the apartment stood my companion, very richly dressed, while servants proceeded to and fro, busied in arrangements. The servants were all habited in rich oriental costumes of white, long flowing robes edged with gold and purple. They all wore foreign costumes, as I fancied, of an Egyptian habit, and their aspects were dark, sallow, and evidently foreign.

"You will make a sensation" I said, "if only through your slaves. You will be conceived to be at once wealthy and eccentric."

"I know your people. You have seen. And now I depart."

The vision disappeared at the waving of his hand.

"Will you go with me or follow."

"I will follow. It is, perhaps, quite as well that you should not appear to be too intimate with me. I can contribute nothing to the success of your career here."

"Ah! but who knows that?"

"I am sure of it. In the first place, my dear Sir William, I am *not* wealthy—nay, I am positively poor; and I am a small man of letters. Now literature is not in fashion here. We have some literary clubs here, but they are what is called Mutual Admiration Societies; the more intelligent gather to amuse and praise each other; and the deficient class to acquire, by contact, if possible, not the knowledge or wisdom, but the reputation of it, as a blockhead runs through a college wall, and sets up for a professor. Not half of these people could parse you an English sentence, but then—the most ignorant give the best suppers. The feast that follows almost compensates for the dullness of that dialogue which precedes it."

"I know all about them. Well, follow me soon, and you may make some new studies for future scenes in comedy."

With these words he disappeared. As soon as he was gone, I lighted my pipe and looked around for that bottle—that Breast of Bacchus—in order first to see if it still gave forth from its fountains. But it was gone. It disappeared as suddenly as its owner. I thought this rather a scurvy trick of Sir William, but remembering his assurance that it was the only bottle which he had brought with, I naturally concluded he would find sufficient use for it in entertaining his expected visitors. We shall see that such was the case.

I smoked my pipe with all the phlegm of a Mussulman, and I tried to be as philosophical as a Yankee Brahmin on a tour through Mammon. But in vain. My thoughts were all disordered—my brain bewildered, not by what I had drunk, but by what I had seen and heard. Another draught of the Persephone-Platonic would probably have yielded me a proper and delicious sedative. As soon as my pipe was empty, I threw off my dressing gown, made my toilet in some haste, and then set forth for the grand reception at the Spread Eagle.

CHAPTER 6
First Reception

The spacious and splendid parlour in the suite of rooms assigned to Sir William Wisp was crowded when I entered, and by just such persons as were well known to be always the first to welcome the distinguished stranger on his arrival in Mongrelia. The mayor was present, of course, a man of little bulk of body but ineffable self esteem; grave as an owl, in the assertion of which he deemed to be dignity, but as stupid as an ostrich; with one merit of the ostrich, however, that of being an enormous feeder. Several of the aldermen were present with him, each of them being distinguished by a new suit of clothes, and a ribbon in his button hole. The visit was an unofficial one, however. It seems that the question had been debated the night before till a very late hour, whether they should go in a body, each with his staff of office; or whether they should drop in, one by one, thus avoiding any committal, whether to Sir William himself or to the governing authorities; for, as it was sagely suggested by one of the aldermen, "Who knows what the nature of this man's mission may be. There are several suspicious things attending his appearance here. By some persons it is thought that he is a Fenian leader, and I know that Colonel Crotchet, who is more than suspected of being the head centre here, was closeted with him to a late hour last night."

Another rumour by another member was to the effect that the mission of Sir William was of even deeper significance. It was shrewdly suspected that under the auspices of the British Government, he was seeking to make up a colony of the discontented whites of Mongrelia, for the resettlement and restoring of the abandoned bogs of Ireland. The British Consul had been seen the night before, full of anxiety and beer, hovering around Sir William's quarters till a very late hour, and it was known that three professional detectives in his employ had been called in to the consulate at dark to receive his instructions.

The result of these revelations and conjectures, to say nothing of a score besides, all equally significant and all equally absurd, was to compel a pause in their demonstrations, and to persuade them to a mere call of courtesy, each rather as an individual than an official, though it was also understood that they were all to make it clear to the comprehension of the eminent guest that his visitors were the magnates of the city.

"We are to drop in upon him," said one who was a barkeeper, "promiscus-like, and every man is to paddle his own canoe."

"Of course, said the mayor with dignity, "as the civil head of the city, I shall be announced to him with my official title."

To this all parties were agreed, and there, in the parlour of Sir William, every man of them was assembled with many others, not so distinguished officially, when I made my appearance. I had sent up no card, never once having thought of it; but to my surprise one of the servants of Sir William, standing at the curtain announced me in loud accents,

"Mr. Richard Silex."

Sir William rose on the instant, and made a step towards me. Now it had so happened that the ear of Sir William had been already taken possession of by one of those polished snobs and sycophants who fasten upon society in all regions and by smoothness and smirk, coupled with great presumption, contrive to thrust themselves upon great people with the twisting and the turning, the alternate expanding and contracting, and the final tenacity of hold which distinguishes the leech. Of this class of toadies, he was perhaps one of the most proverbially distinguished in all Mongrelia. He was as servile as Boswell to his Oracle, but contrived to monopolize him. If possible, he suffered no others to pass between him and his victim. He, alone, knew what the oracle would deliver and could tell it if he would; and a third party being present he had always something to whisper in the ear of his patron. When away from him he always had a late letter, just received from the great man, which he read to you and everybody besides under injunction of secrecy. He had then for twenty years taken possession of half the eminent statesmen, politicians, divines, and men of letters in the confederacy—of all who would suffer it, and who would condescend to write a civil answer to a letter crammed with flatulent eulogiums.

Such was Counsellor Gregorius Gander. He was amicable, however, and was generally supposed to be harmless. He was smooth and specious, and had a sort of lax eloquence which flowed freely enough in dilating upon commonplaces, and which always seconded your suggestions, no matter what, by a speech—*vox et praeterea nihil.* Men of this description, men of great vanity, in brief, are always amiable and at least conciliatory and solicitous. It is their policy to be so. It is only by this process that they can procure the acclaim which they desire. Nothing is more easy than to win the heart of vanity. You have but to feed it. So long as you do so, you will find it amiable, but beware of it, if once you permit yourself to cross the path of vanity. You will then discern that it is the most vindictive and malignant beast that ever ranged through that tangled forest of thorns habited like flowers which we call society! Vanity never forgives any outrage upon its *amour propre.* It never permits you to atone. You may soothe anger, you may pacify rage, you may win the honest enemy to affection and life long trust, but nothing that you can do or say can ever mollify the coxcomb whom you have once taken by the beard.

To resume. The moment I was announced, and the host had arisen to welcome me, the parasite leaps to his feet, and with a soft, seductive, but patronizing manner, exclaimed, approaching me also—

"Suffer me, Sir William to introduce to your acquaintance my friend, Mr. Richard Silex, a gentleman, Sir—"

How he would have finished the sentence may be conjectured, but he was not suffered to do so. Sir William replied—

"I thank you, Mr. —ah." and he paused, as if the name of the courtier had been forgotten. The latter, with flushed cheeks, supplied the desired name.

"Thank you, Counsellor Gander. Thank you, but I have had the pleasure of knowing Mr. Silex before. We are old acquaintances. Come Silex, here's a chair—" pointing to one beside him. In another instant, and ere I was well seated. Counsellor Gander lifted his own chair from its position, passed behind the rear of his host, and planted himself beside me, and began at once to whisper, or rather murmur in my ears. I had been assigned a new importance in his eyes. I was intimate and specially recognized by the great man.

"And so," said Gander speaking only partially *sotto voce,* "you are intimate with the Baronet?"

I simply nodded my head. He proceeded.

"What a splendid fellow he is! What a figure, how magisterial—how symmetrical, with what a carriage. And was there a more noble countenance? The *contour* is magnificent—inimitably fine—and with such sweetness blended with so much dignity and character. He meets my ideal of what Pericles was in the day of his supreme rule over Athens, when the destinies of the world rested upon his genius, and the beauties of Aspasia reposed upon his bosom, &c."

It was no easy work to arrest the Counsellor when once embarked upon the vaporous sea of his eloquence. If the whole company was not edified by his speech, it was sufficiently audible, at least, to the ears of Sir William, who gave me an arch glance, and addressed himself the next moment to his Honor the Mayor, who had challenged his attention having something himself to deliver. What this something was related to myself, though I did not know of it till afterwards.

"You know this young man, Sir William—this Silex?"

"Oh! Yes! I have known him a very long time."

"Indeed! But you never have been in this country before."

"Oh! frequently."

"Ah! travelling *incognito.*"

"Sometimes."

"And you met him then."

"Yes, but I did not then make his acquaintance. I did not then know or conceive his merits."

"Ah! his merits. Pray, of what nature are these merits?"

"What! are you not familiar with his writings?"

"Writings! Well I have heard that he makes verses, and conundrums, and things of that sort; but nobody thinks anything of him here."

"Is it possible! Can it be that you have never read his 'Lamia,' his 'Endymion,' his 'Aglaus,' his 'AEnone,' and all those several fine and beautiful transfusions from the Greek which contributed so large a part of my intellectual treasure in the wilds of my mountain home."

"I confess, my dear Sir William, that I know nothing of these writings, and I doubt if one person in a thousand of our people even heard of them even by name."

"It is very astonishing. Let me ask your Honour a few questions."

"Certainly, Sir William, I will answer them, if I can."

"Well, Sir, supposing that you, as mayor of this city, or your aldermen, were in want of a first rate blacksmith, would you know where to find one."

"Easy enough."

"Well, a machinist."

"Just as easy."

"Bricklayer, carpenter, ditcher, well digger, pumpborer, any of the crafts?"

"Find any number of them for you tomorrow."

"Good! Did you need a beverage, ale, wine, julep, cocktail, would you be able to find a restaurant who could supply you?"

"Scores of them. In fact, Sir William, there is hardly a useful citizen in town whom I do not—hardly an occupation of a useful kind which I cannot reach at any moment, without needing a direction."

"And you have in Mongrelia no uses for the Fine Arts? And you could not find me a Professor of the Fine Arts, if I desired a few pictures?"

"No, Sir William, unless photography is a Fine Art. We have precious little, I confess, for any of them. We have a dozen or two of sign painters, and more than three score of pastry cooks."

"And your acquaintance, then, is wholly confined to what you conceive to be the *useful* classes—the butcher, the baker, the cook, the mechanic, the hole digger, the pumpborer, machinist &c."

"Ah! acquaintances! That's another thing. No, Sir William—we have our *gentry. Our acquaintances*—our *intimacy,* I should say—is chiefly among *them.* We have, here, Sir, as noble an aristocracy as any in the world, Sir. I say it proudly, Sir William, that even in your country, no more accomplished gentlemen could be found. The best blood, Sir, of the best families of Europe courses through our veins!"

(Great Sensation)

Here the voice of Counsellor Gander chimed in. He had with difficulty foreborne until his Honour had got through with his patriotic sentences.

"And, Sir William, this nobility in blood is amply sustained by the grace and beauty, the charm and manner, the delicacy and accomplishments—in brief all the fine qualities which distinguish these gentlemen. Nothing, my dear Sir William can exceed the courtesy, the polish, the fascinating charm, which pervades society throughout Mongrelia. This is the acknowledgement of all noble gentlemen, like yourself, who have visited us from Europe. Nay all have borne the same testimony, and you, too, I take for granted, sprang from the highest sources, and the purest fountains of blood, with a genealogy of the longest roll, you too, I am persuaded, will before you leave us, bear a like testimony to the native nobility of my country. However shortened in fortune, however defeated in our strife for liberty, we bear within our bosoms the hearts that never fear, within our being the souls that live on in hope that the redeeming trumpet will come at last."

(*Hear! Hear!*)

But the orator was not permitted to speak, nor the audience to hear anything further in this vein. Suddenly upstarted a burly red faced and great bellied person in the undress uniform of a Brigadier, who, darting a fierce glance at the last speaker, following it up with a defiant look around among the company, rolled out in rotund and sonorous sentences, a reply which was meant to be potent in its effects upon the company:

"I will not hear—I will not permit any language that seems even to squint at the dishonor of my country's flag!—"

"Oh! d—n the flag!" was the irreverent outburst from an unknown quarter of the room.

"Who said that?" was the imperious demand of the Brigadier.

"Strip off your shoulder straps, and you shall know your man" was the answer from the same unknown quarter.

"I demand to know the speaker. Let him stand forth, if he be a man."

"What! to have a Provost marshal at my heels. Oh! spoons!" was the reply.

The military man raged; he could see the smiling in every face.

"Sir," said he to the Baronet, "I presume that you can answer for your guests."

"It is quite enough for me to assume for myself, General Gobbo; and I am not disposed to engage in quarrels not my own. Still, Sir, as an Irish Baronet, I do not always object to vicarious issues, and if you insist upon it—"

"Pistols for two," said the unknown voice—"but see that your man strips to the buff and throws off his iron breastplate."

"Gentlemen," quoth the host in his most gracious manner, "let there be no more of this. We are not to quarrel and fight, because our rhetoric sometimes flies a pinch beyond the bounds of caution or even right reason. I can answer for Counsellor Gander, I think, that he means no slight to the flag of your country or any flag. Nay, feeling sure that his merits would entitle him to some such high position, I am satisfied that he would do this flag infinite honour were your government to make him a Chief of the Freedmen's Bureau, or afford him in some other superior office, to find vent for the proper exercise of his genius. Pray, resume your seats, gentlemen, and let us hush all doubts and disputes about loyalty in some generous wines, which you will find of the oldest, and I trust, of the best."

With the wave of the hand he gave a signal, and a servant appeared, made a low salaam, and placed a simple bottle—evidently mine—my Persephone-Platonic—upon the table. A troop of servants, all in their Egyptian costume appeared following, each bringing in a salver with two goblets. The size of these goblets filled me with apprehension. But I endeavored to stifle my fears by according a full faith to the assurances of Sir William that, under his will, his vessel was inexhaustible.

"Wines, Sir William," quoth an old citizen and wine merchant, "are our particular boast in Mongrelia. It is found here, Sir, that Madeira ripens to a more exquisite richness and mellowness than in any other regions. The sun seems to assimilate its nature, and it acquires in our attics and cellars a virtue so peculiar that, doubtless, you are aware, it is frequently sought after by your European princes and nobles, and that they are sometimes supplied from private cellar, where the wine has been in bottle for eighty years."

"Hardly find one of those cellars now. Dried up. Done and gone, and you may say with Shakespeare—

> but the lees
> Is left this vault to brag of."

"Drunk up by Sherman's soldiers. The rascals, who did not know the virtues of the liquor they swallowed. Rot gut was too good for them, and the scamps would have preferred it."

So said the unknown voice. The Brigadier rose to his feet.

"Another insult to our country's flag. An atrocious slander upon the champions of liberty!"

"Oh! Shut up, Spoons."

"Gentlemen," interposed Sir William—"these pleasant witticisms, I beg you to forbear for other occasions. As a visitor to your city, a foreigner, and not a subject to your flag, I could wish that every allusion to it or to your local conflicts may be forborne. I am not prepared to sympathize with any expressions of political opinion which may exist among yourselves. Let me entreat you to a taste of my wines. Your Honour," addressing the Mayor—"Shall I be permitted to fill for you?"

The mayor bowed. To me turning, he said—

"Silex, will you join us? You have already tasted of this wine and may testify to the company."

To the servants—a look, and they passed about the bottle, and returned at moments, as it were to have it refilled.

Having had my previous experience of the liquor, I could very well anticipate the effect it would have upon the company. Repeated draughts followed the first, and soon the Mayor and Counsellor Gander were in close embrace, both having attempted to pass their arms about the neck of Sir William, but, as he eluded them with easy dexterity, they found themselves in the grasp of each other. And, it so happened that, in this general era of good feeling induced by the liquor, the *entente cordiale* was unwittingly established between the Brigadier and the Unknown who had mocked and defied him sitting at his very elbow. The Mayor then toasted the host, and the host responded with his usual grace. In the midst of the scene, it found a startling interruption by the announcement of several ladies, one the President of the "Loving Kindness Society," another of the "Seamstresses Intellect Development Society," a third of the "Infant School for the Early Development of Psychological Gifts," a fourth for the "Restoration of Woman to the Divine Heights for Which She Was Endowed," a fifth for the

"Amelioration of the Condition of Unmarried Women," who have passed the fifth period of possibility. The presidents of each of the societies enumerated, heading committees of three at least, were all waiting below for admission.

"Gentlemen," said our host—"Stay not upon the order of your going, but go at once." And he bowed them out, holding me back as they disappeared, a movement which Counsellor Gander beheld with ineffable disgust.

"I will join you," said Sir William, "as soon as I have dismissed these women. I must give them a report. Lord," said he—and before I could say, "all my Eye, Betty Martin," the table was covered with the most exquisite viands of every known and many unknown varieties. The door opened—I beheld a crowd of antique faces, none of which were gems, and removed by the backstairs.

Explanatory Notes

Note: the first number refers to the page in the current volume. The second and third numbers refer to the manuscript page and the line on that page.

Page **128**; ms. page 1, line 2: "Time travels . . . stands withal."—Shakespeare, *As You Like It,* act 3, scene 2, lines 305–8. Rosalind, disguised as a man, is in the forest speaking to Orlando, who does not recognize her.

Page **128**; ms. page 2, line 1: "You know . . . and finally to Hell."—Goethe, *Faust,* part 1: "Prelude on Stage," 231–43. Johann Wolfgang von Goethe (1749–1832) was a German writer, artist, and politician.

Page **128**; ms. page 3, line 5: *rectus in curia*—Latin, right in court. A person who is innocent or acquitted from a legal standpoint and who possesses full legal rights.

Page **128**; ms. page 4, line 1: charlatan—a person who deceives others for personal gain. In the nineteenth century, the word was closely associated with spiritualists who preyed on unsuspecting victims by claiming they could communicate with the spiritual world or with the deceased.

Page **129**; ms. page 4, line 5: Saul—the first king of Israel. In I Samuel, Saul banishes all the mediums from Israel and outlaws sorcery and divination, but he later seeks out the Witch of Endor, a medium, so he can communicate with the prophet Samuel.

Page **129**; ms. page 4, line 5: Socrates—Greek philosopher (469–399 B.C.E.) whose major works often focus on the relationship between material and spiritual phenomena. He was especially interested in how one discerns between true and false gods.

Page **129**; ms. page 4, line 6: Witch of Endor—a spiritual medium during the reign of Saul, the first king of Israel. In I Samuel, Saul banishes all mediums from Israel but later seeks to communicate with the dead prophet Samuel. While in disguise, Saul goes to the medium and asks her to summon Samuel, who foretells of his death in battle.

Page **129**; ms. page 4, line 6: John Faustus or Faust—the protagonist of a popular German legend. Faustus is a scholar and conjurer who sells his soul to the devil.

Many versions of the legend exist, including one by the English playwright Christopher Marlowe, but the best known is the tragic play, *Faust,* by nineteenth-century German writer Johann Wolfgang von Goethe.

Page **129**; ms. page 4, line 6: Michael Scott (1175–ca.1232)—a Scottish priest, mathematician, and scholar who was known for his writings on astrology, alchemy, and the occult. After his death legends circulated widely about his magical powers as a sorcerer.

Page **129**; ms. page 4, line 6: Machiavelli—an Italian statesman. Niccolò Machiavelli (1469–1527) is best known for his political treatise *The Prince,* which describes how rulers gain and maintain control of their countries.

Page **129**; ms. page 4, line 7: Reverend Edward Irving (1792–1834)—an ordained minister in the Church of Scotland, renowned for his unique preaching style and for his ministry among the poor. He was removed from the church in 1832 because of his controversial views on the Holy Spirit and spiritual gifts. He is regarded today as a historical precursor to Pentecostal movements in the late nineteenth and early twentieth centuries.

Page **129**; ms. page/line 5.8–6.1: slave of the Lamp and the Ring—reference originally from "Aladdin and the Enchanted Lamp," a Middle Eastern folktale that features two different djinns, or genies, one who is summoned by rubbing a ring (the "slave of the ring") and the other who is summoned by rubbing a lamp ("slave of the lamp").

Page **129**; ms. page 6, line 8: en rapport—French, in a state of rapport or in a sympathetic, harmonious relationship.

Page **129**; ms. page 7, line 1: Bancroft's *United States*—work authored by George Bancroft (1800–1891), an American historian and politician who served as U.S. secretary of the navy under James K. Polk. Bancroft's ten-volume *History of the United States* was one of the most influential histories of America written during the nineteenth century. Simms criticized Bancroft and other New England writers and historians for diminishing the pivotal role that southern colonies played in the founding of the new nation.

Page **129**; ms. page 7, line 2: Freedmen's Bureau—the Bureau of Refugees, Freedmen, and Abandoned Lands, established as part of the War Department by an Act of Congress in March 1865. The bureau assisted freed slaves with food, clothing, medicine, and education during the postwar years. It also was responsible for determining ownership of confiscated lands and property in the former Confederate states.

Page **129**; ms. page 7, line 2: Mongrelia—see the introduction to "Sir Will O' Wisp." Historically the term often referred to regions in the Far East (Eastern Russia and

Mongolia). It also was used more broadly in reference to countries or peoples who were ethnically or culturally mixed.

Page **129**; ms. page 8, line 3: Mephistopheles—the demon in Goethe's *Faust.*

Page **129–30;** ms. page 8, lines 4–5: Dr. Dee—John Dee (1527–ca.1608), an influential scholar in the court of Queen Elizabeth I. Renowned for his expertise in mathematics and science, Dee was also known for his interest in spiritualism and the occult.

Page **130**; ms. page 10, line 2: Maccaboy—a rose-scented snuff whose name derives from Macouba, a tobacco-growing district in northern Martinique.

Page **130**; ms. page 10, line 3: Scottish mull—originally a Scots variant of mill, the term referred to a snuffbox in which tobacco could be ground to powder, or snuff. It was eventually extended to any small tin box or container for keeping snuff.

Page **130**; ms. page 10, line 4: George Buchanan (1506–1582)—a Scottish historian and scholar; also an early proponent of the Protestant Reformation and a critic of the Catholic monarchy in Scotland.

Page **130**; ms. page 12, line 1: sternutatory—any substance that causes sneezing. It also refers to any drug, usually in the form of powder, that is used to stimulate sneezing.

Page **131**; ms. page 13, line 6: Cuvier—the French naturalist Georges Cuvier (1769–1832), an early pioneer in the field of paleontology and among the first scientists to study the connection between living organisms and fossils.

Page **131**; ms. page 13, line 6: granivorous—animals that feed on seeds or grain.

Page **131**; ms. page 13, line 7: *on dit*—French, an item of gossip or hearsay. Literally means "it is said" or "they say."

Page **131**; ms. page 15, line 2: moustache . . . *a la Napoleon*—a type of moustache where the facial hair is grown in relatively thick such that it can be styled into separate points on both sides of the face. It was popularized among French soldiers during the Napoleonic Wars (1799–1815) as a sign of virility and was later adopted by soldiers, businessmen, and politicians throughout Europe and the United States.

Page **131**; ms. page 16, line 2: *salon les regles*—French, following the rules of fashion.

Page **131**; ms. page 16, line 3: Brummel—Englishman George Bryan (1778–1840), better known as Beau Brummel, an authority on clothing and fashion who is credited with popularizing the suit and tie as conventional clothing for men.

Page **131**; ms. page 16, line 3: *imprimatur*—Latin, to stamp or to imprint, as in printing a book. In this context it means to sanction or to authorize, as in a stamp or imprint of approval.

Page **132**; ms. page 18, line 4: *genus irritabile vatum*—Latin, "the irritable race of poets." The phrase is from the *Second Epistle* by the Roman poet Horace.

Page **132**; ms. page 19, lines 6–7: negro melodies, as Jim Crow, Coal Black Rose, Clare De Kitchen—part of the minstrel tradition that began in the early nineteenth century, these songs were included as part of elaborate theatrical performances by white performers in blackface and portrayed African Americans in stereotypical fashion as simple minded, superstitious, lazy, and violent.

Page **134**; ms. page 26, lines 2–3: Shakespeare . . . unnecessary words—Simms may have in mind these lines from *Henry V*: "For Nym, he hath / heard that men of few words are the best men; and / therefore he scorns to say his prayers, lest a' / should be thought a coward: but his few bad words / are matched with as few good deeds" (act 3, scene 2, lines 1163–67).

Page **135**; ms. page 28, line 6: Belial—originally a Hebrew word meaning without value or worth. It is used in later Jewish and Christian texts as a synonym for Satan or the personification of evil. For example in 2 Corinthians 6:15, Belial (or Beliar) the prince of darkness is contrasted with Christ, the light. Belial appears in Milton's *Paradise Lost* as one of the fallen angels.

Page **135**; ms. page 30, line 1: Yankee Brogue—*brogue,* usually referring to an Irish accent, used here broadly to refer to regional accents in New England.

Page **135**; ms. page 31, line 4: *dum vivimus vivamus*—a Latin phrase associated with Epicurean philosophy that means "let us live while we live."

Page **136**; ms. page 35, line 6: *Lacryma Christi*—or Lachryma Christi, literally the "tear of Christ," the name of an ancient Neapolitan wine produced on the slopes of Mount Vesuvius in Italy. The name comes from a legend that Christ, in sorrow over Lucifer's fall from heaven, shed his tears on the land and gave divine inspiration to the vines that grew there.

Page **136**; ms. page 36, line 5: *recherché*—French, exquisite choice, but also carries the connotation of being excessively affected or pretentious.

Page **136**; ms. page 37, line 7: puffs—overly excessive or meaningless praise; also a person or thing that is insubstantial or inconsequential. Simms seems to have both contexts in mind here.

Page **138**; ms. page 45, line 4: Lapland witch—Lapland, a region in northern Europe that extends across the northern areas of Norway, Sweden, and Finland and into Russia's Kola Peninsula. Lapps or Laplanders, the indigenous population across this region, were associated in European folklore with supernatural and occult practices. In Milton's *Paradise Lost,* Lapland witches are present at the imminent ritual sacrifice of a child (II, ll.613–26).

Page **138**; ms. page 47, line 6: Brother Beecher—Henry Ward Beecher (1813–1887), a prominent New England clergyman, abolitionist, and social reformer. His sister, Harriet Beecher Stowe, wrote *Uncle Tom's Cabin,* an abolitionist novel that Simms severely criticized.

Page **139**; ms. page 49, line 4: Pylades and Orestes—two boys in Greek mythology, cousins who are raised like brothers by Pylades's parents. After Orestes's mother, Clytemnestra, murders his father, Agamemnon, Orestes returns home with his friend Pylades to avenge his father's death.

Page **139**; ms. page 50, line 4: cambric needle—a lightweight, closely woven, white cotton fabric sewn with a small needle; it was first made at Cambrai in Flanders.

Page **139**; ms. page 52, line 2: "The Black Crook"—considered by many historians to be the first American musical, debuted on Broadway in September 1866, and ran for a record-breaking 474 performances. Set in Germany during the 1600s, it incorporated elements of Goethe's *Faust* and featured elaborate special effects and a chorus line of one hundred ballerinas.

Page **139**; ms. page 54, line 2: the elect—the doctrine of election, most closely associated with French theologian John Calvin (1509–1564), a major figure in the early Protestant Reformation. The doctrine posits that God in his absolute sovereignty predestines some humans for salvation (the elect) and the rest for damnation.

Page **140**; ms. page 59, line 6: Harun al-Rashid—Islamic caliph, or ruler, of a large Arab territory that encompassed most of modern-day Iraq from 786 to 809. Harun was renowned as an enthusiastic patron of the arts and sciences. His palace in Bagdad was legendary in the West for its opulence and splendor.

Page **140**; ms. page 60, lines 2–3: Those gay creatures . . . clouds—from John Milton's masque, *Comus,* which was first presented in 1634. In Greek mythology Comus or Komos is the god of festivals and revelry. The actual lines from the masque are "I took it for a faery vision / Of some gay creatures of the element / That in the colours of the rainbow live / And play i' th' plighted clouds (298–301). Simms quotes these same lines in his short story, "Sweet William—A Tale of Faerie," published in *Martin Faber, The Story of a Criminal; and Other Tales,* vol. 1 (1837).

Page **140**; ms. page 60, line 3: plighted—pleated or folded.

Page **140–41**; ms. page 60, line 5: *dolce far niente*—Italian, literally means "sweet doing nothing." A phrase that evokes the feeling of indulgent relaxation or blissful idleness.

Page **141**; ms. page 60, line 6: Thomson's "Castle of Indolence"—Scottish playwright and poet James Thomson (1700–1748) published his long allegorical poem "Castle of Indolence" in 1748. The poem is critical of those who waste away their lives in pursuit of luxury and idle pleasures.

Page **141**; ms. page 60, line 8: piquant—pleasantly stimulating or exciting to the mind.

Page **141**; ms. page 61, line 3: lute of Apollo—Apollo, the Greek god of music, said to have invented the lute, a stringed instrument similar to a small guitar.

Page **142**; ms. page 67, line 2: "Who drinks beer, thinks beer"—from *The Sketch Book of Geoffrey Crayon* (1820) by Washington Irving: "They who drink beer will think beer."

Page **142**; ms. page 69, line 4: *nom de société*—French, name or appelation used in public.

Page **142**; ms. page 70, line 2: Spread Eagle Hotel—an eagle with outspread wings, which is a heraldic emblem that was incorporated into the Great Seal of the United States. The term "spread eagle" referred to excessive exaggeration of American superiority. The term "spread-eagle oratory" first appeared in print in 1858.

Page **143**; ms. page 70, lines 5–6: my chattels . . . my heart—from Shakespeare's *The Taming of the Shrew,* in which Petruchio exclaims in reference to Kate, "She is my goods, my chattels; she is my house, / My household stuff, my field, my barn, / My horse, my ox, my ass, my any thing" (act 3, scene 2, lines 1596–98).

Page **143**; ms. page 71, line 1: Loyalists—colonists who remained loyal to the British monarchy during the American Revolution.

Page **143–44**; ms. page 77, line 1: "A bargain . . . to unlearn!"—this section was cut and pasted into the manuscript from a printed copy of Simms's short story "Jack-O'-Lantern" from the *Southern Literary Messenger.*

Page **144**; ms. page 78, line 2: Matthew—English deist Matthew Tindal (1657–1733), who defended the value of human reason and natural revelation over supernatural revelation.

Page **144**; ms. page 78, line 5: blood-pudding—a dark-colored sausage made from animal blood, suet, grains, raisins or currants, and spices. Also called black sausage or black pudding.

Page **145**; ms. page 81, lines 1–20 "I congratulate . . . you will"—this section was cut and pasted into the manuscript from a printed copy of Simms's short story "Jack-O'-Lantern" from the *Southern Literary Messenger.*

Page **146**; ms. page 83, line 4: Irish Chronicles—a collection of ecclesiastical annals recording events in Ireland from 432 to 911 A.D.

Page **146**; ms. page 83, line 5: St. Patrick—the patron saint of Ireland, Patrick (ca. 387–ca. 460) was born in Roman Britain and became a Catholic priest and missionary among the Celtic tribes in Ireland.

Page **146**; ms. page 84, line 1: Yankees at Bull Run—Simms is referring to the Second Battle of Bull Run, which was fought August 28–30, 1862, near the city of

Manassas, Virginia. The battle was a decisive victory for the Confederate army under the leadership of General Robert E. Lee and sent the Union army in retreat to Washington, D.C. One of the first major land battles of the Civil War was fought in the same area on July 21, 1861, and is referred to as the First Battle of Bull Run.

Page **146**; ms. page 84, line 2: *Scandalum Magnatum*—a public speech or written work that defames a political figure, a nobleman, or a person with social prestige. In England the act, which was repealed in 1887, was a criminal offense punishable by law.

Page **146**; ms. page 84, line 3: seven deadly abominations—according to Proverbs 6:16–19, there are seven abominations against God: haughty eyes, a lying tongue, hands that shed innocent blood, a heart that devises wicked plans, feet that make haste to run to evil, a false witness who breathes out lies, and a man who sows discord among brothers. In more recent Christian traditions, the seven deadly sins commonly recognized as wrath, greed, sloth, pride, lust, envy, and gluttony.

Page **146**; ms. page 86, lines 7–8: proverb . . . of the Devil's brewing—Simms is referring to an American proverb, "As well to eat the devil as to drink his broth," or, alternately, "If it is wrong to eat the devil, it is wrong to drink his broth."

Page **146**; ms. page 87, line 1: salver—a flat tray of silver or other metal used for serving drinks or food.

Page **146**; ms. page 87, line 1: cate—an edible delicacy or treat. In Middle English the term, taken from the French, referred to food that was purchased.

Page **147**; ms. page 89, lines 4–5: Ram's Horn . . . Jericho—Joshua 6:1–27 describes the first battle of the Israelites during their conquest of Canaan. The walls of the Canaanite city of Jericho were destroyed when the Israelite army marched around the city blowing their trumpets.

Page **147**; ms. page 90, line 2: Kickapoo Lighter—the Kickapoo or Kiikaapoi were a Native American tribe, living in the Great Lakes region of the United States. During the nineteenth century, they were relocated to territories in the American Southwest.

Page **147**; ms. page 90, line 3: Puritan Standish—Myles Standish (ca. 1584–1656), an English military officer who travelled with other Puritans to the new colony at Plymouth. He served as the colony's first military commander and later served as assistant governor and treasurer.

Page **147**; ms. page 91, line 2: Samson _____ Samson's last name is illegible in the manuscript.

Page **147**; ms. page 93, line 4: Fenians—the Fenian Brotherhood was an Irish Republican organization founded in the United States in 1858 by John O'Mahony and Michael Doheny. Members were known as Fenians and supported Irish independence.

Page **149**; ms. page 100, line 4: Arabian Nights—refers to *One Thousand and One Nights*, a collection of Persian, Arabic, and Indian folktales. *Arabian Nights,* the first English language translation of the collection, was published in 1706.

Page **149**; ms. page 102, line 1: Curse of Cassandra—in Greek mythology, Cassandra, the daughter of the king of Troy granted a gift of prophecy by Apollo that became a curse when she rejected Apollo's advances. He cursed her so that no one would believe her prophecies. She appears in the Greek playwright Aeschylus's tragedy *Agamemnon,* where she is murdered by Agamemnon's wife, Clytemnestra.

Page **151**; ms. page 110, line 7: Samuel . . . witch—a spiritual medium during the reign of Saul, the first king of Israel. In I Samuel, Saul banishes all mediums from Israel but seeks to communicate with the dead prophet Samuel. While in disguise, Saul goes to the medium and asks her to summon Samuel, who foretells of his death in battle.

Page **151**; ms. page 110, line 9: Paul—in describing his conversion to Christianity, the Apostle Paul (ca. 5 C.E.–ca. 67 C.E.) says he beheld a vision of the resurrected Christ and heard his voice speaking directly to him.

Page **151**; ms. page 111, line 3: Apollonius of Tyana—a first-century Greek philosopher and spiritualist who was said to perform miracles.

Page **151**; ms. page 111, lines 5–6: Caesar . . . at Philippi—in Shakespeare's *Julius Caesar,* Caesar's ghost appears to Brutus before the Battle at Philippi with a warning that his army will be defeated (act 4, scene 3).

Page **151**; ms. page 111, line 7: *rari nantes in gurgite vasto*—Virgil, "a few swimming in the vast deep" (*Aeneid* 1:118).

Page **152**; ms. page 112, line 5: Richard the Third—In Shakespeare's eponymous play, King Richard is haunted by the ghosts of his victims and driven toward madness.

Page **152**; ms. page 112, line 5: Your great master of dramatic fiction—William Shakespeare.

Page **152**; ms. page 113, line 1: Hamlet—in Shakespeare's eponymous play, Hamlet is visited by the ghost of his murdered father, the king, who demands that he avenge his death.

Page **152**; ms. page 113, line 1: Horatio—Hamlet's closest friend and confidant.

Page **153**; ms. page 120, line 5: clod poles—derives from clod pate (head) and is used to refer to a dense-headed or dumb person.

Page **153**; ms. page 123, lines 2–3: the turning of tables, the rapping on floor and wall—activities that were popularly associated with spiritual séances during the nineteenth century.

Page **154**; ms. page 123, line 4: Gordius—the Gordian Knot of Greek mythology that was cut by Alexander the Great after hearing an oracle promise that whoever could undo it would be the next ruler of Asia. The term is synonymous with trying to unravel a complicated problem.

Page **154**; ms. page 124, line 2: *seriatum*—Latin, one after another.

Page **154**; ms. page 126, line 5: Job—reference to the biblical Job who is tested by Satan but never renounces his faith in God.

Page **154**; ms. page 127, line 1: Mammon—associated in Hebrew and other languages with wealth and possessions. In the New Testament, Mammon refers to a false god that is associated with materialism and greed. In Milton's *Paradise Lost,* Mammon is one of the fallen angels who follows Satan in rebellion against God.

Page **155**; ms. page 131, line 3: daughters of the horse leech—the phrase is from Proverbs: "The horseleach hath two daughters, crying, Give, give" (30:15). A large blood-sucking leech that attached itself to the lips and mouths of horses; the phrase refers to anyone who is excessively demanding or who takes needlessly from others.

Page **155**; ms. page 131, line 6: Moloch—appears in the Old Testament as one of the gods of the Phoenicians and the Canaanites who was associated with ritual human sacrifices. In Milton's *Paradise Lost,* Moloch is one of the fallen angels who follows Satan in rebellion against God.

Page **156**; ms. page 138, line 7: Madeira—a wine grown on the island of Madeira in the Mediterranean. Popular in Europe and America, it was used to toast the signing of the Declaration of Independence and served at George Washington's inauguration. One of Simms's favorite wines, he refers to it frequently in his writings.

Page **157**; ms. page 142, line 1: *remollient*—French, emollient; softening, mollifying, weakening the resolution of.

Page **157**; ms. page 144, line 2: *sic transit gloria mundi*—Latin, "thus passes the glory of the world."

Page **158**; ms. page 148, line 3: *eidolon*—an unsubstantial image, specter, or phantom. The term appears in Goethe's *Faust.*

Page **158**; ms. page 149, line 4: Dromios—Dromio of Ephesus and Dromio of Syracuse, twin brothers in Shakespeare's *Comedy of Errors.*

Page **159**; ms. page 154, line 2: Mussulman—an archaic term for Muslim.

Page **159**; ms. page 154, line 3: Yankee Brahmin—refers to wealthy, aristocratic New England families whose origins date back to the earliest founding of the British colonies in North America.

Page **161**; ms. page 161, line 1: Boswell to his Oracle—Scottish author James Boswell (1740–1795), remembered in literary circles for his ground-breaking biography of Samuel Johnson, his "oracle."

Page **161**; ms. page 162, line 6: *vox et praeterea nihil*—Latin, "a voice and nothing more." Simms's friend Henry Timrod published a poem with this phrase as its title.

Page **162**; ms. page 164, line 1: *amour propre*—French, "self love." In this context Simms probably has in mind the concept developed by François de La Rochefoucauld, Jean-Jacques Rousseau, and others that describes a self love derived only from the opinions of others that renders people incapable of ever being truly happy.

Page **162**; ms. page 164, line 4: coxcomb—originally a cap in the shape and color of a cock's comb that was worn by a court jester or fool. Shakespeare uses the term with this meaning in *King Lear* and *Taming of the Shrew.* In the nineteenth century the word also was associated with superficial, fashionably dressed gentlemen.

Page **162**; ms. page 166, line 5: *sotto voce*—Italian, "under voice," means intentionally lowering one's voice for emphasis.

Page **162**; ms. page 167, line 4: Aspasia—bore Pericles one son who became a general in the Athenian army and had a significant influence on Pericles' success as leader of Athens.

Page **163**; ms. page 169, line 5: Lamia—a poem written by John Keats in 1820. In Greek mythology Lamia was a serpentlike demon who devoured young children. Simms's poem "Lamia—The Beautiful Sin," was published in his collection of poems *Areytos or Songs and Ballads of the South with Other Poems* in 1846.

Page **163**; ms. page 169, line 6: Endymion—a poem written by John Keats in 1818. It is based on the Greek myth of Selene, goddess of the moon, who falls in love with the shepherd Endymion. Simms wrote a sonnet that drew upon the Endymion myth, published in his collection of poems *The Vision of Cortes, Cain and Other Poems* in 1829.

Page **163**; ms. page 169, line 6: Aglaus—in Greek mythology a beggar from the region of Arcadia whom the Oracle at Delphi pronounced as being happier and more content than the king of Lydia.

Page **164**; ms. page 175, line 3: undress uniform—an ordinary duty uniform that was less colorful and elaborate than the full dress uniform reserved for ceremonial occasions.

Page **166**; ms. page 181, lines 7–9: "but the lees . . . brag of"—a line from Shakespeare's *MacBeth***,** "The wine of life is drawn, and the mere lees / Is left this vault to brag of" (act 2, scene 3, lines 93–94). Here MacBeth laments that the wine of life has been poured out and only the dregs (the fermented "lees") remain.

Page **166**; ms. page 185, line 2: *entente cordiale*—French, an agreement between political powers.

Page **167**; ms. page 188, line 2: "all my eye, Betty Martin"—the phrase "All my eye and Betty Martin," meaning something is complete nonsense or unbelievable. Its origins are unknown, but the phrase appears in nineteenth-century slang dictionaries. While not proven, some scholars suggest the phrase has its origins in an earlier Latin prayer.

APPENDIX

Jack-O'-Lantern: A New-Light Story

"*Manager.* You know, upon our German stage, every one tries what he likes. Therefore, spare me neither scenery nor machinery upon this day. Use the greater and the lesser light of heaven; you are free to squander the stars; there is no want of water, fire, rocks, beasts and birds. So spread out, in this narrow booth, the whole circle of creation; and travel, with considerate speed, from heaven, through the world, to hell."

GOETHE, *The Faust*

It is scarcely the best policy to begin the work of confession on one's first entry into the world, where, now-a-days, if men confess any sins at all, it is only such as are sufficiently equivocal to pass for virtues; but as my aim is a moral one, and my hope the reformation if this very infirmity among mankind, I know no better mode of beginning, than to put myself right in court, by a frank avowal of the matter which has brought me into it. Start not, therefore, ye devoutly pious—frown not, ye saints of the tabernacle,—and wring not your hands, ye godly dames, who form societies to help unto grace and gravy, the infinite number of wise young men, who are possessed of the spirit, and lack all other possessions,—when I boldly declare into ye, that, like Saul of old, and the Witch

"Jack-O'-Lantern: A New-Light Story." By Eyes-In-Glass. Chapter I. *Southern Literary Messenger* 4.5 (May 1838): 336–39.

*And, possibly, chapter last, since I cannot be certain that the taste of the reader will so highly approve of my devil as my own does. Time will show. I will bind myself to no conditions. If the mood suits me—and the "Messenger"—there will be more words to this argument. The public shall be made wiser, if they have the wit to desire it. I shall be happy to serve and enlighten them, but I will not throw pearls away upon—those who do not know how to wear them. I' faith, I had nearly written out the proverb in full, and there were no good policy, my gentile public, in that.

of Endor, John Faustus, Michael Scott, and possibly, the Reverend Edward Irving, I have a familiar—in plain language, a devil; one of those active and intelligent spirits, who from sympathy, animal magnetism, or some other equally unintelligible cause, attach themselves to the fortunes of that grub-worm, man, for his special comfort and edification; conveying him the news—canvassing morals, (and *par parenthese,* the devil has a particular interest in this department of human economy,) and, altogether, affording him a mass of information not yet attainable even by the most adroit practitioner in *clair-voyancing.* How I became familiar, with this familiar, is, the gentlest of all possible readers—without becoming too familiar—none of your business. He came to me, suffice it to know, not as visiters from the unsubstantial world usually come, reeking with smoke and stinking of antimony; there was not even a flourish of trumpets—not a breeze or breath of music—to intimate his approach. Never was coming more innocent and unimposing. I made use of no sort of incantations; none of your sculls and circles—grim, grinning jowls, skinned bats and withered frogs, encircled me; and, except the proverbial devil of the printing office, I do not remember to have ever had before the slightest communication, from or with, and of the hotly-quartered gentry. Nor did I solicit, the honor of a visit, (rhyme is a devilish propensity,) but uninvited, uncommanded—I will not say, undesired—he stood before me; nay, there I am wrong, he stood behind me, such was the unobtrusive modesty of his approach at first; and a sound was the first notice which I had of his near neighborhood. My devil first made my acquaintance in the shape of a sound. But that, gentle reader, was no vulgar sound, though not an unfrequent one since the discovery of Maccoboy. My snuff-box lay beside me, on the table, and from its capacious treasury, I had just withdrawn, betwixt my forefinger and thumb, a generous pinch of the titillating dust. Applied to my nostril, it had promptly done its office in provoking a most relieving and liberal sneeze. What was my consternation to behold, in the next moment, another sneeze behind me—a sneeze, as it were, the very *fac-simile* and echo of my own. Such, at first, I was almost persuaded to believe it, but a repetition of the explosion soon convinced me that it was not the sneeze of humanity, and I clearly comprehended the operation of my Maccoboy upon the sternutatory organs of an infernal. "Ha!—tshe—tshe—tshe—ha!—ha!"—was the melodious acknowledgement which my visiter gave to the potency and general excellence of my tobacconist; and the sympathy which his nostril thus seemed to exhibit with my own, half removed the feeling of disquiet and apprehension which his first annunciation had occasioned me. In an instant I turned to confront him, and a moment's glance sufficed to set my heart at ease and silence all my annoyances.

On looking at him, I felt, of a sudden, all the freedom and familiarity of a long acquaintance; and this feeling, the moment I had discovered his quality, forced upon me the unpleasant conviction that I had been no better than I should be. His face was by no means remarkable. Such a face I have often seen. It was rather Gallican in its contour and general expression. A disposition to laugh at all things seemed its predominating feature, but there was a slight sinking at the corners of the mouth, which denoted a habitual sneer, and a fondness for sarcasm, which was strongly opposed to the general benevolence of his other features. The cheeks were full, fat and rosy, but the eyes were rather small and the chin degenerated apishly. His figure was good enough—his person, though diminutive, was perfect. I cast my eyes with some curiosity towards his feet, but they were perfect also; and in a fashionable square-toed boot seemed even handsomely formed. There was nothing like club or hoof to offend my sensibilities or alarm my fears, and I wondered at our grandams who could tell, and really believe, such discreditable stories. My devil, on the whole was really a comely fellow. I have seen the editor of a ladies' gazette, a far worse looking man, and infinitely less of a gentleman.

With that divine instinct which we have never denied to the devil, while denying him all other virtues, he readily discerned my annoyances and saw that his coming had put me out; but with that felicity of manner which it would be equal folly in us to deny to a person so proverbially persuasive, he took special care in what he said, not to suffer me to see that he ascribed my discomposure to any other cause than the natural irritability of an author at being described in his daily scribblings. I was at this time busily engaged upon a new work, calling for all my taste and research, no other than a collection of the most fashionable negro melodies, such as Jim Crow, Coal Black Rose, Clare De Kitchen, and other pieces of like national and moral interest, with a copious appendix of illustrative notes, such as might well become a work of so much magnitude and interest.

"I see that you are busy, Mr. Silex, and I would not willingly disturb you at this moment."

"Pray, proceed, sir—I have time enough to spare, and will wait upon you."

He drew a chair as he said these words, and with the air of a man resolved, under all circumstances, to be as good as his word, he prepared to take a quiet seat in a corner, and give himself up to meditation.

"Beg pardon, sir" said I, "but you will find it tedious—may I be honored at once with the purpose of your visit."

"That is soon told," said he in reply; "I see that you know me."

Here I expressed a little reluctance, and prayed for more direct information.

"I cannot deny," was my response, "that I have a shrewd guess, but—" There I paused.

"Which is perfectly correct, sir; your instinct is not less good than mine in matters of this sort, and there needs no formality between those already acquainted. Besides, there is something less than civil—certainly less than social—in calling folks continually by their titles of dignity. I freely confess to you a willingness to dispense with mine. It operates against me, and sits heavily upon me at certain seasons. I am, like many princes of old, and some of the officers of penal justice in modern times, infinitely more fond of a snug disguise, and a good humored *nom de guerre,* than of the solemn ceremonial which follows upon and announces the presence of superior attributes. At present, sir, as I see you still somewhat at a loss, you will do me the favor to recognize me under one of my many names—the most innocent and least imposing, perhaps, among them—and whenever you may deem it necessary to call me by a name at all, which I trust will not be often the case, to know me as Jack-O'-Lantern. I shall certainly be willing to give you all the light I carry, should you require it. Jack-O'-Lantern is a common acquaintance, and nobody should be seriously alarmed or annoyed at his presence. You, I know, who are a poet and philosopher, will readily show yourself above all idle superstitious fancies; and you will soon find, upon doing so, that if I have few virtues, I have many uses; and my more imposing names of sovereignty thrown out of the account, there can be no objection to the employment of my services."

"Your services, My John O'-Lantern?" I exclaimed with some wonder, in the sudden commotion of my thoughts, not exactly knowing what to make of this sort of introduction—"Your services!"

"Ay, my services," he replied; "I propose to serve you, because I see that you need my help, and because I have somehow taken a liking to you. You smile, but I am above jest in this. I am serious. In my friendship for you I have sought you out, and I am resolved to become your friend, companion, assistant, anything, whether you will or no! You want an amanuensis, and considering the color of the work on which I see you busy, perhaps I am the very person of all the world whom you should soonest choose. But I insist not on this. Take me in what capacity you please. I am an actor of all work, as the comedians call themselves. I can be a boon companion, a grave counselor, a curious penman, and a dapper valet. Make me what you please, with a will, and rely on me to be the thing which you most desire. I will take no refusal; you must employ me."

So liberal an offer, so graciously volunteered, was not to be rejected idly. He saw me hesitate, and threw in certain additional suggestions.

"My library is large and various; I see that you are busy, and sometimes at a loss, in your search after authorities. You correspondence is extensive; let me give you a taste of my skill in assisting you to answer some of these letters."

He turned over a pile, seated himself at the table, and with a pen that seemed rather to stream over the paper than to rest upon it, he wrote almost in a breath the most admirable and fitting replies to the greater number of them. To a politician wanting a vote, and giving a dinner accordingly, he wrote a brief but comprehensive eulogium upon the arts of the cuisine, and concluded with an acceptance to his invitation, premising only that my wine for the current month was Lachrymae Christi. To a lady of fashion whose billet for the next *soiree* was rather a summons than a solicitation, he pleased a rule to reject all invitations for Friday, but complimented her at the same time upon the *recherché* fold of her missive. To the editor of a weekly magazine who begged for contributions, for which he promised to pay in praises, he wrote an essay on independent criticism. To a tailor soliciting custom and proffering extensive credits, he penned an order for a claret colored coat, such as the man wore who seized on the New York arsenal, and kept it for the whigs against General Arcularius and his man Friday. There was one letter which he was about to open, but as if he knew the contents already, or saw from the glance of my eye that he was now on forbidden ground, he paused in his progress, and I availed myself of the interval to acknowledge his powers, and relive him for the present from their farther exercise.

"Enough, Mr. O'-Lantern, I am quite obliged to you. You are indeed a valuable acquisition, and really I know not how I shall requite you."

"Requite me—I ask no requital, Mr. Silex—none. The pleasure of serving you is enough for me."

"Indeed! Truly you are becoming disinterested in your old age. You have not always toiled thus unprofitably, and with so little regard to self. If report speaks truly, you have usually been a severe expectant—a rigid exacter of your dues. You have done nothing for nothing."

"Report has done me wrong," he said coolly. "I have always been a much scandalized person among men, I assure you."

Never did injured mortal look more in need of sympathy. I felt myself getting lachrymose.

"What!" I proceeded, "and is your love in my case so great that you are willing to do for me those things for which you have exacted the eternal and unmitigated toils of other men, not to speak of their sufferings?"

"I do not understand you, really," was his reply, and he certainly looked at a loss when he spoke those words.

"'Pon my soul," I continued, "either you are exceedingly dull, Mr. O'-Lantern, or I have been grievously imposed upon in the histories I have heard of you. Is it really possible that you intend to serve me for nothing? Do you really want no compensation? Do you ask nothing of me in return?"

"Nothing."

"What! Shall there be no bond between us?"

"Bond! For what? Speak out my dear master that is to be, and tell me your real difficulty."

"Well, in plain terms then Mr. O'-Lantern, do you not want to bind me, body and soul, in return for these services? Do you not want a mortgage of my soul?"

"Your soul, indeed, what do I want with it? Bless your stars, my dear Mr. Silex, that thing is entirely out of fashion now. I have more souls than I know what to do with—they are positively rotting on my hands. I wouldn't be burdened or bothered with an increase on any terms; and next to the mistake which you have been led into by your grandmother on the subject of my character, is that monstrous error which you men seem to entertain as to the value of the article you think I trade in. Souls, indeed! The very idea is absurd. No, sir, if I wished for anything at your hands, it should be the breeches you have worn. Now I think of it, sir, I will have to pay for my services. You shall pay me in old breeches; you shall contract to give me all your breeches after a month's wearing them, and I will trust to your generosity, should you ever get married, to throw in occasionally a petticoat of your wife's. These shall be my terms. I ask for no other. Keep your soul, and do what you please with it; I would'nt have it as a gift. But your breeches, sir—your breeches; and in the event of your wife's; these you shall give me, if anything, in return for my services. What say you to these terms?"

"A bargain," I exclaimed, delighted with the humor of the fellow, not less than his generosity. "Breeches and petticoats! You shall have them all! Why, Mr. O'-Lantern, you are the very pink of liberality, and I rejoice at your coming. Pray resume your seat, and let us talk over this matter, that it may be the better understood between us. There may be something covert and equivocal in it, after all. You gentlemen of the lantern are apt to hang out false lights for the temptation of the unwary, and I am resolved to see that you have no occult signification in what you say, before I sign this agreement. It may be my soul, after all, that you're driving at, in aiming at my breeches. I know many men whose souls never go beyond their breeches, and though I trust that mine is not of this sort, yet I would take every precaution against involvements. I will have legal advice first in this business."

"You are right, my dear sir," he replied promptly, "take what precaution you please, and be satisfied before you proceed a single step in this matter. I have no disposition to deceive you—indeed, I am not a proficient in the arts of falsehood. I know many a lawyer who would put me to the blush for incompetence, and might, if lying were a prime requisite in my dominions, usurp their sovereignty. Even if your soul were in your breeches, there would be little danger if its loss; all you have need to do is to shake them well before giving them to me, and unless it be a very sleepy or a very adhesive soul, it is physically impossible that it should stick there long after the shaking."

"But the instrument, itself! How would you have it drawn up? Possibly you may desire that it should be written with my blood; if you do, I must tell you—"

His immoderate laughter silenced me.

"Another pinch of your Maccoboy," he said, helping himself. "I see you have been among the Germans. These are diabolical fancies I confess, and to my mind, rather dirty ones. I pray you, my dear master, look on me as one having a tolerable taste, and rather delicate stomach. These blood-pudding imaginings are my abomination. I deal differently with my friends. Leave the drawing up of the instrument to me, and keep your soul and blood to yourself. I would not rob you of a particle of either. The breeches will content me,—the breeches; and, mark me! An occasional petticoat, whenever you may think it necessary to bring home Mrs. Silex."

"You shall have them—that you shall," was my answer.

The deed was drawn out in the twinkling of an eye, and the contract signed and delivered. Nothing could exceed the delight of Jack upon his installation into office as my servant of all work. His joy broke out into tumultuous expressions the moment the papers were completed.

"I congratulate myself, my dear master, as well as you, on our mutual acquisitions. There is nothing so distressing as being out of place; I have been trying for sometime to employ a master after my own heart, and my rapture is now excessive at having found him."

"A double-edged compliment," I muttered to myself, with a slight shiver. He beheld and divined the sensation.

"Ay, I see," he cried playfully, "you are still unassured. You do not conjecture my value yet. But let me convince you. Say, what shall I do for you? It is proper that I commence my duties forthwith. Let me know them. I am ready now. I have no trunks to remove. My wardrobe is already here. As for my bedding, I want none. A chink in the chimney will yield me a sufficient sleeping place, and your saving in candles, alone, will be no small item. You have only to set me above the chimney-piece when you want a light, and I will burn at both ends to please you. In food I am moderate. A fricasseed frog is the utmost that my stomach will bear, and in wine I am a single bottle man. In supplies I am a prime commissariat, and you would find me valuable for this quality, even if my consumption were greater than it is. To speak with due modesty, you will find me a wondrous acquisition; and will soon wonder how you ever did without me before."

"I nothing doubt it, Mr. John O'-Lantern."

"Plain Jack, if you please, Mr. Silex. John O'-Lantern will do for visiters and state occasions, when we go into company. Between us, and at our own fireside, a little more familiarity is best, and plain Jack more agreeable to my ear than any other epithet. And now, sir, shall I being in the coffee? Your usual supper hour is at hand."

"If you please, Jack," was my answer; and yet, I had some qualms of stomach, not to say conscience, as I thought of the proverb which denounced all liquor, however pleasant, of the devil's brewing. While I thought thus, the coffee urn was hissing on the table, and to do my new retainer lean justice, I assure you, I never drank a better cup of the purple beverage in my life. As a cook alone, he deserved new breeches daily; we shall see, as we get on, that he displayed other qualities which entitled him to far higher rewards; but of these—anon.

INDEX